# Social Theory and Social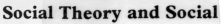

# Social Theory and Social Welfare

Peter Taylor-Gooby and
Jennifer Dale

Edward Arnold

© Peter Taylor-Gooby and Jennifer Dale 1981

First published 1981 by
Edward Arnold (Publishers) Ltd
41 Bedford Square, London WC1B 3DQ

**British Library Cataloguing in Publication Data**

Taylor-Gooby, Peter
  Social theory and social welfare.
  1. Public welfare – Great Britain
  I. Title    II. Dale, Jennifer
  361.6'0941       HV245

ISBN O 7131 6332 1 Pbk.

Filmset in Compugraphic 10/11 pt Plantin

Printed in Great Britain by Richard Clay
(The Chaucer Press) Ltd, Bungay, Suffolk.

# Contents

# Preface

The current crisis, and possible radical reconstruction of social welfare in this country has been accompanied by a spate of books discussing the welfare state from a theoretic standpoint. These can be grouped loosely into two categories: the work of writers such as George and Wilding (1976), Mishra (1977), Room (1979) has as its main concern the review, analysis and application of the range of available theoretical approaches to the subject. Hall *et al.* (1975), Gough (1979), Pinker (1979) present a detailed discussion from a particular standpoint — marxist political economy, pluralist theory or a Durkheimian notion of citizenship, respectively. This distinction is one of emphasis: to a lesser extent the writers of the former group discuss the problem of choice between theory. Those in the latter consider briefly the justification of their standpoint.

Our contention is that theories necessarily rest on unargued presumptions. All understanding must start somewhere. Premises that are unstated are often as significant in shaping the directions and conclusions of discourse as the considerations that are. Any application of a theory must also pay attention to the foundations of that theory. The first part of this book (by Peter Taylor-Gooby) attempts to tackle the range of theories available by grouping them into general approaches, resting on different background assumptions, and making a reasoned choice between them. The second part (by Jennifer Dale) develops the perspective which appears to offer the most fruitful possibilities of explanation. The themes of market, state, need and crisis are analysed from a marxist standpoint.

The intention of the book is to apply this theory to the welfare state in context, as a justified method of understanding, rather than taking the foundation of the theory for granted. It is hoped that this will go some way in the direction of reconciling the two kinds of approach mentioned above, integrating the breadth of a perspective that considers the variety of possible theory with the power of an analysis from a particular standpoint.

Peter Taylor-Gooby,
University of Kent,
Jennifer Dale,
University of Manchester,
March, 1980.

# Acknowledgements

Our gratitude is due first and foremost to Ian Gough, without whose advice, encouragement and scholarship this book would not have been written. Peggy Foster, Vic George, Norman Geras, Norman Ginsburg and Nick Manning also made generous and perceptive comments on the manuscript. Joseph Lakeman contributed a sense of proportion to the first section. Errors and shortcomings are our exclusive responsibility.

# Part I

Approaches to the Welfare State

# 1

## The domain of social administration studies

### Introduction: the starting point

This book is about social administration. Social administration is traditionally defined as the study of social arrangements for meeting need (cf. Mishra, 1977, p. xi; Forder, 1974, p. 11; Carrier and Kendal, 1973, pp. 209–10 list authorities who have held this view). Definition characterizes something by seizing on key features. This runs the risk of imposing tunnel vision by fiat. One may get so used to the blinkers of a particular approach as to forget they're there. The above definition is a starting point to be treated with caution.

All societies which contain groups who do not directly produce necessities must distribute resources from producers to non-producers to meet their needs. A peculiarity of modern times is that this process is carried out to a considerable extent by the state. In the UK government agencies expropriate through taxation and borrowing about half (by value) of the goods produced each year and put them to various uses: many of these are often seen as meeting social needs and tackling social problems — social security for the retired, sick and unemployed; health services; free education; social work; council housing; and so on. Net transfer of income between various groups through the differential impact of taxation and social security accounts for roughly half of state activity.

This major economic institution is also a political centre. Weber defined the state by its monopoly of the legitimate use of physical force within a given territory (1948, p. 78). The twin aspects of control through violence and popular acceptability form the poles of most discussions of the topic. Modern governments rely less on overt repression of dissent than on legitimate authority executed through a legal system and backed up by more or less distant threats of coercion. (The reality of the threat should not be ignored by students of the UK; armed force has been used to assure the integrity of a particular social order in Ulster since 1968). In modern British society, state power over family life, child rearing, divorce, employment opportunities and dismissal, housing and planning, education, social security and so on is exercised through law formally originating in parliament. Social arrangements for meeting need other than direct state welfare — principally wage-labour, the purchase of goods through market exchange and non-market transfers through the family — are subject to state regulation, actual or potential. They take place in the shadow of the state.

In deciding which manifestations of need should be met in what way, the state also decides whose needs shall not be met — explicitly (as in the case of the exclusion of most single homeless people from help with housing under the Homeless Persons Act) or implicitly (as in the failure to set up a comprehensive housing service with universal coverage comparable to that of education, health or social security systems). To escape the assumptions built into the traditional language of 'social arrangements for meeting need', our starting point in contemporary social administration studies must be the political process of the regulation of need. This stresses the political concern of the subject and avoids a facile equation of need with the goal of social policy. In principle the process can be analysed at any point along the spectrum of possible interactions of political and economic systems. In practice, the subject has tended to focus on particular social formations wherein capitalist market systems are regulated by democratic political systems. In this chapter we review some of the issues raised in discussion of the welfare state. We go on to discuss some problems that result from the radical ambiguity imposed by the traditional starting point. This confuses the issue by presenting in universal terms an analysis limited by the boundaries of a particular form of society. An uncritical empiricism tends to take existing arrangements for granted.

## The features of the modern leviathan

The material significance of the welfare state, its massive economic impact, has already been suggested. Roughly one-third of the labour force are employed by the state, from postmen to civil servants, from shipwrights to nurses. At any one point in time something like one-half the households in the country receive welfare benefits; just under half of these relying on them as their main means of support. The direct impact of the welfare state in people's lives from the provision of hospitals to education, to care for the mentally sick, to old persons' homes is enormous.

Ideological and cultural effects are also important. Unemployment at the turn of the century meant starvation, charity or the workhouse. Now it means boredom and meagre living. Sickness meant bills and worry. Now it means waiting lists — and so on. The result is immeasurably greater (though by no means perfect) security for (most of) the needy. Since virtually all the working class runs the risk of falling into this category through the social contingencies of marital collapse, retirement, sickness, unemployment, homelessness and so on, this represents profound social change. Whether we see its effect as sapping the moral fibre of the country (Boyson, 1971, p. 9), as the perpetual enhancement of expectations (Hirsch, 1977, pp. 6–7) or as real social advance, the existence of state care has transformed the circumstances which shape people's thinking about their lives.

Something of the scope of the change is indicated by Tressell's fictional description of a house-painter contemplating killing his family and himself at the threat of unemployment in the early 1900s (1955, pp. 92–3). This is no artistic licence. A cursory glance at the contemporary press reveals such family immolation rated about one column inch. In January, 1900 the *Manchester Evening News* recorded half a dozen such cases where poverty seems to have been a major factor including one headed 'Out of Work Suicide'.

Social welfare also imposes controls on society. Social security regulations distinguish those who do and those who do not deserve support. The curtailment of benefit entitlement for those who leave their work voluntarily or are dismissed for 'industrial misconduct' (as it was once put to the writer by an SB clerk. 'Did you leave or were you sacked?') and the denial of benefit to strikers influence the scope for action of workers in the labour market. The provision of benefits to some of the low-paid affects pressure for pay increases. The regulations which ensure that a household head is usually responsible for the living standards of family members defined as dependants encourage a certain household pattern. And so on. The fact of state welfare is of major importance for understanding contemporary political, economic and social relations. It affects the conditions of life of all citizens of contemporary Britain. Two aspects offer a striking contrast — the international spread of state welfare and its historical fragility.

## The spread of state welfare

Welfare states exist in all advanced industrial countries. There are differences in development, coverage, conditions of eligibility, standards of service, relation of state and private services and so on, but state commitment to welfare is virtually universal. Wilensky, on the basis of a close analysis of 64 countries concludes that:

> economic growth and its bureaucratic outcomes are the root cause of the general emergence of the welfare state — the establishment of similar programmes of social security, the increasing fraction of gross national product devoted to such programmes, the trend towards comprehensive coverage and similar methods of financing
>
> (1975, p. xiii).

The ubiquity of state welfare transcends national, ideological and political categories:

> In any systematic comparison of many countries over many years, alternative explanations collapse under the weight of such heavy, brittle categories as 'socialist' versus 'capitalist' economies, 'collectivistic' versus 'individualist' ideologies or even 'democratic' versus 'totalitarian' political systems. However useful they may be in the understanding of other problems, these categories are almost useless in explaining the origins and development of the welfare state
>
> (*ibid.*).

Such evidence has strengthened the plausibility of theories which postulate an iron law of 'convergence' between different social systems, under the influence of technological change, the development of common industrial and world-wide interdependent exchange systems, the expansion of equal citizenship or whatever. As Galbraith puts it, 'given the decision to have modern industry, much of what happens is inevitable and the same' (1969, p. 396).

This approach tends to a determinism that writes human agency out of history, in an account of the development of society free of reference to humans as actors. A stress on common trends stultifies consideration of the different political arrangements of different countries. While socialist and capitalist may be 'brittle categories', the relation of state to private corporation, the making of investment decisions, the range of opportunities presented to citizens for the satisfaction of need and the structure of individual motivation differ between the US and the USSR. Yet to deny the explanation is not to subvert the evidence. Alternative approaches to the development of welfare systems must provide a plausible account of similarities.

## Change and welfare

Examination of contemporary trends writes welfare large. Attention to the past highlights its recent origins. Systems recognizable as state welfare were not apparent anywhere until the last quarter of the nineteenth century. Previous relief arrangements were concerned more with public order and the working of the labour market, and in any case tended to be overshadowed by private charity. In this country the 1834 Poor Law Amendment Act was designed to impose strict limits on public aid, to stigmatize recipients and to ensure that the standard of living of the pauper was below that provided by the lowest wages. Contemporary observers in the 1850s estimated private charitable relief in London as worth at least half as much again as state aid (Woodroofe, 1962, pp. 26–7). Stedman-Jones puts the ratio of state to charitable relief as low as 2 to 7 (1971, pp. 244–5)

In Germany, limited social insurance systems covering unemployment and other contingencies for some groups were set up in the 1870s. Similar systems were enacted in this country during the 1906–14 Liberal administration, to which many writers trace the foundation of the modern welfare state (see Hay, 1975, p. 11). A national system of council housing did not emerge until after the first world war. Education, health services and social security took roughly their present form after the second. In all areas there is continued pressure for change. The comprehensive revolution in education received statutory backing in 1976, only to be reversed in 1980. The NHS and the personal social services underwent thorough-going reorganization in the early 1970s. The emergence of owner-occupation as the dominant form of tenure in the 1960s, and the progressive reduction in state spending on the provision of rented housing in the 1970s has transformed the government's role in housing from a regulator of tenancy to a moderator of mortgage interest rates. From 1978 onwards a transformation of national insurance from predominantly flat-rate to predominantly earnings-related benefits has been introduced.

If the welfare state is a historically recent and dynamic system it may also prove to be ephemeral. It is challenged both by ideological and by practical pressures. In the first area lie arguments from the political left (for example, Marcuse's critique of 'a Universe of total administration', 1964, ch. 2) and right (Powell's assertion that 'the translation of a want or need into a right is one of the most widespread and dangerous of modern heresies', 1972, p. 12) or Seldon's trenchant argument for the 'hiving off' of state services to private enterprise

(1978a). In the second lie the various crises of the state postulated by a number of writers. Central to these are the idea that it is hard to see how the continued demands for extra resources by the state, profits by capital and wages by labour can be reconciled when growth is low and slow (Devine, 1974). In addition, it is suggested that state welfare itself manufactures an expectation of the solution of recognized social problems which it may be difficult for the modern state to fulfill (Hirsch, 1977, ch. 11; Habermas, 1975, part 2, chs. 5 and 6).

Problems ranging from the management of industrial relations to that of deprived inner-city areas, from the control of wages to that of unemployment have shown a peculiar intractability. Such problems are compounded by factors internal to social services. These are generally labour-intensive. Indeed the ratio of medical personnel to patients, teachers to pupils, home helps to population and so on is often used to indicate quality of service. In the recent past, many of these groups have gained substantial wage rises, so the cost of maintaining provision — of standing still — goes up (Bacon and Eltis, 1978, ch. 1). The increasing cost of provision collides with pressure to contain welfare expenditure.

These factors make the future development of state welfare hard to foresee. Since the modern state conditions so much of our lives and our expectations about those lives, it is easy to take the present for granted.

## Values and state welfare

The pervasiveness of state welfare makes it part of the ideological context of our lives. Of prime importance are two interlinked ideas. First O'Connor is typical of a line of writers who argue that legitimation is a major function of the modern state — the justification of the status quo to citizens (1973, ch. 1). What could be more certainly in the common interest than a 'caring society'? The second aspect is contained in the idea of 'democratic welfare capitalism'. State allocation of resources to meet need puts that area of social life firmly in the political arena — the arena of common decision-taking. The development of state intervention in the market — the 're-coupling' of the political system to the economic — generates an increased demand for legitimacy for the continued expansion of the compass of state action (Habermas, 1975, p. 36). Democratic accountability provides this. So a caring society in the common interest is what people want. Success in achieving such an order to the general satisfaction reflects back to justify the system that provides it.

The welfare state is central to our understanding of modern political, economic and social life. Its material development in the growth of social services and the expansion of state spending has been well-charted (Gough, 1979; Sleeman, 1979). Here we wish to focus on the overall requirements for theoretical work in the study of this complex, polymorphous, gentle and ambiguous Leviathan.

All understanding must start somewhere. Argument for the foundations of a theory requires further argument to justify *its* premises, and the regress cannot be continued indefinitely. In practice, the problem that Berger and Luckmann refer to as the 'vertigo of relativity' (1971, p. 17) rarely obtrudes, because unstated presumptions pass unremarked in the shared interest of a particular tradition. Any theory of the welfare state ultimately rests on unargued premises.

In later chapters, we review a range of approaches to state welfare, grounded in different basic assumptions about the nature of society. First, we must examine the major tradition in the area.

## The empiricist tradition in social administration

The subject of social administration has traditionally borne the burden of welfare state studies in this country. The dominant perspective in this field has emphasized practical solutions to practical problems: unemployment, poor housing, the inaccessibility of health care, inadequate wages, lack of educational opportunity and so on confront some people in the colour supplements and others in daily life. This approach reviews piecemeal remedies: an empiricist study of social problems and a pragmatic assessment of state attempts to resolve them. Since theory remains implicit it is hard to identify this perspective by overt allegiance to theoretical tenets: the approach is commonly typified by a catalogue of eminent practitioners. An impressive heritage stretching back through Donnison, Townsend, Titmuss to Beveridge, the Webbs, and Rowntree, Booth and earlier Chadwick, Kay-Shuttleworth and John Simon. Moreover, many authorities conceptualize the approach as a 'field of study' 'an ill-defined but recognizable territory' rather than a discipline (cf. Donnison, 1965, p. 26). It contains a variety of methodologies borrowed from major social-science disciplines united by a common focus — the welfare state — rather than by a common theoretical concern. This begs the question of whether the welfare state, variously interpreted by various disciplines is adequate to serve as conceptual glue. The theoretical issues of welfare state studies can readily escape attention in the confusion.

The outcome is that 'social administration' develops a radical ambiguity. The central tradition in the subject limits its capacity to discuss critically its object — social arrangements to meet need — by imposing the blinkers of the *status quo*. This is not to deny that the subject has had worth as a contribution to human welfare (see Mishra, 1977, p. 19; Jones, 1978, p. 6; Pinker, 1971, p. 92). This chapter is concerned to argue the unaptness of the approach to meeting the problems detailed above — to show how an uncritical empiricism has led to a persistent tendency to analyse social problems and social needs in a way that takes the limitations of state intervention in a capitalist society for granted. The characteristics of the social administration approach will be reviewed. Various accounts of the forces that develop and sustain this perspective will be discussed. Finally some theoretical results of blinkered vision will be set out. Of particular interest is the fact that recent attempts to provide a more thorough theoretical basis for the subject tend to revert to previous shortcomings. The peculiar tenacity of a 'perspective of the state' can only be explained by the suggestion that the forces that moulded this approach remain dominant.

## Key features of the social administration approach

In a clear summary, Mishra identifies five main features of the social administration approach:

> First, concern with national policies and problems; second, an interventionist and prescriptive approach; third, focus on statutory welfare; fourth, a field rather than disciplinary orientation; and fifth, empiricism or concern largely with the facts of welfare
>
> (1977, p. 7).

The tradition has tended to confine analysis to the development of and the problems facing the British welfare state, an approach which weakens comparative studies and tends to ignore the issues of the international interrelation of welfare problems which Myrdal (1960) pointed out. The concern with interventionism and statutory welfare has led to an approach which operates between the poles of maximum and minimum intervention of government in capitalism: institutionalism versus residualism (Pinker, 1971, p. 99). These categories are not uncontested. Mishra points out that state activity could extend

to a normative supplanting of the basis of capitalist economic relations. Moreover, institutional and residual welfare have been understood as bearing other social functions than meeting need: Lenin commented on the pre-World War I reforms 'capable of securing fairly
substantial sops for the obedient workers in the shape of social reforms
(insurance, etc.) Lloyd George serves the bourgeoisie splendidly'
(Quoted in Thane, 1974, p. 541).

The empiricist approach is associated with the field orientation:
since no theory specifies the subject's concerns, the only unifying
force available is that of shared and unexamined presuppositions
about the appropriate area. Unexamined, because if these became
subject to scrutiny, the limits of the field would become a matter that
could only be resolved through theory. Shared, because the covert
consensus is the sole foundation for the subject.

## The perspective of the state

These five characteristics are not accidental, but may be subsumed
under a sixth — the perennial tendency to analyse social needs, and
arrangements for meeting them from the standpoint of the modern
welfare state. Thus nationalism — an international perspective is not
completely absent: international factors are simply considered as
inputs to the extent that they influence domestic events; prescriptive
interventionism — the welfare state can do nothing more or less than
intervene, since capitalism is taken as given: social administration
judges the state's performance within the limits its sets itself; a statutory focus is the clear corollary of a state that operates through law; a
field orientation — in the field of the welfare state. This can only be
defined by taking the welfare state as given; any attempt to move to the
rigorous analysis of a disciplinary approach would open the possibility
of calling the welfare state into question; empiricism — because the
welfare state defines and points the relevance of facts: the challenge of
theory to welfare statism is thus evaded. Forder remarks in the preface
to his study *Concepts in Social Administration*: 'the selection of
concepts is related to a view of the social services as institutions of a
democratic welfare capitalist state' (1974, p. xi). The problem is that
such arrangements are taken as covering the entire range of ways of
meeting social need. Unrealized historical possibilities are blandly
obliterated. The critique of particular political and social arrangements becomes impossible.

## The repression of theory

In the recent past social administration has become more preoccupied with its theoretical naivete. Pinker asserts that the approach 'lacks that body of theoretical material which might give it a greater intellectual unity and perspective' (1971, p. 5). *Social Theory and Social Policy*, with its attempt to focus the subject on a social psychological theory of stigma lies at the threshold of recent theoretical interest in the subject. The recent expansion of literature with an overtly theoretical basis and concern is striking, as a review of recent prefatory declarations indicates (cf. Forder, 1974, pp. xi–xii; Jones *et al.*, 1978, p. 6; Heisler, 1977, p. ix; George and Wilding, 1976, p. 1; Mishra, 1977, p. ix and so on). However, the spread of theoretical sophistication has been matched by a continued regression to the uncritical empiricism and perspective of the state that is the hallmark of the social administration tradition. A good example is the way in which the introductions to succeeding editions of Donnison and his colleagues' excellent standard text (1965, pp. 11–14 and 1975, pp. 1–43) display a continuing development of theoretical insight prefacing substantially the same collection of case studies.

The incorporation of new theory into standard social administration practice (rather than the other way round) is justified in two main ways. The 'handmaiden' view holds that state social services are the brief of the subject and imposes this straightjacket on conceptualization. Thus Forder (see above). Hall *et al.* adopt a more sophisticated version of this approach. They justify social policy case-study from the view-point of government by an argument that defines the political context of the modern welfare state as 'bounded pluralism'. This is an acceptance 'first . . . that in a fundamental sense policy-making is of secondary interest because the really important questions (about the distribution of economic and political power) rarely come within the ambit of social policy. Second . . . social policy is confined to an area of activity that does not threaten the interests of those who hold power' (1975, p. 151). The really important questions and the issues of distribution of power and interest are defined out of the study of social policy, which reverts to considering what the government does, rather than the situation of a particular form of government in a particular form of society.

The second regressive strategy is more far-reaching. Uncritical empiricism is justified by debunking the pretensions of social theorists. Jones *et al.* justify 'a reformist stance' and abandon both Marx on the left and Hayek or Friedman on the right for their 'simplistic theories of history and simplistic theories of man' (1978, p. 5).

Both these arguments are unsatisfactory. The tenacity of an overtly atheoretical practice in the study of social welfare requires explanation. Various accounts will be reviewed. Only by considering the approach in relation to the growth of the welfare state is a satisfactory account possible.

## The resilience of the social administration approach: empiricism versus dogma

Pinker suggests that the present structure of the social-administration approach results (like that of the royal family) from its inability to escape the past. Social policy and administration 'starts as a makeshift rearguard action against the authoritative prescriptions of certain forms of normative theory, which sought to explain and justify a new kind of competitive and industrial social order' (1971, p. 49). The origin lies in struggle against the 1834 Poor Law Amendment Act, which sought to force people to work for any employer on any terms by the rigorous restriction of relief to deterrent workhouses: 'into such a house none will enter voluntarily: work, confinement and discipline will deter the indolent and vicious; and nothing but extreme necessity will induce any to accept the comfort which must be obtained by the surrender of their free agency' (1834 Report, p. 271 quoted in de Schwenitz, p. 123 — in Piven and Cloward, 1974, pp. 33–4). The intellectual justification for such a policy (whatever interests in society it served) was the normative theory of political economy which stressed the paramount importance of the unfettered operation of free markets in meeting human need. Pinker argues that against such Gradgrind utilitarianism a blend of evidence and principle proved effective. For example: 'the growing body of evidence about the plight of the non-able-bodied pauper . . . strengthened the case for building separate hospitals' by the mid nineteenth century (Pinker, 1971, p. 71). In general, the development of empirical social science 'was a major part of the challenge to the claims of political economy' (p. 92). Thus a committed empiricism fed by 'Blue-book' sociology and the investigations of workers such as Mayhew, Chadwick and later Booth and Rowntree gained pre-eminence in social policy studies, by its success in political debate.

There are two kinds of problems with this account of the progress of empiricism with a conscience. First, facts can cut both ways. Rimlinger points out the background to the 1834 legislation was also

empirical: 'the Commissioners gathered an enormous amount of data
. . . the preliminary digest of their findings was designed to show that
the [previous] system was wholly bad. . .' (Rimlinger, 1971, p. 52).

Secondly, the argument begs questions about the mechanism of
policy change in favour of the triumph of reason: it omits any account
of the forces that produce and sustain the body of facts appropriate to a
particular normative theory in the Victorian period, or that reproduce
such an approach now. Alternative accounts of policy change exist.
Thus Rimlinger comments on the fracture of the Poor Law: 'several
principles were involved in the mounting criticism of the existing
order. One was the growing strength of organized labour. . . .
Another . . . was the change in attitude among certain segments of the
middle and upper classes' (p. 57; cf. Stedman-Jones, 1971,
pp. 239–40; Marshall, 1977, p. 32; Thane, 1978, pp. 11 and 17; and
so on). It is important to produce an account of empiricism that
enables us to discuss arguments about the particular circumstances in
which certain facts were associated with change. It is difficult to see
how contemporary debates on whether housing should be provided
through state agencies or the market or on whether it is better to spend
a certain amount of money in raising the minimum school-leaving age
or in providing more nursery education, for example, can be resolved
by 'the facts'. To regard policy change as the triumph of evidence over
dogma is to reduce the background to policy to the considerations that
would influence a reasonable practical and unbiased person: to reduce
history to progress and to give it an 'excessively tidy shape'. Thane
argues that the response to this view has been interpretation of the
history of social welfare as a 'history of social control. This it was and
most reformers made no bones about it until it became politically
unrewarding to do so openly after the second world war' (1974,
p. 540). The approach that writes off failed normative theory as
'dogma' blankets out this kind of perspective: the arguments of losers
are prejudged as prejudice.

## Social administration and government

George and Wilding argue that the close association of social policy
studies with government contributes to the analytic weakness of the
subject. 'Without realizing it, the social administrator, the sociologist
or the economist can become a professional adviser paid by governments to find acceptable solutions to prevailing social problems'
(1971, p. 237). The corollary is that the prevailing social problems

and the acceptability of the solutions are defined by government. (See also Baker, 1979, pp. 204–5.) The association of social administration with the welfare state is more far-reaching than Freire's charge of 'assistencialism' — that the practice of the subject simply props up the system — implies (Freire, 1976, pp. 14–15). The enactment of solutions (based on empirical evidence presented in the form of rational argument) to common problems identified by the political system is precisely the remit of the modern state. Habermas argues that the state, in providing the social (and other) services demanded from it under democratic capitalism 'must collect the necessary sum in taxes by skimming off profits and income, and put it to such rational use that critical disturbances in growth are avoided' (Connerton, 1976, p. 376). At the same time it must prioritize expenditure (including that on needs) in such a way that its actions are seen as legitimate by the electorate to whom it is formally accountable.

The government's decisions must make sense in practical terms and be seen to make sense. The rational discussion of measures to meet needs identified by empirical study in relation to a shared framework of values is a powerful route to this goal. It presupposes consensus on values and on what counts as rational decisionmaking. Breakdown of agreement in either of these areas subverts the state as a democratic institution, as conflict in areas as widely disparate as wage-bargaining and differentials or energy policy, the provision of social security to strikers' families and the role of education shows. If the empiricist study of consensual solutions to defined social problems did not exist, it would be necessary to invent it: democratic welfare capitalism presupposes the social administration approach.

This argument identifies a niche into which the dominant tradition in the subject may neatly fit. It fails to explain the reluctance to develop an explicit theoretical orientation in addition to the service of government demands.

## The consensus on consensus

A third aspect is the tendency to intellectual dominance of consensus and functionalist theories of society. Many recent writers in social administration have pointed to the importance in the recent past of theories which rest on the idea that a common interest of the various groups in society may be secured. Hall and her colleagues point to the prevailing 'assumption that social policy has developed and changed along basically consensual lines' (1975, p. 7). Such approaches have tended to be allied with more or less sophistication to a framework that sees society as consisting of functionally related institutions each with a task that may be identified in its organic relation to the whole. Since their business is elsewhere, the practitioners have tended to pay little attention to these presuppositions. The approach may be criticized from a number of perspectives (see, for example, Giddens, 1976, p. 21; Rex, 1970, pp. 75–6). Three are of especial relevance.

First, discourse on the functional relation of a social system tells us little about how it originated and developed, and little about the different systems that might fulfill the same role. To point out that, in general, education of the work-force is essential to advanced industry doesn't tell us why the state education systems of France and the UK differ in many important respects. The most widely quoted expression of this argument (among social policy texts) is Goldthorpe's essay (1962). (See, for example, Hall *et al.*, 1975, p. 10; Pinker, 1971, p. 103.)

A second point, also powerfully expressed by Goldthorpe, is that functionalism leaves little room for a perspective that sees social events as the collective product of willed and autonomous human action. This argument has been most strongly put among social administrators by Carrier and Kendal (1973).

The third critique stresses the importance of conflict rather than consensus in the maintenance and development of social systems. This approach denies the possibility that an organic social unity might serve as a common interest for social policy to support. The view is well put by Rex (1970, pp. 129–31) among others, but has been little regarded by social policy writers. Among those who adopt conflict critiques of functionalism, a Marxist approach which sees the central conflict of capitalism as between social interests understood in terms of relation to the means of production is almost entirely absent. Thus George and Wilding argue 'in our view it is more realistic and more fruitful to think of society in terms of conflict theory' (1971, p. 238). Their central theme is to examine the role played by dominant values in the control of conflict. But dominant values 'are in fact upper-and middle-class values legitimated by the institutional order and internalized by the whole population' (p. 244) — the values of the better off, rather than those of capital. Similarly Leonard, in a perceptive essay on social work, identifies social conflict between clients and authority, unrelated to any notion of class (1976).

The breakdown of the functionalist concordat has reduced the intellectual credibility of consensus approaches. Two features of the social administration response are of interest: first the failure to develop an adequate marxist challenge to the consensus perspective. This is well documented by Gough (1978). Secondly, the uncritical empiricism of social policy studies has tended to resurface in the reduction of conflict to consensus through the bounded pluralism and the evasion of theoretical argument discussed earlier.

## Applied social science

Several writers suggest that a further brake on social administration has been its link with practical social work. Forder puts it bluntly: 'the study of the social services in Britain, usually referred to as social administration, sprang originally from its place in the training of social workers. It concentrated on those services about which social workers needed to know in order to help their clients and to understand their own role' (Forder, 1974, p. 11). MacRae describes the subject as 'the training of welfare workers and administrators, and the concrete study of individuals suffering social deprivation or disaster' (quoted in Pinker, 1971, p. 4). He goes on to argue that too close an identification of such an applied area with sociology could be detrimental to the development of theory in that subject. Mishra concludes his discussion of social administration with the implication that its character as applied social science militates against the development of an adequate analysis of welfare (1977, p. 19).

The practical concerns of the subject are apparent in Titmuss's careful balance of its contribution to the production of professionals and to the advancement of knowledge in his appraisal of the London School of Economics department (1968, p. 55). This, the first and the pre-eminent department originally directed its efforts to 'those who wished to prepare themselves to engage in the many forms of social and charitable effort' (London University Calendar, 1913, quoted in Titmuss, 1968, p. 15).

These concerns may limit the scope of social administration. However, they cannot in themselves account for an atheoretic predisposition. The welfare state is one of the major social objects of modern times. Why should a theoretic orientation not develop alongside personnel training in the subject that takes this object as its arena?

## The political context

The fifth factor may be found in the peculiarities of the British Labour movement. Many commentators have noted the paradox between the numerical strength of labour and its conspicuous lack of success in achieving socialist political change even by the reformist Fabianism of politicians such as Crosland. Why should a movement that claims to represent the interests of the working class by and large (but not always) accept the 'rules of the game' of bourgeois democracy, instead of implacably opposing capital? (See Miliband, 1973, p. 122; Parkin, 1971, pp. 127–8; Westergaard and Resler, 1975, p. 381.)

In a rhetorical *tour de force* of imaginative history, Anderson attempts to chart the relationship between the development of British class structure and ideology (1965, ch. 1). His brief historical survey emphasizes a union of aristocracy and bourgeois under the 'high noon of Victorian Imperialism', and a working class weakened by defeats in class struggle and unable 'to transform the fundamental structure of British society' (p. 29). At an ideological level, the nineteenth century produced 'a proletariat distinguished by an immovable corporate class-consciousness and almost no hegemonic ideology' (pp. 3–4) – a class concerned to pursue its interest in a social context shaped by factors it took for granted, rather than to transform that society.

Anderson's historical study is open to question, not least because he omits all evidence 'to avoid making the text unwieldy' (p. 13). Thompson's critique (see *The Poverty of Theory*, 1978 — especially 'The Peculiarities of the English') is well known. Hobsbawm also provides an alternative account of the reformism of Labour. This stresses three factors: the history of a century of world supremacy from which the British working class drew advantage; the fact that the movement was formed and moulded at a time when the dominant tradition was that of a reforming liberal-radicalism; and most important the fact that 'in conditions of stable or flourishing capitalism and of official recognition of labour movements a reformist policy is "natural" because it is the obvious and practical policy and a revolutionary policy correspondingly difficult' (1964, p. 341).

Overt struggle clearly has importance in the development of social policy. Marshall points to the significance of the 1886 Trafalgar Square riots in awakening the ruling class to the need for reform (1977, p. 32). The origins of legislation for rent control and for the local authority provision of working-class housing have been variously traced as including the revolutionary threat from the Red Clyde (Moorhouse *et al.*, 1972; for an incrementalist view see Wilding 1972, pp. 3–18). Navarro discusses the role of working-class pressure in shaping the development of health services (1978, p. 140).

Beer traces the commitment of the Labour Party to 'a socialist re-organization of society by gradual steps', rather than by revolution to the 1908 Hull conference (1953, Vol. 2, p. 334). It is against this background that the development of Fabianism and its influence over social administration must be seen. The influence of this approach on the intellectual development of the labour movement may be exaggerated. Pease's claim that they 'broke the spell of marxism in England' rests on the false premise that there was a spell to break (see MacBriar, 1962, p. 347; cf. Anderson, 1965, p. 37). Yet it is perhaps true that 'The Fabians were the first group in the field with a socialism suitable for a nation so prosperous, so constitutional and so respectful of suave and confident authority as England' (MacBriar, 1962, p. 347).

The twofold weakness of the labour movement both as a revolutionary force and as a stimulus to radical theoretical development is reflected in the arthritic empiricism of social administration. Reformism writ small — the Fabian tradition — has exercised a continuing influence over the subject since the Webbs. Of the three representative Fabians discussed by George and Wilding (1976, ch. 4), Tawney and Titmuss exercised a brilliant influence over the LSE department and the development of the subject.

The influence of the Fabian tradition on practical politics has been slight. Crosland's apologetics for the failure of reform under the 1966 Labour government contained in the essay 'Socialism Now' (1974) merely serve to underline the weakness of this ideology in the face of practical matters (like 'the central failure of economic policy' that led to the sterling crisis and devaluation on 18 November 1967). The upshot of the argument is economic growth today and welfare tomorrow (or perhaps next week). Similarly, the Minority Report of the 1905 Poor Law Commission (Webb and Webb, 1909), written largely by the Webbs, has exercised far more influence over social policy courses than over social policy.

The rational reformism that is a peculiarity of Fabianism is founded on the common-sense belief that sense will prevail that Pinker saw as the moving spirit of the social administration tradition. Such an approach has its appeal even for avowed class conflict theorists. George and Wilding find an explanation for the failure of the welfare state to solve social problems in the idea that the egalitarian basis of 'radical' pressure lacks popular appeal (1976, pp. 127–9). Their solution is the substitution of an ideal of social justice (refined by Rawls) as a 'basis for a new and more vigorous egalitarianism'

(p. 131). Rawls's theory is founded on an interpretation of justice as the distribution that free, rational and unbiased people would choose. Yet, if egalitarianism fails to tempt, why should another socialist ideal?

## The perspective of the state — again

Thus social administration as an intellectual practice finds a natural home in a society which lacks a powerful, revolutionary labour movement. A sixth and final aspect to the atheoretic slant of the subject may be summed up in the slogan that it takes the 'perspective of the state'. The state is charged with solving the social and economic problems presented to it in the common interest. It is committed to a consensus view of the social organism — a view that cannot be critically analysed because it is part of the presuppositions rather than the subject-matter of state action. Because problems must be understood as resoluble within consensus, the process of action is reduced to administration rather than politics. Marcuse identifies the resulting 'universe of total administration' as the penetration of the end of ideology into consciousness: the welfare state:

> seems capable of raising the standard of administered living . . . under such conditions decline of freedom and opposition is not a matter of moral or intellectual deterioration or corruption. It is rather an objective societal process insofar as the production and distribution of an increasing quantity of goods and services makes compliance a rational technological attitude . . . . With all its rationality, the welfare state is a state of unfreedom because its total administration is systematic restriction of [factors including] the intellectual (conscious and unconscious) capability of comprehending and realizing the possibility of self-determination
>
> (Marcuse, 1964, pp. 48–9).

From this viewpoint of assumed consensus on goals, the debate about appropriate means may be resolved by reference to the facts. In this sense, facts defeat ideology — within a given framework that determines their relevance. For example, only because the 1834 Poor Law was designed to remove the threat of a starving pauper class without subverting the work ethic, and at minimum public expense, did the fact that most paupers were not able-bodied workshy make the workhouse an irrationality. Deterrence doesn't make people who can't work work, but it may increase their resentment.

The link between government and social administration as sympa-thetic critic and as handmaiden of social policy places it squarely in a perspective that sees social problems as things the state must do some-thing about. The inability of the subject to rise beyond its practical application and its failure to respond to the vigorous questioning of consensus approaches consequent on the breakdown of functionalism elsewhere in social science also follow from this viewpoint. The social context in which working-class consciousness accepts state welfare as the limit of achievement of that class's interest is also moulded pre-cisely to the production of a subject that operates from the standpoint of state welfarism rather than as a critique of that standpoint. The lack of a practical challenge goes hand in hand with the lack of a theoretic challenge.

Social administration is the paper owl of the British welfare state. A number of intellectual developments in the subject result from this status and may be used to illustrate the peculiar direction of its approach. An intellectual liaison with the welfare state results in an inability to construct a critical standpoint which includes an account of popular values. This leads to a particular treatment of ideology and to the reduction of the analysis of need from a critical concept to the discussion of criteria used by the state to ration resources. This follows from the treatment of human welfare as what social policy does, and is coupled with an incapacity to examine aspects of state interven-tionism. It also underpins a cursory treatment of a major issue in ideology — the puzzle of the continuing gap between the expectations assumed to be associated with state welfare, and its evident achieve-ments. In addition, the perspective results in a tendency to interpret marxism in a way that pays little attention to the critical potential of a materialist approach.

## What counts as ideology?

George and Wilding's book (1976) is the most thorough-going recent study of the place of values in theory-building about social policy. The authors discuss the place of commitment to various interpretations of liberty, equality, fraternity and social justice in justifying different ideological standpoints. The interesting feature is that nowhere are the values associated with private property considered. Yet the idea that goods, services and labour must be the exclusive property of individuals, groups, corporations, the state or whatever and that in general they are alienable so that they may be exchanged is basic to the practice of capitalism and thus to that of an interventionist welfare state. Such a state can be seen as concerned to achieve various goals by the protection, regulation and subsidy of interests generated by the private property system as opposed to the subversion of such interests or the expropriation of their foundation. A clear analysis of the foundation of property rights in the ideology of possessive individualism and the implications of these rights for modern society is provided by MacPherson (1962, pp. 263–75; 1978, Ch. 1, esp. pp. 8–10). Similarly Pinker in his discussion of 'the economic ethos of an industrial society' — and it is clear he has in mind a capitalist industrial society — stresses equivalence in exchange. 'We learn to equate money with the protection of individual autonomy. Money gives both buyer and seller instant equivalence' (1971, p. 154). Such equivalence is parasitic on the institution of priced and exchangeable private property. To take this as given is to take the perspective which limits the range of action of the state for granted.

### The reduction of need

Need is a value-loaded concept. Since values are uncheckable beliefs, any definition of need must be essentially contestable. Yet a welfare state is supposed to distribute resources according to some commonly accepted notion of need. The problem for the 'perspective of the state' is to recognize the normative nature of the concept, yet to subvert the possibility of value-conflict. This is achieved in social administration in a variety of ways.

First, reification. The contestability of need is often presented through a much-quoted article by Walton (1969 — thus Forder, 1974, p. 40) which links needs to the values of a given society. Such a treatment links values to the hypostatized entity of society as a whole rather than to the consciousness of groups of people. The possibility of considering competing concepts of need as held by different groups is automatically excluded. Such problems as: on the grand scale, how far should taxation policy aim at preserving the rewards of the better off, as opposed to making living standards more equal? Or on a smaller scale: should Manchester social services department save money by reducing the numbers of home helps or the numbers of qualified social workers? must be decided within democratic welfare capitalism. To consider them in relation to the views of various groups in society opens the way to a discussion of the conflicting interests that particular policies serve. To assume a consensus on values by attributing them to society obviates conflict and reduces the problem of choice to that of a technical administration decision. What practice accords best with the central value system?

This approach smooths the path to a second theme in the reduction of need. However, it is no way essential to it. Need is reinterpreted as rationing; analysis of the social foundations of the various value-positions on any given issue is reduced to the empirical study of the rationing procedures used by the present-day state. Thus Bradshaw's widely referenced article 'The Concept of Social Need' is in fact a useful list of techniques used by policy makers to operationalize the concept. He opens by pointing out that 'it is often not clear in a particular situation what is meant by social need'. The meat of the article is 'four separate definitions used by administrators and research workers' (1972, p. 640). Similarly, Parker lists five rationing procedures in his article on 'the variety of ways in which the problem of scarcity is dealt with by the social services' (in Butterworth and Holman (eds.) 1975, p. 205). His approach takes need as given and 'potentially infinite' — an unanalysed, undifferentiated clamour for resources. Forder in a chapter on the concept of need (1974, pp. 39–57) argues that another way of looking at the problem of defining goals for the social services is to examine 'first the difficulties of defining ideal goals . . . then . . . attempts to operationalize such ideal norms' (p. 39). In practice, 16 out of 19 pages are spent on the review of how governments and social administrators attempt to devise techniques for describing what would count as an adequate level of provision.

Jones and her co-authors achieve the reduction by discussing needs and resources in the same breath. Resource availability is taken as given. The discussion is inevitably of rationing — of making needs fit. The role of values in the definition of need is given half a sentence (1978, p. 33). That of resource constraint takes 8 sides (pp. 34–41).

The discussion of need as the prioritizing of competing claims in the face of restricted resources reduces the issue to a question of administrative rationing, which is precisely what it becomes for a consensual welfare state. The concept is robbed of all subversive content — the possibility that human needs may be such that this form of society cannot meet them becomes unthinkable, as does the possibility that values dominant under democratic welfare capitalism may produce unsatisfiable needs. Yet such conflicts have been identified as a central problem by some writers. MacPherson argues it is a major problem of liberal democratic theory that it defines property right as

an individual right to the exclusive use and disposal of parcels of the resources created by nature and of parcels of the capital created by past work on them. When it is combined with the liberal system of market incentives and rights of free contract, it leads to and supports a concentration of ownership and a system of power relations between individuals and classes which negates the ethical goal of free and independent individual development

(1978, pp. 199–200).

If the treatment of need is reduced to the rationing of property, the possibility of a conflict between a need for autonomy and the ownership principle is ruled out by fiat. In this sense the suggestion by Nevitt (Heisler, 1977, pp. 127–8) and Culyer (1974; Williams's remarks on p. 67 are a clear example) that need be reinterpreted as a sub-species of demand is correct. A radically different concept is being employed.

Julia Parker's approach arrives at the same position by a different route. She recognizes two meanings of need: first, 'a criterion which may be used in a non-market situation for political decisions about supply and about the legal and administrative recognition of need' (1975, p. ix). In other words, need is what the welfare state apparatus says it is. The second sense focuses on 'the objective variations in people's circumstances with respect to standards of health, housing' and so on (p. ix). The standards are those set by experts and the state. Their 'objectivity' is again a denial of value-conflict. This approach is the assessment of conditions identified by government (or its critics) as deserving action. Need is defined from the perspective of the state as what the state sets out (or should set out) to change.

The problems of understanding state intervention in the market discussed earlier on centred on the difficulty of choosing between competing conceptions of state  market and their interaction. The conflation of value-conflicts discussed above inflicts a myopia on the social administration approach that obscures such issues. The possibility of a critique of interventionism as a way of meeting need slips unnoticed out of view, drowned in oceans of 'fact'.

## The weakness of welfare

Nine-tenths of the empiricist social administration tradition is concerned with the charting of facts about the shortcomings of state welfare — from Rowntree's study of York (1902) to Townsend's study of old people's homes (1963), from  Donnison's study of housing

(1967) to Jones's study of community care (1975), from Field's analysis of wealth inequalities (Field *et al.* 1977) to Byrne's study of educational disadvantage (1972). Indeed for Pinker this use of fact (interpreted as theory-free) to confront theory has been the guiding light of the subject. One aspect of this exercise is the assessment of the failure of welfare to live up to the standards it sets for itself. A rare extended discussion is provided by George and Wilding's attempt to account for the failure of social services to achieve the 'explicit aims enshrined in statute or in the speeches of those responsible for inaugurating or restructuring the services' (1976, p. 106). The authors detail the persistent geographical inequalities in health care, the continuance of poverty, the prevalence of homelessness and poor housing and the lack of progress in the extension of educational opportunity. Such clear and lasting deficiencies, they claim, can only be accounted for by structural social mechanisms: 'we see the conflict between the values of capitalism and the ethic of welfare as the underlying reason for the failure of social policy to achieve agreed aims' (p. 129). This passage is striking in its treatment of an issue little discussed elsewhere.

In another study, Miliband lists the history of broken promises to eradicate poverty and poor housing and offers a political account of the persistence of disadvantage. 'Economic deprivation is a source of political deprivation; and political deprivation in turn helps to maintain and confirm economic deprivation' (Wedderburn (ed.) 1974, p. 183). Such a perspective takes us beyond the traditional universe of social administration. 'The truth . . . is that the abolition of poverty will have to wait until the abolition of the system which breeds it comes on the agenda; and this is a question which far transcends the issue of poverty itself' (p. 194).

The limited discussion of the overall failure of welfare is surprising, if only because it is social administration that has itself documented the component parts of the failure. The results are twofold: first the subject is debarred from considering some major ideological issues of democratic welfare capitalism. Here a perplexing problem is how the welfare state gets away from diswelfare. How do people think about state welfare in such a way that the disjunction of practice and promise goes largely unremarked? Democracy assumes a correspondence of promise with people's wishes, and (in the long term) of policy with expectation, all things being equal. Explanation of a lack of unrest at the weakness of welfare may rest on a multitude of factors from false consciousness to inertia, from self-interest to ignorance, yet room for an account should be left.

Secondly, the capacity of the subject to develop a theory of the welfare state is crippled, if one of the more important features of that institution — its need for legitimacy — is excluded from analysis. A recent discussion of case-studies argues that one of the most important factors contributing to a social policy decision is the relative legitimacy and feasibility of and support for the various courses of action open to government (Hall *et al.*, 1975, concluding chapter). This is certainly correct, in that the various inputs into the policy-making machine may be categorized under these heads. We might turn the process on its head and inquire how it comes about that a system which produces a performance/promise gap in welfare is legitimate, feasible and enjoys support? To provide an answer to this question would take us beyond the viewpoint of the state to consider how people come to think about their society in a way that produces this paradox.

## Marxism in social administration

The perspective of the subject leads to a particular interpretation of marxism. This is particularly clear in discussion of Marx's materialist method and of the views of writers in the marxist tradition on the state. The waters are further muddied by limited acquaintance with Marx's work. Thus it is suggested that Marx 'working in the British Museum Library from 9 'til 7' was unlikely to have been aware of the social achievements of mid-Victorian England (Jones *et al.*, 1978, p. 4). Such a remark plays down the empirical analysis that informs Marx's work (for example, *Capital*, Bk. 1, chs. 9, 10 and 15, 1976); it also reveals the peculiar piecemeal and personalist empiricism of social administration. As if one could not comprehend social reality as well through the medium of the finest library in the world as by social action. In any case, far from being a bookworm swot, Marx was the 'dominant personality' on the General Council of the International Workingmen's Association from 1864 onwards (McLellan, 1978, p. 21).

Marx's method has been variously interpreted. We cannot hope to do justice to the debate here. Suffice to state the 'guiding thread' of marxist materialism as expressed in the 1859 Preface.

> The sum total of these relations of production constitutes the economic structure of society, the real foundation on which rises a legal and political superstructure and to which correspond definite

forms of social consciousness. The mode of production of material life conditions the social, political and intellectual life processes in general

(1968, p. 181).

The social administration school in general has tended to interpret marxist social theory in such a way as to destroy the link between the intellectual and the material, to present conclusions without foundation. George and Wilding present a marxist 'ideology' of state welfare as a union of particular values of liberty, equality and fraternity with a conflict theory of contemporary social formations: an interpretation compounded by their choice of peripheral proponents of marxism as paradigms. In a famous passage Lenin neatly summarizes the source of Marx's ideas in the integration of French socialism, German materialist philosophy and English political economy (1963, Vol. 1, pp. 66–70). The social administration approach ignores the analysis of capitalism that makes socialist values appropriate to the future development of history. Similarly, Rein describes marxism as an 'explicit moral position' (1977, p. 78).

Mishra alone among social policy writers presents Marx's view of the basis of social relations and people's ideas about those relations in relations of production coherently and sympathetically (1977, pp. 63–4). Yet there are weaknesses in his treatment of the state. He constructs a continuum of residual, institutional and normative models of social policy, corresponding to *laissez-faire*, citizenship and marxist social theory (pp. 12–13). The job of the continuum is complex, serving to relate intellectual positions and to sketch out a theory of how welfare states develop. The result is to obscure both the gulf between idealist and materialist analyses of society and that between bourgeois and marxist viewpoints on the relation of state and economy. The state cannot finally resolve the social problems rooted in the relations of production Marx terms 'modern industry' because the state is itself the product of those relations.

Mishra compounds the problem by attributing to marxists the view that equal welfare can only be achieved when collective consumption is brought under 'communal, e.g. state, control' (p. 122). Significantly, he wrenches the slogan 'to each according to his need' out of context. Marx used it in his Critique of the Gotha Programme to characterize a 'higher phase of communist society' when, among other things, division of labour had ceased and scarcity had been abolished. Mishra applies it to the Soviet Union from 1917 onwards.

Further problems result from the view that marxism reduces the state to the status of an institution that can only operate directly in the short-term interests of the capitalist class. Thus Pinker claims marxism sees the welfare state as simply 'a bourgeois deceit, subverting or delaying the process of socialist revolution' (1971, p. 44). Later he argues 'social reform rather than repression has made marxist social theory an irrelevance in advanced industrial societies' (p. 181). The idea that state policy is the result of a conspiracy of the powerful has its merits and is in some cases probably correct. However, to attribute it as an *a priori* principle to marxism is to ignore the emphasis of this school on the contribution of class struggle to achieving social reform, a facet elaborated for example by Mishra (1977, p. 75) or Saville in Butterworth and Holman (1975, p. 57) or Navarro (1978, *passim*) — although these writers differ both in their views on its relative significance in contemporary events and its potential. Typical of confusion in this area is the way in which Hall and her colleagues confuse class conflict and elite theories of social policy change (1975, pp. 140–51). The latter puts the burden of policy development on the dominant minority, the former finds the motor of change in a society-wide balance of forces.

The difficulty which social administrators experience in accommodating marxist thought lies in the challenge it offers to the approach which operates simply from the viewpoint of government. To take materialism seriously would be to licence on the one hand the view that needs may be systematically and socially produced by agencies beyond the control of the state in democratic welfare capitalism; and on the other hand that the state as a product of material relations may be unable to meet them. To allow scope to class conflict in influencing state action would be to move beyond the consensus approach.

## You can't get there from here

The traditional social administration approach is irrevocably committed to a piecemeal and uncritical empiricism that has value as a watchdog and buttress for the welfare state. It encounters difficulty in theorizing social arrangements to meet need adequately, because it takes a particular form of society for granted. This theme goes hand in hand with the unselfconscious attempt to construct theory from facts as given. Empiricism finds difficulty in transcending the status quo to achieve an independent and critical standpoint. In the next three chapters we review a range of approaches resting on different and conflicting prior assumptions that attempt this task.

# 2

## Accounts of social issues

In this and the next chapter we undertake a review of theories relevant to the understanding of state regulation of need. This takes us in two directions: focusing on the present and the particular we consider theorizing of the grist of state welfare — the issues that become recognized as social problems. Widening our approach to the most general level, we consider the welfare state as a whole. This distinction is heuristic rather than analytic. The two levels interpenetrate. In one sense, state welfare is the sum-total of action taken to resolve issues identified as social problems. The stubborn persistence of such issues is at once a rationale and an indictment of the welfare state.

The political form of state welfare means that policy is consciously directed to mitigate problems. This rubs our noses in the necessity of producing accounts that will guide practical action. At the same time, the historical fragility of the welfare state as a form of society makes theory that can suggest its future and pronounce a judgement on it desirable. Such theory contains within it an account of the structure of interests in society, and the particular interests that particular policies serve. For convenience, theories of social issues and of state welfare — the welfare state writ small and large — are discussed in separate chapters.

### Normative and explanatory theory

The state is an agency for collective decision making about social action. If such action is to be rational, it requires theory about the processes and structures with which it deals. In the area of social policy, explanatory theory is especially important: if we can provide an account of how a circumstance identified as demanding action arises, it is in principle possible to do something about it — to tackle it at root. In the vexed area of inner-city problems, for example, a feature of recent initiatives has been the attempt to carry out research, in order to guide future action. (For a discussion see Community Development Project, 1977 pp. 9–16.) The problem that immediately arises, of course, is that we are embarrassed by a surplus of theory. A clear example is provided by the Home Office sponsored Community Development Projects of the early 1970s. The original brief contained the implicit assumption that the problems of deprived areas

> can be blamed partly on the apathy and abnormality of local residents and partly on the incompetence of local government; the solutions lie in self help . . .; and more sensitive services by the local authority
>
> (Coventry CDP, 1975, p. 3).

However, the CDP team developed a completely different perspective:

> the area has not lacked public attention: it has featured as a priority for comprehensive urban renewal in every major plan published by the local authority since the war. A good deal of public money has been invested in trying to improve the physical condition of the housing and the environment and in providing compensatory and additional social and community facilities . . . . The persistence of areas like Hillfields in a prosperous and progressive city like Coventry is a clear indication that neither economic growth nor enlightened social administration by themselves are sufficient to eradicate urban problems
>
> (Coventry CDP, 1975, p. 63).

In practice it is hard to see how we are to choose between the two perspectives. The fact that previous initiatives failed to resolve the problems of an area like Hillfields does not demonstrate that they are the product of processes beyond social policy control. In any case, the complexity and messiness of a particular social context mean that adequate experimental verification of theories is impossible. The assumptions that underlie competing approaches are more like different ways of looking at reality. How to choose? For rational policy-making, a choice, implicit or explicit, is essential.

The choice of a theory, of a particular characterization of social systems and processes, is irremediably normative, for such systems are themselves human productions, and not objective entities. Robinson puts it well:

> to look at a system from the outside implies that it is not the only possible system; in describing it we compare it (openly or tacitly) with other actual or imagined systems. Differences imply choices, and choices imply judgements. We cannot escape from making

judgements and the judgements that we make arise from the ethical preconceptions that have soaked into our view of life

(1964, p. 19).

This is the essence of Pirsig's argument in *Zen and the Art of Motorcycle Maintenance*:

value, the leading edge of reality, is no longer an irrelevant offshoot of structure. Value is the predecessor of structure. It is the pre-intellectual awareness that gives rise to it. Our structured reality is preselected on the basis of value and really to understand structured reality requires an understanding of the value source from which it derived

(1974, p. 284).

Attention to normative judgements plays a central part in any understanding of theory. To put it another way, explanation must start somewhere, if it is not to be circular. Not everybody necessarily starts in the same place. Yet an explicit or implicit theory about the origins and nature of social problems as a guide to policy is an urgent necessity. Does this mean that: 'in the end, if the end comes, we just have to beat those who disagree with us over the head; let us hope the end comes seldom'? (Mills, 1970, p. 89.)

It is worth noting that the intellectual problem of relativism of theory, which perplexes many academics (see Lukes, 1974a, p. 186; Emmet, 1966, ch. 5; Gallie, 1956, p. 179; Carrier and Kendal, 1973) hardly stultifies political debate. A further twist is added by the fact that different approaches to a problem may be seen as serving different interests in society. Thus original statements described the national CDP as 'a neighbourhood-based experiment aimed at finding new ways of meeting the needs of people living in areas of high social deprivation' (Home Office, 1970, p. 1). Some CDP workers understood the projects in a radically different way: 'in the final analysis, the 'deprivation initiatives' were not about eradicating poverty, at all, but about managing poor people' (CDP, 1977, p. 63). This approach stemmed from a theory that analysed modern capitalist society as containing conflicts of interests and saw the production of urban deprivation as part of such conflict. The problem of the inner-city from the capitalist viewpoint is that such deprivation may lead to a breakdown of law and order and challenge to propertied interests. A clear example of how different theories situate social action in relation to different interests is Marx's claim in his Inaugural Address to the Workingmen's International Association that legislation to control working conditions in factories represented a victory of the 'political economy of the working class' over the 'political economy of the middle class' (Marx and Engels, 1962, p. 489).

The theories of society held by Marx, by the CDP writers and by the official originators of CDP each suggest that modern society contains different interests relating in different ways. Thus a study of the explanation of issues tackled by social policy must include discussion of the range of accounts of the structure of interests in the modern welfare state. The first area will be tackled in this chapter and the second in chapter 4.

Approaches to both may be conveniently grouped under three headings: first, an individualist approach, which minimizes or denies the significance of over-arching social factors in generating the issues regarded as problems. Problems tend to be seen as properties of persons or small groups originating within those individuals. The welfare state is a mistaken intervention in the freedom of the majority.

Secondly, a reformist approach which allows room for the social production of social problems and thus for the generation of welfare state policy to mitigate these social causes, but sees solution as possible within the framework of democratic welfare capitalism.

Thirdly, a structuralist approach which sees problems as the result of the operation of that form of society, and suggests that it is in general impossible to resolve them within it. This classification will be illustrated in this chapter by reference to what is arguably the most generalized form of deprivation in a society where money is the principal medium of exchange — poverty.

## Three perspectives on social policy issues

Sir Keith Joseph, Secretary of State for Social Services, wrote in 1972: 'why is it that, in spite of long periods of full employment and relative prosperity . . . deprivation and problems of maladjustment so conspicuously persist?' His answer, in general, was; 'do we not know only too certainly that among the children of this generation there are some doomed to an uphill struggle against the disadvantages of a deprived family background? . . . many will not be able to overcome the disadvantages, and will become in their turn the parents of deprived families' (Sir Keith Joseph, 1972).

Conversely a recent National Consumer Council report on means-tested welfare argues that we can only effectively tackle poverty if we change the way the whole benefit system is run: 'Far from Britain being a nation of scroungers . . . people are not claiming hundreds of millions of pounds to which they are entitled in law . . . we are asking for a Beveridge-type review . . . to outline a plan to reconstruct our tax and social security systems to work in such harmony that, according to need, they give as well as receive' (NCC, 1976, p. 80).

Ralph Miliband, a marxist political scientist, concludes an essay on the politics of poverty; 'But the truth — the bitter truth — is that the abolition of poverty will have to wait until the abolition of the system which breeds it comes on the agenda; and this is a question which far transcends the issue of poverty itself' (Wedderburn, 1974, p. 194).

These quotations typify three different ways of looking at social problems. A problem may be understood in terms of the individuals who suffer it and their immediate social influences — in the example above, the family. It may be seen as the result of inadequacies in the services that are supposed to cope with it. Or it may be regarded as a necessary outcome of the workings of a particular kind of society.

Poverty is a major problem. Roughly half of all the resources spent on social programmes by the government take the form of social security payments. We shall look in detail at the three kinds of explanation of why some people are poor. First, some facts.

Roughly one in four households in the UK are dependent on national insurance benefits, mainly retirement pensions, widows benefit, sickness and unemployment benefit. Something like 1.1 million people in addition are solely dependent on means-tested supplementary benefit. These households are defined as poor by the state welfare system — they get benefits designed to relieve poverty. Official figures indicate there are nearly 1 million more households scraping an existence below the poverty line because they don't claim the benefits they have a right to.

There are probably as many explanations as there are people of why these particular individuals came to be classified as poor — how they lost jobs, became redundant, retired, whether they claimed all they were entitled to and so on. That is not our concern. We are interested in explaining the existence of the poor *as a group*. But what do we mean by poverty?

If poverty is the lack of the necessities of life, it is clear that the proportion of the population affected has fallen dramatically over the last 100 years. In the 1890s Booth discovered that just under one third of the population of London had 'barely sufficient means for decent independent life', (quoted from an article in the *Pall Mall Gazette* by

Holman, 1978, p. 3). In modern Britain very few people experience such a degree of want, although its worth bearing in mind that even under the welfare state old people still sometimes die of cold (see Fox *et al.*, 1973).

More recent researchers have emphasized a different view of poverty. Being poor is being unable to keep up with the standard of living considered normal in the community as a whole. This idea is sanctioned in the government's attempts to keep welfare benefits in a more or less constant relation with the standard of living. If we think of poverty in this way, a remarkable feature of our society is the persistence of inequality, in spite of the colossal programmes designed to mitigate it. Two of the most careful recent researchers write 'overall income disparity appears to have remained remarkably stable; at particular times even to have increased. Inequality today plainly cannot be dismissed as a matter of "frills" when the richest one per cent of the population take as much of all income as the poorest third or so' (Westergaard and Resler, 1975, p. 51). What we have to account for is the rugged persistence of the poor as a group.

### Individual explanations

Can poverty be explained in terms of individual make-up and the effect of immediate social environment on the poor? Good examples of attempts to do this are the view that income, intelligence and heredity are closely linked, the idea that poor families are 'problem families' and, most important, the cultural view of poverty.

These approaches are well reviewed by a number of writers including Holman (1978, chs. 2 and 3) and Townsend (1979, ch. 2). In brief, we may point out that in respect of the first idea the suggestion of an hereditary explanation of income differences has been strongly criticized by for example Block and Dworkin (1974) and Rose *et al.* (1973). In any case, no normative conclusions would follow if such a link were demonstrated. As Jencks argues, if inequality is due to factors over which people have no control, perhaps we should try 'to devise insurance systems which neutralize the effects of luck' in the genetic lottery (1973, p. 8), rather than regard inequalities as justified.

The view that poverty is the result of individual inadequacy perpetuated through a 'problem family' syndrome is criticized by Jordan, who assembles evidence to show that indicators of inadequacy such as alcoholism, family breakdown and delinquency do not correlate well with poverty (1974, pp. 6 and 7); see also Coates and Silburn (1970, pp. 54 and 102).

Cultural views see the poor as showing a relatively stable set of attitudes and beliefs that tend to reproduce their poverty. In the UK the most important cultural explanation has been the 'cycle of deprivation' theory associated with Sir Keith Joseph, Secretary of State for Social Services, 1971–4.

Sir Keith argued that inadequate parenting tended to produce children who were permanently disadvantaged. They failed at school, got the worst jobs, experienced unstable and unsatisfying marriages and family lives, and produced a further generation of children who were ill equipped to seize the opportunities offered by our society. This approach links together some of the ideas that underlie the problem family view with those of the culture of poverty. A vicious circle compounded of emotional immaturity and the continually justified expectation of failure perpetuates itself. The cyclical idea sparked off a major government-sponsored research programme and lay behind some of the social-policy innovations of the period. How adequate is it?

Like all cultural views it's based on the thesis that the poor are somehow different from you and me. They are — they have less money — but it is difficult to point to other differences. We have already argued that the deviance attributed to problem families is not typical of the poor. On the other hand, many poor families are 'normal'.

Similarly, it is hard to demonstrate that the poor have anti-school or work attitudes that seal their own fate. Both Hill (1973) and Marsden (1975) found that the unemployed and those in low-paid work displayed a striking will to work. Antagonism to the school system can equally well be explained as a result of the way it treats low achievers than as an attitude picked up at home. In a recent study, Paul Willis argues that schools provide little official reward to academic failures. This encourages the growth of a counter-culture among them, consisting of attitudes which suit them to low-paid, dead-end jobs. 'In the sense . . . that it is their own culture which most effectively prepares some working-class lads for the manual giving of their labour-power we may say that there is an element of self-damnation in the taking on of subordinate roles in western capitalism. However, this damnation is experienced, paradoxically, as true learning, affirmation, appropriation and as a form of resistance' (1978, p. 3).

The most difficult problem for cycle-of-deprivation theorists to surmount is the weakness of the cycle. Such evidence as exists indicates that intergenerational transmission of poverty is uncertain. Indeed, there is much stronger evidence than the children of the rich inherit privilege, than that the children of the poor inherit disadvantage! (see Madge and Rutter, 1976, pp. 19, 27 and 48). It is interesting to note that Sir Keith Joseph, commenting on the results of research into the cycle-of-deprivation thesis declared himself 'slightly humbled and relieved and glad', that 'it turned out to be a pretty negative piece of analysis' — in other words, mistaken (*Guardian*, 18 July, 79).

Accounts of poverty that focus on the poor and their immediate surroundings have particular implications for policy. If poverty is seen as the outcome of individual factors or of the operation of a minority group sub-culture, the suggestion is that a minimal policy is adequate. This justifies either a lack of action, on the grounds that the majority have no responsibility for the poor, or small-scale paternalist policies directed at particular sub-groups identified by theory. Individualism opposes large-scale institutionalized welfare.

In the shift between individualist and reformist perspective, we cross what Mills termed 'the most fruitful distinction with which the sociological imagination works'. This lies between 'personal troubles of milieu' located within the character and immediate personal relations of the individual, and 'public issues of social structure'. For example:

> when in a city of 100,000 only one man is unemployed, that is his personal trouble, and for its relief we look to the character of the man, his skills and his immediate opportunities. But when in a nation of 50 million, 15 million are unemployed, that is an issue . . . the correct statement of the problem and the range of possible solutions require us to consider the economic and political institutions of the society . . .
>
> (1970, p. 15).

We shall group sociologically aware accounts of social problems into two classes: those whose focus is on the reform of institutions within prevailing structures, and those which transcend this perspective to view recognized problems as themselves aspects of the operation of those structures. The institutional approach implies particular systems may be changed and adapted to resolve problems without damaging implications for the form of society as a whole. The structural approach understands the link between different institutions as much closer, and questions whether worthwhile reform can be achieved by piecemeal change.

## Institutional reformism

This standpoint focuses attention on the inadequacy of welfare state agencies in doing the job they are supposed to do. Take housing. 1919 electioneering spawned the slogan 'homes fit for heroes'. In the mid-1930s, Sir Hilton Young, Minister of Health, declared 'twelve months hence, the slums should be falling five times as fast . . . five years is not an unduly long time to cure an evil that has been growing for a hundred.' In the mid-1950s, Duncan Sandys, Minister for Housing, spoke more cautiously of an estimated one million slum homes. 'We should aim at breaking the back of the problem within ten years.' (Quotations from Samuel *et al.* 1962). Official figures from the Housing Condition Survey put the number of unfit houses in England and Wales at about one and a quarter million in 1971. George and Wilding paint a similar picture of the failure of health, social security and education services to live up to the aspirations of those who planned them (George and Wilding, 1976, ch. 6).

If the welfare state is to tackle poverty, it must redistribute resources. Revenue is raised by a bewildering variety of means, including income tax, VAT, national insurance contributions, and spent (among other things) on an even more complex array of services and benefits. We all pay tax, even if it is only on the goods we buy. The majority of households receive some form of state benefit. To calculate the redistributive effect of the welfare state, it is necessary to work out how much people in various income groups get back, compared with what they pay in. Estimates unfortunately have to be based on the answers given in sample surveys about the services and benefits people use and these can be notoriously misleading. Moreover, dubious judgements are involved in working out how much in cash terms a service like the NHS or education benefits a family.

Taking all these shortcomings into account, an impressive summary of the evidence (Nicholson in Wedderburn, 1974, p. 78) indicates that the welfare state, taken as a whole, does tend to reduce inequality to a modest degree. The Royal Commission on the Distribution of Income and Wealth (1979, p. 81) concurs. Direct cash benefits are highly redistributive, benefits in kind such as council housing or the health service rather less so. This effect is counterbalanced by indirect taxation, such as rates and VAT, which is particularly prone to take proportionately more from the poor than the rich. By and large, the welfare state has rather more effect in redistributing to those with larger families and hence greater needs from smaller households, than from well-off to poor. Of particular interest is the way in which this modest redistributive impact does not seem to have changed much over time (p. 79).

Titmuss was the first to stress that it is a mistake to concentrate exclusively on the impact of state benefits. Occupational welfare schemes (mainly private pensions) and fiscal welfare — the jungle of tax allowances which people may claim for various expenses — also have the effect of redistributing income. This is unfortunately a shadowy area where hard and fast evidence is thin on the ground. Titmuss lists some of the benefits that may be available as perks to the upper-middle-class executive — cars, housing, holidays, private health care, school fees, cheap loans, and so on — a far cry from the Durham miner's allowance of concessionary coal or the binman's 'knockings'. One study of benefits to managerial staff shows clearly how their value relates to status in the job hierarchy. In 1978 the cost to the employer of superannuation and fringe benefits expressed as a percentage of pre-tax income was 36 and 37 per cent for Managing and General Directors respectively, 33 per cent for Manufacturing Managers but only 18 per cent for General Foremen (Royal Commission on the Distribution of Income and Wealth, 1979, p. 53).

Retirement pensions are perhaps the most important item. State pension schemes have always taken good care to leave ample scope for private endeavour. One reason for this is the enormous financial power of the schemes. By the end of 1974, private pension funds owned over a quarter of the quoted shares in UK industry (Fogarty, 1976, p. 25). No government in its right mind would threaten the stability of the economy by tampering with such a large chunk of investment. Kincaid estimates from official figures that the various tax concessions and guarantees add up to a government subsidy for these schemes one and a half times as great as that going to state pensioners. (Kincaid, 1978). We know that the schemes tend to cover higher earners, and it is certainly the highest earners who get the highest pensions. This is a colossal redistribution away from the poor, an effect exacerbated by the general tendency of the better-off to live and therefore enjoy pensions for longer.

The most striking evidence against the redistributive view is contained in the report of Townsend's monumental empirical study. On his estimation the better-off fifth of the population in terms of net disposable income also 'received the highest money value of other types of resource. Their advantage in respect of imputed income from assets and from employer welfare benefits is striking, though not surprising, but they also had a higher value of social services in kind' (Townsend, 1979, p. 233).

Relative to income, social services in kind made up a greater proportion of the receipts of the poor. Taken with the Royal Commission discussion of the incidence of taxation, this finding shows the extent to which redistribution in the welfare state is limited, and is focused on cash benefits. What about the situation of the margin? Do the people with the worst problems get better welfare?

When we contrast the contemporary situation with that of 100 years ago, there are dramatic differences. The alternative for the unemployed labourer is no longer the workhouse or starvation. The grim choice for the widow is no longer charity, relatives or separation from her children in the workhouse. To assess the adequacy of contemporary poor relief, we must first examine how the social-security system for the poor works.

Social security is traditionally divided into a contributory sector — national insurance benefits — and a non-contributory sector. In the former area, the most important benefits are retirement pension, widow's benefit, sickness and industrial injury benefit and unemployment benefit. In the latter most benefits are allocated to those who can prove need through a test of means.

Contributory benefits are by and large paid to people who have an adequate contribution record and are in the circumstance covered — retirement, unemployment or whatever. Their relation to poverty is the relation of that contingency to poverty. People may be in need and lack the contribution record, like the unemployed school leaver. Equally, their need may not be covered by the insurance system, like the single parent. The gaps in the system are papered over by means-tested welfare. It is on the adequacy of this system, directly linked to proof of need, that the efficacy of the system as a whole depends. How well does means-tested welfare meet need?

There exists a vast range of means-tested benefits. Over forty schemes are administered by central and local government for needs ranging from the cost of dentistry to legal aid, from educational maintenance to rent and rates, from chiropody to school meals. Here we concentrate on supplementary benefits, designed as the name implies to bolster up the national insurance system by supplementing the incomes of those below a poverty line laid down by government.

There are two kinds of problems with supplementary benefits from the point of view of the poor. First very large numbers of those entitled do not claim. Just under one million households fell into this category in 1976, forfeiting about £250 million, according to the rather conservative estimate of the SBC official report for 1977 (p. 27). The reasons why people do not claim are obscure. Certainly ignorance of entitlement, the inconvenience of making a claim and producing supporting evidence, the humiliation of discussing one's personal affairs with often insensitive officials and means-test stigma all play a part.

The second problem is the numbers excluded from the scheme of last resort. Those in full-time education and work are excluded. The scheme was never devised to make student grants or poverty wages up to a reasonable level. Administrative decisions have also excluded those living with a partner who might be expected to support them. In practice this rule bears heavily on single women, who may be refused on suspicion that they are living with a man. Some 8,000 women with 6,000 dependent children were denied benefit in this way in 1974 (S.B. 1976). Benefit is also curtailed for strikers, those with high rents, those who are judged to persistently refuse work, those who left their last job voluntarily or as a result of 'industrial misconduct' and so on.

In all, although statistics are hard to obtain, it seems likely that the benefit system fails at least one million families at the margin, and probably many more. Writers who explain poverty in terms of agency deficiency are concentrating on this kind of inadequacy. A whole tradition of writing about the welfare state has been concerned to chronicle such shortcomings and suggest piecemeal remedies. The underlying and often implicit idea is that the welfare system is on the right lines, but that tinkering, tampering and fine tuning are needed to get it to solve the problems better. This conception is often found in the social administration tradition.

Sometimes this perspective suggests supplementation of existing policy. An example of an approach which backs up income-maintenance measures with an attempt to change the context in which these measures operate is provided by recent positive discrimination experiments. Both the Educational Priority Areas recommended by the Plowden Report (1966, ch. 5) and the Community Development Projects set up in 1969 tackled what were seen as causes of deprivation confined to particular areas — in the one case, poor educational facilities, and in the other inadequate and chaotic social and welfare services and a breakdown in community organization. However as Halsey points out:

> a constructive synthesis seems to have emerged . . . that the 'poverties' to which urban industrial populations are prone must be understood to have their origins in both situational and cultural characteristics of those minorities which suffer disadvantage and discrimination, and to have its cures in both economic and cultural reform not only at the local or community level but also in the total structure of society
>
> (in Wedderburn, (ed.) 1974, p. 130).

It is hard to see how extra resources for hard-pressed schools or greater coordination of housing, educational and personal social services can operate as more than a marginal amelioration of poverty problems in particular localities. The argument linking education and deprivation stated by Plowden was that:

> from some neighbourhoods . . . there has been a continuing outflow of the most successful young people. The loss of their enterprise and skill makes things worse for those left behind. Thus, the vicious circle may turn from generation to generation, and the schools play a central part in the process both causing and suffering cumulative deprivation
>
> (para. 132).

It might equally be claimed that improving the schools even to the point where the most able teachers were readily retained, would simply accelerate this process, by improving the qualifications and thus the capacity of able youths to find work elsewhere. Rather more bitterly, the Community Development Programme has been condemned as empty rhetoric — 'like the emperor's new clothes' (CDP, 1977, p. 63). The argument is that no amount of piecemeal, low-budget policy will make much difference, when the root cause of poverty lies in structural factors of the British economy. There is no necessary reason why all available labour should be needed and technological advance may act to displace it.

In general then, we may question how adequate an account of social problems it is that puts them down not to shortcomings in the people who suffer them, but in the services that are supposed to tackle them.

## Problems of institutional reform

Two problems: first, where does the approach take us? To suggest administrative deficiency as the root of social malaise implies that administrative reform is the solution. However, in practice, administrative changes may tend to benefit administrators or providers rather than the users of services. Rationalization closed outlying sub-post offices, and SB offices and absorbed smaller units into the District General Hospital in the early 1970s. How far old-age pensioners who have to take a bus-ride to cash their pension or those who need to visit relatives in hospital see this as progress is a good question.

The history of social policy is dotted with resolutions for the greater coordination of services. The Goschen Minute of 1869 encouraged the multitude of private charities to organize themselves under the central regulating agency of the Charity Organization Society. In 1969, the essence of the Seebohm committee report was a call for the coordination of local government welfare services in a unified social services department, and their more effective interaction with outside agencies. An administrative solution to the problem of delivering human services might be thought appropriate from a committee chaired by a banker. Townsend makes the telling point that among the large numbers of experts and social workers consulted, not a single consumer of social services was included, (Townsend, 1970). A recent report on 'obstacles to an effective working relationship between DHSS local offices and the Social Services Department' in Islington found that 'a major cause of the breakdown of relations was inadequate means of communication in areas of disagreement' (DHSS/Islington Borough Personnel Dept, 1978). It is not clear that reorganization has helped the providers talk about the receivers of services any better.

The second problem is that reform operates in a political climate. Any measures have to be made appealing to MPs and to political parties. Events outside the sphere of welfare may nullify the best of intentions. The determination to prune welfare budgets in the wake of the 1975 economic crisis has threatened several projects, including the new Child Benefit scheme, grants for people to improve their homes, and nursery education.

We have already reviewed evidence on the resistance of social problems to the onslaughts of the welfare state. The nature of constraints on welfare effectiveness remains mysterious under an agency analysis. By the way the problem is understood, we are compelled to look for episodic, contingent explanations of failure. Problems such as poverty have a remarkable capacity to endure the assaults of government policies. Such and such a deficiency in the social security system that can be rectified by sensible policy-making might account for piecemeal variations in the level of poverty. There is an uncomfortable feeling of coincidence about an explanation of consistent events that appeals to the repeated accident of various administrative failings.

Neither of these arguments amounts to a knock-down refutation of the institutional account of social problems. They do show that it rests on a view of society that claims there are no fundamental obstacles to the resolution of problems. All that is required is the adaptation of the present set-up. They also make it worthwhile seeking a more comprehensive account. For this we turn to structuralist approaches.

## Structuralist accounts

This approach tends to see the underlying cause of social problems in the way in which society is constituted as a whole. Major barriers lie in the way of satisfactory solutions. This is not to suggest that all recognized problems are insoluble. For example, it would be unwise to claim that it was in principle impossible for British society to take steps to house the 33,750 households applying to local authorities as homeless in 1976 (*Social Trends*, 1979, p. 154) although certainly not all these were in fact satisfactorily housed. Structuralism tends to advance two claims: first that the way in which society is constituted tends to militate against successful resolution of the sum total of serious and recurring recognized problems. Secondly that while certain states of affairs may be recognized as problems by various groups or by official bodies, their continuance may serve the interests of powerful groups.

Thus, the esteem in which private property and access to it through the market is held; the way in which large-spending areas like housing tend to function as economic regulators and thus become vulnerable to interruption for economic reasons unrelated to housing need; and the way in which state provision on demand would threaten the private housing market, all militate against the fortunes of the homeless. They can be provided for, but only in inconvenient and unhappy ways. Moreover, this state of affairs suits an economic system which gives the tone to society. You have to work and pay for what you get.

A perspective that serves as a bridge between institutional reformism and a structural approach is provided by Titmuss's emphasis on the 'diswelfares' of modern society:

for many consumers the (social) services . . . are not essentially benefits . . . at all; they represent partial compensations for disservices, for social costs and social insecurities which are the product of a rapidly changing industrial urban society. They are part of the price we pay to some people for bearing part of the costs of other people's progress: the obsolescence of skills, redundancies, premature retirements, accidents, many categories of disease and handicap, urban blight and slum clearance, smoke pollution and a hundred and one other socially generated disservices

(1968, p. 133).

For Titmuss, this is an argument in favour of social services. He does not consider whether the mechanisms that produce diswelfare are likely to militate against the provision of compensating welfares or outrun the capacity of the state to provide. Marshall comments in an essay reprinted by Butterworth and Holman that 'it identifies the cause of the damage as structural — located in the economy — but does not suggest ways in which social policy itself might induce any remedial structural changes' (1975, p. 42). This confronts us with the essential issue of a structural approach: a structural basis provides a powerful account of the continued existence of problems despite state welfare, but it also suggests that the way in which social policy may overcome obstacles is far from clear.

The third perspective on poverty sees it neither as the result of individual psychological malaise nor as the effect of inefficient agencies, but as the inevitable result of the operation of a particular kind of society. It is important to be clear about the status of this kind of explanation. Structuralists would not deny that agencies are failing to meet need. The essential difference between this view and the institutional view is the reason given why the agencies fail. From a structuralist perspective the reasons are not casual, accidental or contextual: they are built into the very bones of society. The implication is obvious. Without some kind of fundamental change the problem is not going to be solved. Any claim to solve it within the present system is self-contradictory.

Such a view fits in neatly with Vaizey's summary of the facts about poverty:

while the general level of income has risen dramatically since 1900, the spread of incomes has only narrowed at certain times: and there is no serious evidence that the spread has narrowed since 1950. There seems to be some sort of social mechanism which constantly throws out at the bottom . . . a predetermined proportion of poorly paid people (1973).

The problem is to find the mechanism. It's not clear why we can't all become better off. Groups like teachers, coal-miners, policemen and property speculators have achieved substantial rises in living standards since 1950. Is there a convincing reason why this process cannot be generalized?

Most impressive is the fact that we act as if it can. Most definitions of the state agree that governments have a monopoly on the justifiable use of force. The government represents a common interest in law and order and democratic decision making against sectional interest and power. This idea suggests that governments can (if they wish) exercise a degree of control over economic systems. In that case they should be able to do something about poverty.

The view that the government can have a tremendous influence on the economy is accepted all the way across the political spectrum. Free-marketeers on the political right attribute many ills to the state throwing its weight about. 'The result of all this extra state interference financed by taking over 50 per cent of the gross national product in taxation has been . . . rampant stagflation, that is to say stagnation in production and raging inflation which further destroys belief in the future. The moral fibre of our people has been weakened', (R. Boyson, in Butterworth and Holman, 1975, p. 384). The Fabian socialist tradition, to the left, has concerned itself with drawing up manifestos for interventionism to achieve desirable social ends. A good example is Crosland's call for 'a sharper delineation of fundamental objectives, a greater clarity about egalitarian priorities and a stronger determination to achieve them' as he sets out a programme including the redistribution of wealth and the nationalization of development land, (Crosland, 1974). A structural analysis of social problems confronts major traditions in thinking about welfare.

Structural accounts focus on the extent of inequality throughout society. The bland assumption of the 1950s that state welfare had led to a levelling off of social differences has been exploded by so many studies that it is not worth repeating the evidence. (See for instance, Coates and Silburn, 1970, ch. 1; Westergaard and Resler, 1975, pp. 31–7; Royal Commission on the Distribution of Income and Wealth, 1979, p. 75.) Some groups are better paid, housed, educated, and healthier than others. It is the cumulation of all these inequalities in desirable attributes that has led social scientists to talk of differences in chances in life in general being distributed on a class basis. 'To him that hath shall be given . . . .' Stratification has a strong tendency to perpetuate itself from generation to generation. 'Movement up and down the ladder is inhibited by sharp inequalities of opportunity. There is certainly no automatic inheritance of position; but inheritance is a powerful influence on the life-chances of individuals' (Westergaard and Resler, 1975, p. 312).

In a stratified society, the poor simply occupy the bottom rung of the ladder. Holman argues that they carry out three important roles that benefit the rest of society and particularly the most advantaged members.

### Legitimation

The inequality of power and privilege for the rich and of disadvantage and risk for the poor can be simultaneously justified by the idea that the poor are to blame for their own poverty. The feckless poor deserve their condition, and the relative prosperity of the rest of us is a sign of good management rather than good luck. In addition, the image of the shamed scapegoat claimer reinforces and justifies the work system. Piven and Cloward conclude a close analysis of the humiliating way in which relief claimers in the US are treated: 'the main target of these rituals is not the recipient who ordinarily is not of much use as a worker, but the able-bodied poor who remain in the labour market. It is for these people that the spectacle of the degraded pauper is intended' (Piven and Cloward, 1974, p. 173).

### Stabilization

In a major study of social attitudes to inequality, Runciman argued that discontent is linked to expectations rather than to the actual size of the gulf separating different groups in society. Revolution unlike poetry is not wrung from the oppressed by want, but by unsatisfied expectation. If the working class as a whole is split up by the way in which people regard the poor; if as Rhodes Boyson claims 'the reliable and industrious worker looks with irritation and animosity at his idle fellows whom he helps to maintain' (Butterworth and Holman, 1975, p. 382), pressure to change an unequal system is as likely to be reduced as increased by poverty. The poor become scapegoats for their problems and a distraction from the real targets for political action.

*The marginal labour force*

The poor also provide a useful labour force for unpleasant jobs — the night-cleaning of office blocks, bus conductors, labouring and so on. These jobs also predominantly recruit women, migrants and other marginal workers. They will accept low-paid, inconvenient and uncertain work because of their weak position in the labour market. In times of boom, they can be called on to supplement the industrial work force — in slump they tend to be expelled from the country, returned to work in the home or, in the case of the poor, put on relief. The fact that a reserve army of labour is available also weakens the bargaining position of workers generally.

The core of a structuralist approach to poverty is that the poor form an integral part of a social system that serves the interests of the rich and powerful. The existence of the poor helps to keep that system running smoothly. Yet just to show that what is a social problem for some people can serve to benefit other groups in society, by keeping an unequal system going, does not answer some basic questions. How has this situation arisen? Why is it so difficult for governments to do something about poverty? What exactly are the obstacles? There are two kinds of structuralist answer to these questions. I shall call them the political conflict and the marxist view, though they are thoroughly confused in much discussion.

## The conflict view

This approach rests on the idea of an elite group or class that has the power to engineer the consent of the ruled to a social structure that serves elite interests. The ruling class is at the apex of the pyramid, on the top rung of the ladder. It is benefitted by the stratified nature of society. It can also strive to convince the rest that the ladder ought to be there, that its a very good kind of ladder, very easy to climb, and that the lower rungs are quite nice rungs in their way, and thoroughly well suited to those who sit on them.

The trouble is that in a modern democratic society the advantaged, property-owning groups — big buinessmen and so on — do not actually rule as a class. Most of the time they're far too busily absorbed in the innocent and engrossing pursuit of more wealth. So how do they accomplish the trick of getting elected governments to act in their interest, by not getting down to the job of redistributing wealth and income? The problem is made worse by the fact that the trick has to be worked in secret. If the mass of the people found that a government supposed to serve the common interest in fact served a class interest they might justifiably feel their faith had been misplaced. Three explanations of how government is constrained exist.

First, the idea of the elite. It is easy to show that top businessmen, and people who hold key positions in government as politicians and civil servants, the higher judiciary, top-ranking army officers and so on tend to come from similar social and educational backgrounds, (see Westergaard and Resler, 1975, p. 258). For this reason it seems likely that they will have similar attitudes and beliefs and will tend to act to help each other. However, the idea of an elite is inadequate. Labour Governments with determinedly egalitarian manifestos and a powerful mandate have on occasion been elected, for instance in 1924 and 1945 in this country. Why have they not succeeded in getting more radical programmes through?

A second strand to explanation lies in the limits of government action. The argument is that while a government is free in principle to represent the will of the people, in practice it is constrained by the working of the economic system. This operates in at least two ways. First the economic system is international: people buy, sell and invest in a world market. International agencies such as the International Monetary Fund and other powerful nations will tend to bring pressure to bear on any government that seriously challenges business interests. In any case, any capital that can will tend to be invested abroad, where the challenge from government is less.

Secondly, it is hard to see how far governments can go in redistributing without opposing business interests. Taxation of the rich at the rates required to bring about redistribution, with strong anti-avoidance legislation, will kill off the profit motive. A secure and adequate welfare system will erode work incentives. A society which gave people who did not work as much as it gave some (at least) of those who did, yet relied on work (which is not generally regarded as much fun) to provide the necessities of life, would not get very far.

These two kinds of argument can be woven together to give an account of the structural limits to welfare. Yet it is seriously lacking in some important respects. The relationship between business and government looks suspiciously like a conspiracy against the masses. Public conspiracies like the Poulson affair or the Bay of Pigs invasion of Cuba are uncovered from time to time. It seems strange that the total conspiracy of cynicism in high places remains unmasked. Yet the idea that more equality is a practical proposition remains extraordinarily powerful among some academics and politicians.

A third leg to the tripod is provided by the idea of values. The values we are here interested in are shared ideas about the right way for society to be governed and for people to live and relate to each other. The democratic myth — the view that governments are responsive to the will of the electorate and independent of economic interests — has considerable influence. If people tenaciously believe that the state is independent of the class system they're unlikely to see social policy as necessarily linked to the maintenance of that system. Such attitudes disguise the working of elite sympathy and economic constraints on government.

Equally important is the work ethic. The idea that the right means of support is income derived from work is clearly strongly entrenched in our society. The treatment meted out to welfare 'scroungers' by the press amply testifies to this. This value sets close limits to the field of operation of social policy. Complex safeguards have to be built into the system to ensure that unemployed claimers are not better off than they would be in work, and to encourage them to work if at all possible.

Such attitudes constrict the field of acceptable welfare measures in a democratic society. At the same time the viability of highly redistributive welfare, which might challenge them, is weakened. The full extent of stigma — a feeling of shame or humiliation at being on the receiving end of state welfare — is unknown. Evidence exists that at least a quarter of old-age pensioners who fail to take up their SB entitlement do so for this reason, (Ministry of Pensions and National Insurance, 1966, para. 203). Most writers would agree that stigma can only be understood in terms of values rooted in our economic relations. We live in a world where nothing is free (except air) and it is right to pay the price. Free state welfare for the needy is therefore charity and runs the risk of shaming the recipient, because its something for nothing.

The existence of attitudes such as these helps to bolster up the position of the ruling class and impose strict limits to the scope of welfare. It is easy to see how those on the bottom rung of the ladder find the system that offers them poverty acceptable, where democracy masks the constraints on social policy. Similarly, a welfare state which cannot offend the work ethic is unlikely to be able to do a great deal to advance equality. The class system which serves the interests of an elite is perpetuated.

An interesting variant of this kind of approach is presented in

Townsend's master-work. The explanation of poverty is rooted in class relations which affect the 'relationship between the production, distribution and redistribution of resources on the one hand and the creation or sponsorship of styles of living on the other. One governs the resources which come to be in the control of individuals. The other governs the "ordinary". . . expectations . . . the denial or lack of which represents deprivation' (1979, p. 917). It is the interaction between who has what and what everyone is expected to have that accounts for poverty. The concept of class used here is complex, involving both economic power and ideological and cultural leadership. It constitutes a social structure (or rather 'structuration' — the influence of patterns of economic relations on non-economic structure). 'The pattern of their interrelationships reflects and perpetuates the basic value system and not only the economic class structure of society' (p. 91).

What is interesting is that, despite the massive accumulation and intricate analysis of original data, the account of the social outcome of this unequal structure of resources and its legitimation requires development. Resources affect life-styles: but 'society has to . . . integrate its members . . . different institutions, including the Church, the media and various professional associations . . . endeavour to universalize . . . standards . . . it is society which defines the nature and level of the threshold of activities and consumption which it expects its members to attain' (p. 924). The reliance on the reified abstract society which imposes living standards below which the poor fall is not an explanation. Why do people think in a way that allows this imposition? And (more important from a policy studies viewpoint) how does it come about that social practices that fail to eliminate poverty — social policy — are legitimated? From Townsend's perspective these represent a failure in universalization. Yet presumably many people see them as in the common interest. Why is a failure to impose common standards accepted?

These structuralist perspectives require an account of prevailing values governing political action. For these we must turn to a marxist perspective.

## A marxist approach

Marxist approaches to the values that govern democratic political action rest on a materialist method. This stresses the overriding importance of the social relations which people enter into to produce what is necessary to keep society going, in determining all other aspects of society. Because the relationship between humanity and nature — the appropriation of raw materials and their fashioning into manufactured goods to be distributed and consumed — is clearly an essential feature of production, this method has given marxism a central focus on economic and politico-economic areas of social life. However, the basic point of the approach is that society is to be viewed as a totality — an integrated whole — each part of which can only be understood in relation to the others.

The values of political life must be tackled as part and parcel of the rest of social life. Marx argued that the form of state encountered among 'conditions of modern industry' is radically different from that produced by previous social forms. 'The abstraction of the state as such was not born until the modern world, because the abstraction of private life was not created until modern times. The abstraction of the political state is a modern product' (Marx, 1975, p. 90). The peculiarity of the capitalist market system is that people's economic relations become autonomous from the body of society. In prior social forms, the dominant kind of social relationship had been between individuals in such roles as feudal serfs, barons, slave-owners, slaves. These roles have in-built political as well as economic and social aspects. A slave has no rights, is removed from politics: a serf is tied to the lord in a complex structure of relations, economic, political, juridic and military. With the advent of the market in labour, the individual is freed, as it were, from the chains of feudalism, to labour where he will for the best price he can get. Employers hire through unconstrained choice. Commerce is unfettered by the pre-existing obligations and restrictions. The relations of people to the material necessities of life in a complex structure of rights and obligations were transformed by the new ideology of goods as alienable private property, which could embody both accumulated and deployed wealth. The location of the individual in a stable and hierarchical world-order evolved into the status of the free person, responsible principally to self and immediate family, and owed no obligation. The dire necessity of freedom corresponded to a structure of choices appropriate to the wage-labour system.

As the market develops, social relations become increasingly a matter of individual will constrained only by inhuman economic forces: the impersonal process that Adam Smith conceptualized as the 'hidden hand' of the market. The result of this process taken to its logical conclusion is the uncaring pursuit of self-interest — the war of each against all that underlay Hobbes's contemporary analysis. Individuals may choose to band together in groups for mutual protection in areas where their separate interests overlap — price-fixing, labour unions, consumer associations and so on. Each of these institutions, however, is dominated by the theme of mutuality of self-interest, and contains no principle of unity beyond it.

The will of self-interest is a private will. The overt intermingling of structural political power with the religious, economic, social, military and legal ties of feudalism recedes, although institutions sedimented in culture may continue to play a powerful role. Of most importance is respect for the family, an organizing principle of peculiar defensive strength that retains a vital role as a bastion of care. Minor areas are the formal endurance of church and monarchy.

Corresponding to the transformation in economic relations is a reordering of political relations — the abstraction of political life from the newly 'privatized' economic realm to which Marx refers. The advent of democratic forms as individuals separated from the politicized roles of feudalism demanded entrance to government presses the question: how is the role of the abstract state to be understood?

A democratic state must function as overriding power-holder in society, and reflect common (or at least majority) interest. In this sense it is set against the individualist sphere of the market, and its principles are other: a centre of power as opposed to a framework of conflict; a system of common interest as against the struggle of private interests. If the duality of society is taken at face value, strict limits to the legitimate activity of the state in capitalist society appear. The only common interest that can be reconciled with the system of private interest is private interest writ large: the role of the state is to protect the structure of private interests that is the market. The integrity of this system demands non-intervention. The political mandate becomes the preservation of the system as a whole: the minimalist role of guaranteeing the rule of law and the enforcement of contract inherent in the notion of private property, with perhaps a little paternalist welfare for the incompetent at the margins of the system.

Such a *laissez-faire* ideal has never been realized. The progress of capitalism has led to state intervention on an ever-increasing scale. Built into the conception of legitimacy sketched out above is the justification of state action which is seen to buttress the market, resolve crisis and aid growth. The inroads of state on market autonomy require apology in relation to these larger goals. For much of social welfare this is readily provided: health services, education, housing and social security can be seen as helping to produce a contented, healthy and well-trained workforce, able to pursue individual interest more effectively and permit the system of self-interest to achieve ever greater mutual success. If no such justification is available, social policy must fight an uphill struggle against the ideas about the role of the state inherent in its position in capitalist society. These prove major obstacles in the struggle of progressive working-class groups to achieve recognition of their interests. Thus the abstraction of state from market imposes a particular tendency on its capacity to recognize issues as meriting public policy, and on the kind of action that tends to be seen as legitimate. This limit derives from the ideology of the state nourished by a market system.

A second ideological influence exists. The abstraction of the public sphere of the state from the private sphere of the market is parallelled by a further distinction within the depoliticized economic realm. Archetypically, this is the anarchic interaction of individuals in the pursuit of private interest. It contains, however, a fundamental division when viewed from an alternative standpoint. Society may be seen not from the standpoint of the individual, but holistically, as an unconscious collective enterprise. In the capitalist market, people interact through industrial undertakings to produce a greater and greater product each year. Investment of wealth in production produces profits which further expand the system: capitalism is dynamic.

> The bourgeoisie, during its rule of scarce 100 years, has created more . . . colossal productive forces than all preceding generations together. Subjection of nature's forces to man, machinery, application of chemistry to industry and agriculture, steam-navigation, railways, electric telegraphs, clearing of whole continents for cultivation, canalization of rivers, whole populations conjured out of the ground — what earlier century had even a presentiment that such productive forces slumbered in the lap of social labour?
>
> (Marx and Engels, 1972, p. 37)

What Marx would have made of North Sea oil, Voyager or World War III we can only guess.

Marx analysed this dynamism in terms of a theory of surplus. The product of society as a whole increases because capitalists are able to extract unpaid labour from the workforce. His theory suggests that this proceeds not from fraud or capitalist conspiracy, but from the fact of free market exchange. He argues that under normal circumstances the value of the amount of goods a given amount of work at an appropriate technological level produces exceeds the price of that work. Society may be analytically divided into two groups: capital and labour. In an objective sense these groups have opposed interests: the existence of the one depends on the exploitation of the labour of the other.

This objective viewpoint is not conveniently available to the individual member of society. The market system itself obscures the relations of production. The social element disappears, screened out by the focus on the motive-force of individual interest:

> where commodity production prevails, relations between persons really do take the form of relations between things .... A moment's consideration of the defining relations of capitalist society — capitalist/worker, producer-of-/consumer-of-commodities is enough to verify this. For the capitalist, the worker exists only as labour-power, for the worker, the capitalist only as capital. For the consumer, the producer is commodities, and for the producer, the consumer is money
>
> (Geras, 1972, p. 293).

The collective viewpoint is confused by the equation of individual interest with money — with command over resources, which in this society take the form of commodities. This reduces relations with others to relationships with things with a money-value. Issues tend to be recognized from a standpoint which takes the individual perspective of the market for granted. A powerful ideological tendency acts to hinder people realizing their interests as class interests. Issues again tend to be thought about in a way that takes the institutions of capitalism and the limited role of the state in relation to them as a given. This is not to deny that collective interest can be recognized. However, it does point to the ideological bias against seeing mutual interest as anything more than a contingent coincidence of individual interest. Class action in pursuit of common interest is borne down, not only by the superior physical power of capital that we pointed to in the discussion of political conflict theory, but also by the countervailing strength of this ideology.

Marxism stresses the complexity of capitalist society in the limits it lays down for state action. Citizens are likely to think about the issues over which social policy is made in a constraining way. The dominance of market relations separates the political from the economic and characterizes interest as individual. In addition, the role of people in the collective reproduction of society and the structural conflict of interests inherent in that role is confused. The interests that are brought to the state and inform the framework of democratic political action are likely to take the market system, and its inequalities, for granted.

This is not to claim that values that serve capitalism are dominant *because* they serve capitalism. Rather it is to suggest that such values are part and parcel of that form of society. Society is a collective human production. To describe a social form as a whole is to presuppose that the values relevant to the element that gives it its character (from this viewpoint, economic relations) are dominant. This does not imply that such values form an unbreakable determination of human action. The recognition of how current beliefs and the structures that constitute their correlative exercise power sets the stage for the discussion of social response (see, for example, Miliband, 1977, chapter 6, or Corrigan and Leonard, 1978, pp. 143–56).

In this way structuralist accounts of welfare issues seem best able to explain the central paradox of the welfare state — that social services seem not to solve social problems, but to contain, rather than obliterate them. However, the mere appeal of an explanation is not a convincing ground for adopting it. Each of the three approaches reviewed suggests a different characterization of 'the poor'. From the individualist perspective, they are those with maladaptive attributes. From the reformist perspective, they are unlucky, on the receiving end of social mechanisms that need government intervention, or institutions that require change. From the structuralist perspective, they are members of groups in a weak bargaining position, because their work or their non-working status is little valued in the ideology of a particular social whole.

Each account also contains a different recipe for action. Individualist accounts demand that we concentrate attention on changing individuals. Agency accounts suggest that we should tinker with the social services to find a better approach. Structural accounts claim the root of the problem lies with the social system. We should encourage the tendencies to radical change in society. How to choose?

## The choice between frameworks

First, it seems reasonable to claim that individualist approaches square least well with the facts. Attempts to account for poverty by some factor peculiar to the poor such as hereditary membership of a 'problem family' or participation in the culture that generates a 'cycle of deprivation' cannot explain the imperfect fit between the relevant characteristic and the problem. Many poor people do not share the quality, many who display it are not poor. However, no such convenient empirical test for the other two approaches exists.

It might be thought that a technique loosely analogous to experiments in natural science would solve the problem. We can see if our explanation is correct by finding out if it works in practice. This idea lay behind the explosion of 'action-research' projects in the late 1960s and early 1970s. Action research in this sense is the monitoring of the effectiveness of a bit of social policy (the action) by seeing if it produces the result you want when tried out (the research). An example is the attempt to find new ways of combatting urban deprivation through Community Development Projects.

There are two difficulties. First as Marris points out 'social policy cannot avoid questions of power and interest', (Jones *et al.*, 1974, p. 250). Even if the plan works, so long as it harms the interests of powerful groups (and if it is redistributive, it will) it is a political rather than a scientific question whether it gets put into practice. Rein points to an even more fundamental problem (1977, ch. 2). Society is just not like the natural world. It consists of people who have free wills. Just because a certain input — perhaps a particular reform of SB — produced a certain output — say higher take-up of the benefit — doesn't mean it's going to do so next time round. People can change their minds and act differently.

We are left with a choice between structural and institutional approaches that rests on plausibility and judgement. The different approaches involve fundamentally different ways of looking at society, at what governments can and should do and how people see the welfare state. Institutional reformism suggests greater freedom of action for the government and a much more optimistic outlook on the possibility of resolving problems. Structuralism stresses the class divisions in society. Social problems involve society as a whole. The group directly affected is the symptom, not the cause. The state is part of society, and the way in which society is made up crucially affects how far governments can go in tackling problems.

The next chapter projects our problem to a more general level, by considering the abstract theorizing of philosophers, statesmen and political economists about the welfare state as a form of society seen in the span of history, rather than the immediate practical problems that confront those concerned with running it.

# 3

# Normative theories of the welfare state I — Individualism and reformism.

In these chapters we consider the range of available theories of the welfare state as a whole, using a classification broadly similar to our treatment of theories of social issues. Discussion of the nature and desirability of state welfare at this level of generality presupposes an account of welfare — of what serves human interests. It also involves the theorizing of how economic and political systems work to link social action to anticipated effects in a particular form of society. We shall argue that the overall perspectives of individualism, reformism and structuralism serve to integrate different accounts of human interests, and of economic and political systems. These perspectives in turn depend on presuppositions of method — of how to start on the task of understanding the welfare state. The problem of choosing between methods forms the subject of chapter five. Since we wish to review a comprehensive range of theory in brief compass, we shall attempt to mention salient positions using the statements of major figures as illustration, rather than to discuss all significant writers on the subject.

George and Wilding (1976) provide perhaps the most useful (and certainly the most comprehensive) guide to normative theory of state welfare. Their framework groups writers into four categories: anti-collectivists, who oppose the interventionist state; reluctant collectivists, who are torn between suspicion of centralized authority and recognition of the need for economic planning and social reform; fabian or reformist socialists; and marxist socialists. Each group represents a loose constellation of values (that specify the goals of social action) and theories (that give an account of how state and economy work). Thus anti-collectivism is an association of concern for liberty, inequality and competition with consensus political and *laissez-faire* economic theory.

This approach may be criticized in detail and in method. In detail: the particular categories and the choice of representative individuals may be questioned. Thus Pinker (1979, p. 239) argues that George and Wilding exaggerate the caution with which Beveridge and

Galbraith viewed collectivism. Laski, Strachey and Miliband are not representative of modern marxist thought. Indeed one recent writer on the state (Therborn, 1978 p. 27) describes Miliband's early work on the state as completely bypassing the problem of political organization.

In method: the union of values and descriptive theory appears to be more than the contingent matter these writers imply. It is hard to see how Friedman, having analysed society into atomic individuals and their external economic relations, could suggest any other human interest than the integrity of individualism (in other words, liberty) and any other role for the state than the preservation of that individualism through a minimum of interference. The problems that arise from lack of consideration of the way in which methodological standpoint unites values and explanation are clearest in George and Wilding's account of marxism. The radical distinction between the idealist approach of most other theory and the materialist basis of marxist analysis is glossed over. We hope to sidestep the first kind of difficulty by the use of particular writers simply to illustrate more general argument, and to clarify the relation between presuppositions of method, and the theoretical and ideological perspectives of the various writers. The issue of method is the lynchpin of our approach. We now discuss individualist, reformist and structuralist approaches to the welfare state.

## Individualism

The variety of interpretations of this concept are well analysed by Lukes (1973). For our purposes it underlies the view that holds collective action through the state in the regulation of economic system, in particular for welfare ends but also as part of more general management, to be undesirable, at any rate above a certain minimum level. Three kinds of arguments need to be considered: those based on the primacy of individual liberty; those that stem from a rigorous methodological individualism; and those that base themselves on contingent claims about people's desires and motives.

## Friedman on liberty

The first approach finds its most recent forthright statement in Friedman (1962). 'This book's . . . major theme is the role of competitive capitalism — the organization of the bulk of economic activity through private enterprise operating in a free market — as a system of economic freedom, and a necessary condition for political freedom' (p. 4). The problem of modern society is 'how to coordinate the economic activities of large numbers of people' (p. 12). Friedman argues that this is possible only through two methods — coercion 'the technique of the army and the modern totalitarian state' and voluntary cooperation which will tend to take place when people see that a transaction is to their mutual advantage. If cooperation without coercion can be achieved, it is through an unfettered 'free private-enterprise exchange economy'. Friedman states (but does not argue) the idea that freedom is 'an end in itself' (p. 8 — see also p. 12).

State interference must be kept to a minimum. There are in fact three plausible roles for government: the maintenance of law and order and the general framework of 'rules of the game' (p. 27); the mitigation of the overspill of neighbourhood effects (where 'the activities of one party have repercussions for others for which it is not feasible to charge or recompense them' (p. 30); and paternalistic provision for the irresponsible, especially children and idiots (pp. 33–4). State action beyond these limits involves unjustifiable coercion.

Friedman's argument is characterized by down to earth practicality. The justifications for state activity are discussed on a commonsense basis — quite where the line is drawn between the irresponsible and the free citizens, or how far the government should go in controlling pollution are issues to be resolved by practical argument, and by the circumstances of particular cases. It should be noted, however, that Friedman is alive to the issue that neighbourhood effects might well serve as justification, in practice, for a high level of intervention. Who can draw limits to how far the transactions of A and B have unaccounted repercussions for C or even Z? He points out that government action to overcome neighbourhood effects is likely to itself create further neighbourhood effects. Thus the Clean Air Act of 1956 may well save some 1,000 lives a year in Greater London (the number of deaths plausibly attributable to smog — see Hall *et al.*' 1975, p. 406). Evidence assembled by Social Audit indicates that 'the quality of air near Coalite plants is poor and may well contribute to ill-health' (Social Audit, 1974, p. 39). Similarly it has been argued that planning controls on office building in London in the late 1960s acted against the common interest by inflating the market value of existing premises and diverting capital from productive industry to speculative development. Thus property formed the fastest growing sector of pension fund investment between 1960 and 1972, expanding by a factor of four when the funds as a whole increased by a factor of less than three (Counter Information Service, 1976, pp. 8–9).

Friedman's willingness to consider the circumstances of instances makes his book a commonsense counterpart to the rigorous a priori argument of Nozick (1974).

Nozick's view is that 'a minimal state limited to the narrow functions of protection against force, theft, fraud, enforcement of contracts and so on is justified; that any more extensive state will violate people's rights not to be forced to do certain things, and is unjustified; and that the minimal state is inspiring as well as right' (quoted in Lukes, 1977, pp. 191–2).

This claim rests on an argument that opposed an 'entitlement' to an 'end-state' theory of justice. It is just that people should have what they are entitled to — namely what they have 'mixed their labour with' (worked to produce) and what they gain through free gift or voluntary exchange. To deprive some people of their entitlements in order to transfer them to others is unfair, however much one desires the end-state of a particular distribution. State welfare intervention is illicit.

Lukes points out that this argument rests on a view of the world that is 'radically pre-sociological, without social structure, or social and cultural determinants of and constraints upon the voluntary acts and exchanges of its component individuals' (1977, p. 194), in short, an abstracted individualism. MacPherson points out that the social structure of capitalism imposes obvious restrictions on the free contracts a rational person will make. The separation of labour from the means of production through private ownership radically limits access to what people need to use in order to survive. Social structure contains an inequity of power, that Friedman ignores. (1968, p. 98). It is also hard to see how entitlement to the produce of labour is to be apportioned by the market. Many people interact to get North Sea oil into petrol tanks. It is not clear that the rewards paid, for example to divers (who also enjoy preferential tax arrangements — see Hansard, *Written Answers* Vol. 943 col. 259) and forecourt attendants correspond to contributions to that effort, but rather to factors like the relative demand for their labour. In any case, the social factors that Nozick omits are likely to enter into anyone's judgement of contribution. Thus Coates and Silburn point to evidence that dissatisfaction with reward is not evenly spread among the working class, and that a sense of exploitation is associated with factors including feelings of class solidarity and general awareness of the extent of social inequality (1970, pp. 153–5).

The nub of Friedman's formal argument is the idea that the free coordination of human activity may be achieved through the motive of self-interest, and that this may be achieved in an ideal typical market where people will exchange when it suits them. This argument implies an approach to political relations that stresses consensus and an approach to economic relations that stresses the idea of balance or equilibrium.

There is no essential conflict of interests in free market capitalism, because individual actions in the pursuit of self-interest can be complementary:

> The US has continued to progress; its citizens have become better fed, better clothed, better housed and better transported; . . . All this has been the product of the initiative and the drive of individuals cooperating through the free market . . . . The central defect of (government) measures is that . . . they fail to resolve what is supposedly a conflict of interests . . . not by establishing a framework that will eliminate the conflict . . . but by forcing people to act against their own interests
>
> (p. 200).

Political intervention is itself the source not the symptom, of conflict: it 'tends to strain the cohesion essential for a stable society' (p. 23).

The argument for the stability of the free market economic system is not directly stated (presumably because Friedman recognizes no evidence of instability), but is implied in the provision of alternative accounts of the generation of recurring social problems and economic malaise. These are due to the interventions of 'men of good intentions and good will who threaten to reform us'. On pages 197–9 a summary of the counterproductive effects of progressive income tax, monetary reform, housing programmes, social security legislation, the protection of labour unions and other measures is presented. No overall theory of the causes of recognized social problems as such emerges. However, the attribution of juvenile delinquency to problem families (p. 180), the assertion that a large part of inequality results from differences in endowment of human capacities (p. 163) and the assertion that qualities recognized as meritorious and 'deserving' owe much to genetic inheritance (p. 166) are reminiscent of the individualist accounts discussed in chapter 2. It is difficult to see how else someone who regards the free market as a successful balance of interests could account for situations in which interest is not served. It is symptomatic of Friedman's individualism that the great depression is seen primarily in psychological terms as 'the most severe banking panic in American history' and thus as needlessly exacerbated by the failure of a state agency (the Federal Reserve Board) to act to restore confidence in the fiscal system.

The clearest expression of the limitations of Friedman's idea of the individual lies in his lack of any notion of structural power. Thus freedom is defined — negatively — as the absence of coercion. 'Political freedom means the absence of coercion on man by his fellow men — the fundamental threat to freedom is the power to coerce by monarch, dictator, oligarchy or momentary majority' (p. 15). The role of government is 'to prevent the coercion of one individual by another' (p. 27). The idea that economic transactions are voluntary if people are free to enter 'any particular exchange' has already been mentioned (ch. 1). Any idea of power as an aspect of social structure rather than of the individual or group is absent. The social relations of private property and market exchange force people to engage in the latter to get access to the former to meet their needs. This restriction on freedom is unaccounted in Friedman's framework. Similarly, the way in which the historical development of social structures influences their stability cannot be introduced. Stability to Friedman is simply an abstracted relation between people. There is no room for social structure as constraining the individual.

## Hayek: the pure form of individualism

The development of Hayek's thought (and jargon) forms a fascinating field of study in itself. For our purposes, however, the critique of the modern state founded in a formal methodological individualism constitutes a continuing theme. The main developments of the theory are four: Hayek's later work sets his analysis of society in a framework of the historical development of human civilization (a panorama of history equivalent in scale to marxism), and not a simple appeal to the value of liberty; this is allied to a theory of human progress through confrontation with the challenge of the unintended consequences of human action (1979, epilogue); state welfare is treated more sympathetically; and the analysis of basic concepts (rules, law, social justice, social order, etc.) becomes ever more rigorous.

For our purposes the essential theme is individualism, stated in the early essays (1949, p. 6) as

primarily a theory of society, an attempt to understand the forces which determine the social life of man . . . this argument is directed against the properly collectivist theories of society which pretend to be able directly to comprehend social wholes . . . as entities *sui generis* which exist independently of the individuals who compose them.

This critique of collectivism in social theory rests on the 'indisputable intellectual fact . . . that man cannot know more than a tiny part of society' (1949, p. 14). If we accept this proposition, Hayek's argument that it is best not to meddle where you don't know becomes persuasive. 'In a Great Society in which the individuals are to be free to use their own knowledge for their own purposes, the general welfare at which government ought to aim cannot consist of the sum of particular satisfactions of the several individuals for the simple reason that neither those nor all the circumstances determining them can be known to government or anyone else' (1976, p. 2). The outcome is on the one hand a negative appraisal of human rules for social organization and on the other a positive respect for the spontaneous and uncomprehended development of social order: 'So long as men are not omniscient, the only way in which freedom can be given to the individual is by such general rules to delimit the sphere of action in which the decision is his' (1949, p. 19).

It can never be advantageous to supplement the rules governing a spontaneous order by isolated and subsidiary commands . . . this is the gist of the argument against 'interference' or 'intervention' in the market order . . . The spontaneous order arising from each element balancing all the various factors operating on it . . . will be destroyed if some of the actions are determined by another agency on the basis of different knowledge and in the service of different ends

(1972, p. 51).

The conclusion is a subtle and powerful critique of state welfare as fundamentally wrong-headed. Since society cannot be known as a whole by any individual, the concept of social justice is only meaningful in a negative sense, in terms of the application of equal rules to everyone across the board (1976, p. 97). Any attempt to use social justice as a justification for interference within economic relationships rather than in the construction of a common framework for those relationships is likely to cause confusion. It is in principle not possible to know what the results of interference in the balance of a spontaneous order will be since it consists in an incomprehensible multitude of interacting individual relationships.

Hayek betrays a similar concern that society should achieve human freedom to that of Friedman. This however is interwoven with an explicit concern for human welfare. Individualism is defined (1949, p. 20) as: 'the endeavour to make man by the pursuit of his interest to contribute as much as possible to the needs of other men'; a minimum of government action in the utopia 'Great Society' (1976, p. 2) will secure: 'conditions in which individuals and small groups will have favourable opportunities of mutually providing for their respective needs'. The rigorous individualist claim that social planning and economic management is logically impossible is paralleled by enthusiasm for the free market: 'only because the market induces every individual to use his unique knowledge of particular opportunities and possibilities for his purpose can an overall order be achieved that uses in its totality the dispersed knowledge which is not available as a whole to anybody' (1968, p. 30). This argument is at once more subtle and more powerful than that of Friedman. The market is not only the sole route to freedom: it is also the best route to welfare, and if you respond by appeals to social justice as a basis for intervention and management, you're talking (literally) nonsense. Elsewhere Hayek argues that such nonsense is dangerous: the idea that 'the same representative body lays down the rules of just conduct necessarily leads to the gradual transformation of the spontaneous order of a free society into a totalitarian order' (1972, p. 2).

In a similar vein to Friedman, Hayek countenances the resolution of neighbourhood overspill (1979, p. 43) and the provision of defence and security (p. 54) as legitimate roles of the state. Surprisingly he is prepared to go further in the sphere of welfare. He argues for redistribution to 'those who cannot make their living in the market, such as the sick, the old, the physically or mentally defective, the widows and orphans — that is all people suffering from adverse conditions which may affect anyone and against which most individuals cannot make adequate provision' (pp. 54–5). This is the thin end of a fat wedge.

Assessment of Hayek's argument must ultimately rest on discussion of the individualism of method on which it is based. The essence of the argument is that since (a) society consists of people and people are individuals and (b) an individual can only know so much and certainly not all of society, (c) society cannot be known. Therefore, on the negative side, (d) talk of the management of society by the state rests on a mistake, and it is not possible to apply judgements (such as that the modern British welfare system is just or unjust) to society as a whole. On the positive side, (e) the free market leads to the best possible coordination of resources. However, it seems that none of the last three points follow from the preceding statements.

Thus Mill presents an individualist perspective: 'human beings in society have no properties but those which are derived from, and may be resolved into, the laws of nature of individual man' (1846, vol. 2, p. 543). This, however, is a prelude to the discussion of all social phenomena 'in terms of facts about individuals', including their consciousness of society, rather than the assertion of the inscrutability of society — see, for example, the discussion of Political Economy (pp. 576–8). Lukes (1970) gives typically lucid discussion of individualism of method. If the point is that social phenomena are to be analysed in terms of the individual's perception and conception of them and this includes ideas about social relations, as in Mill's version, it is hard to see what the particular contribution of the doctrine is. If a stronger version, that concepts referring to collectivities are meaningless, is advanced (and this seems to be Hayek's view) the doctrine suggests rigid restrictions on explanation. Are these justified? Certainly in everyday social practice we seem to have no difficulty in using collective concepts. Consider the shared social meanings that constitute the authority of a judge or the process of trial by jury, for example. Lukes points out that such ideas, in practice, may well be more readily comprehensible than the individualist motives of the criminal (1970, p. 80).

The individualist constraint on explanation seems an unnecessary hindrance. Let us consider two concepts — power and legitimation.

From an individualist standpoint, power has to be understood in terms of the relations of particular actions. This may be plausible in consideration of a soldier coming at you with a fixed bayonet. However, in most social settings the power of, for example, the police (and, more so, the environmental health officer) is to do with shared values, in this case, respect for civil authority and the idea that law and order represents a common interest, as much as it is to do with the coercive ability of big boots and the apparatus of the law. A strict individualist interpretation would seem, if it is to have any point, to restrict us to the latter account.

Similarly a discussion of the power of child care officers (as they then were) over their clients concludes:

The coercive aspects of the casework relationship are not . . . due to

the lack of professional training or the personalities of the officers
. . . . The coercion stems from the . . . position of the agencies
which gives them enormous power over clients. Child care officers
are authority figures.

(Handler, 1968, p. 487).

Authority results not simply from the capacity of social workers to do
things to people they don't want (like threaten to take children away
from their home) but also from the expectations and values attached to
their social role.

It seems that the legitimacy of a particular form of society rests (at
least) on the fact that considerable numbers of its members have
similar favourable beliefs about it, and that this shared opinion
contributes to the formation of institutions which socialize the young,
incorporate or control deviants and generally contribute to the continuance of that social order. A strict individualist would be left to
observe these events without being able to devise a conceptual structure to link them together.

The individualist restriction on the construction of theories about
society seems an unnecessary encumbrance. We do try to understand
society. The point, however, that social theory can never attain cer-
tainty is well made. The application of ideas in this area is subject to
irresoluble dispute. To deny any place for politics on these grounds
seems a counsel of despair.

## Practical preferences: the Institute Of Economic Affairs

The third apology for free market capitalism rests its case on empirical
evidence rather than theoretical analysis. This approach is well illustrated in the work of the Institute for Economic Affairs. Practical
argument is intertwined with the assertion of values. The general
editor of the IEA's influential Hobart paper series writes
(Hutchinson, 1970, p. 10):

a distinguishing characteristic of the series and the main thrust of
the Hobart attack consists in advocating and advancing the use of
price and market mechanisms and competitive forces, based on an
underlying philosophy which starts from a strong preference for
the decentralization of initiative and for the revival or extension of
freedom of choice for individuals as buyers and sellers or
consumers and producers.

In practice this philosophy lies concealed behind detailed micro-economic analyses ranging from airport location to advertising, from negative income tax to the national health service, from libraries to land. These discussions may be distinguished from the analytic arguments of Friedman and Hayek by their stress on contingent factors — particularly the inefficiency of state provision and the claim that most people don't want it. A detailed critique of the IEA arguments is provided in Collard (1968) and a more sympathetic appraisal in Judge (1979).

The inefficiency argument is well put by Seldon, the IEA's editorial director (1978a). The argument in brief is that state provision is only necessary in the case of public goods which have 'the essential characteristic . . . that they cannot be refused to people who refuse to pay and who would otherwise have a "free ride" if they were not required to pay' (p. 17). Thus national 'defence' protects (?) all citizens regardless of who actually pays for it; pollution control benefits everyone whoever provides it. In these cases, were provision to be made through a free market, people who had any sense would not contribute, secure in the knowledge that action by someone else would inadvertently serve their interests. Coercion by the state is therefore justified.

However, only about a third of British state expenditure is on such services. In all other cases, Seldon argues, it is more efficient to charge for services through a market system since this provides more revenue (people will pay more if they can see what they're getting for their money); it enhances consumer sovereignty since people will have real choices between alternative suppliers; and it reduces the unnecessary expense and ill-feeling of tax collection. Leaving aside the question of whether the last advantage is outweighed by the unnecessary expense and ill-feeling of fee collection, these arguments, if used with moderation, have some force. They are backed up by a circumstantial account of the special interests and mistakes that have given rise to the modern bloated state.

The argument that many people don't really want state welfare is put by Harris (IEA General Director) and Seldon (1979). This book discussed the responses obtained in a series of sample surveys over the period 1963–78. The most striking finding is that in the most recent survey some 60 per cent of respondents favoured the idea that individuals should be allowed to contract out of state health and education provision and seek salvation in the private market (pp. 50 and 53).

The methodology of the surveys has been repeatedly questioned (by, for example, Townsend, Crossman and Forsyth — see Harris and Seldon, 1979, pp. 16 and 103). In particular, the phrasing of some questions seems restrictive. The issue that concerns us here is where exactly such pragmatic arguments take us in normative theory of the welfare state. It may or may not be the case that free market services would be more cost-effective, people would be prepared to pay more through the market than through taxation, and that people would by and large prefer such a system. In fact evidence on none of these points is as conclusive as the IEA claims. Comparative work may well indicate that free market services are less cost-effective (see Titmuss, 1973, pp. 177–8); the problem of how to make the good health and employment risks subsidize the bad ones becomes doubly pressing if people pay for what they get (Titmuss, 1974, pp. 96–9) and some evidence suggests a high level of satisfaction with state welfare services (Abrams, 1973, p. 43). In addition, several writers argue that markets impose additional unaccounted costs, such as the stigma accompanying inability to pay (Titmuss, 1974, ch. 3).

The point about the IEA analysis is that such weight is placed on consumer opinion. Issues of false consciousness — of whether people are the best judges of their own interests — or the extent to which participation in a market society may mould people's views on the best ways to pay for welfare do not arise. In this the implications of a purely individualist approach to liberty that rests on the ideal of the unconstrained person are apparent. In addition, there may be an element of circularity in arguments for the extension of free markets that rule out of consideration social costs that cannot be accounted in such a system.

The majority may support free market health care. Subservience to their interests may be deleterious to those of the small unhealthy minority who would be faced with high bills. Since the cost of health care rises with age (costs to the NHS of those aged over 75 were estimated at an average of £400 a head, as against £95 for the population at large in 1975–6, *Social Trends* 1979, p. 143) we may wonder how far the elderly infirm and similar 'bad risks' would be able to get satisfactory free market health insurance cover.

The practical arguments incorporate micro-economic and micro-political analysis into the assertion of values that are broadly similar to those of Hayek and Friedman:

> The failure of the half-century experiment in state control over welfare is now making it politically profitable for new policies that

will win support by returning to the sovereign people their freedom to spend their own money on education, medicine and other services of their choice

(Harris and Seldon 1979, pp. 199–200).

The goal is freedom as choice. Seldon's critique of welfarism boils down to the statement (1978a, p. 59) 'you pays your taxes but you gets no choice'. This notion of choice corresponds to Friedman's ideal of the uncoerced individual.

All three approaches detailed above rest on an individualism that links free market and freedom and leads to the conclusion that freedom of individual action is the ultimate goal of society. Since there is nothing in the social world but individuals and since no obstacles to the recognition or realization of their interests in commercial inter-action are admitted, it is hard to see what could count as common interest other than non-interference — the absence of coercion. The free market will achieve a timeless balance and a conflict of interests at the political level is unnecessary. One is reminded of Veblen's satirical characterization of this concept of a person as:

a lightening calculator of pleasures and pains who oscillates like a homogenous globule of desire of happiness under the impulse of stimuli . . . self-imposed in elemental space, he spins symmetrically about his own spiritual axis, until the parallellogram of forces bears down on him, whereupon he follows the line of the resultant . . .

(quoted in Lukes, 1973, pp. 139–40).

The absence of any idea of social structure — the sumtotal of relations — acting to mould motives or influencing chances in life, means that the origin of problems must lie with the individual. This conclusion is given an added twist by the assertion of Friedman and Hayek that well-intentioned government action will only make things worse. The denial of the categories of ideology and of any significance to the collective render this perspective pre-sociological.

Next we move beyond 'individualist' theories of the welfare state to two groups of theories that consider society and the way it is organized as producing both collectivities of interest and problems for its members. First we examine some examples of the approach that suggests problems may be resolved by institutional change within the overall structure of democratic welfare capitalism.

## Reformist approaches to state welfare

A reformist approach is one based on a theory that suggests problems are soluble by action within the existing structures of the welfare state. This presupposes theories about these structures and how they relate to problems. The category covers a wide and varied field of writers. As we have argued earlier (ch. 2) academic discussion of social policy in the dominant tradition that takes the 'perspective of the state' tends to fall within it. However it also includes other writers whose central concern has been wider than social policy. We shall discuss four approaches: the reluctant interventionism of Keynes and Beveridge; normative consensus exemplified by Tawney and Titmuss; the revisionist socialism of Crosland and Donnison and the critical political economy of Galbraith. These cover a range of work that may be classified in several ways. For example, the second and third groups may be amalgamated as Fabians (George and Wilding, 1976 ch. 4). This however lays us open to the problems pointed out by Trotsky when he observed unkindly that the distinctive feature of Fabianism was that it was 'the most boring form of intellectual creation' (Deutscher, 1964, p. 204). More generally, Fabianism represents a fluid and varied tradition rather than a rigorous school of thought.

Similarly, the economic foundations of Galbraith's analysis may be seen as marking him off as a critic of advanced capitalism, rather than of specific political or social relations. This obscures the essential feature linking his perspective to that of the other writers. Although he claims that the problems of modern society are formidable and the outcome of the working of major institutions, the thrust of his argument is an appeal to resolve them by determined action within existing structures.

The common standpoint is an idealist approach to the analysis of society. This has two aspects: the view that society consists of a plurality of structures or institutions united by a relatively weak linkage, so that one may be changed without major repercussions for others; and the view that change is to be achieved through change in convictions. These rest on the notion that social reality ultimately rests on ideas — the collective motivations, aspirations, norms and values of its members. Piecemeal change through the creation of motives by intellectual conviction is possible because the make-up of society is constituted through the bundle of ideas governing institutions that exists in peoples minds. If the structure of ideas can be changed, it is in principle possible to reorganize society appropriately.

This standpoint has room for the collective creation of ideologies as structures of ideas that may have a certain power. If people believe shop-lifting is wrong they will tend to uphold the institutions of trial and punishment. Thus power may rest on a basis beyond the individual. Both consensus and conflict views of political relations and disequilibrium and equilibrium views of economic relations are compatible with it, though there seems to be no recent example of a writer on state welfare who is not an individualist who holds the view that capitalism left to itself is a stable economic system. The idealist basis ensures that political conflict and economic problems are subject to mitigation by conscious action through the state. This school provides a powerful foundation for proponents of state welfare in the service of human interest.

The opposing perspective, materialism, tends to see society as a totality of relations, strongly influenced by brute facts of human existence beyond conscious control. These facts stamp a consistent character on the whole of society. This leads to a strong structural account of the genesis of problems, a tendency to deny the possibility of resolving them within the social whole in which they originate, and the linkage of accounts of interest at economic and political levels into a unity. Change in the system as a whole is required to solve problems. The difference between these two perspectives is contained in the respective slogans, 'If you don't think, you can't eat!' and 'If you don't eat, you can't think!' recommending different views on the primacy of ideas and material production relations in the continuance of civilization.

The link between idealism and reformism is that of a sufficient but not necessary condition. The view that society is to be understood at the level of ideas and to be changed by change in ideas could as well lead to an advocacy of national or sectional interest as of welfare, of totalitarianism as of democracy, of brain-washing as of rational conviction. However, when applied to democratic welfare capitalism idealistic approaches lead to reformist conclusions. Materialist approaches contradict these conclusions.

## Keynes and Beveridge — recipes for intervention

The work of Keynes dealt a major blow to the equilibrium theory of the economics of capitalism: the idea that in the long term the demand and supply for anything would be balanced by the price mechanism, so that resources would be used in the general interest where they were most needed. He demonstrated that there was no inherent reason why the balance of supply and demand should be achieved at the level of the maximum utilization of available resources. Thus depression is not simply a minor aberration of adjustment but a continuing hazard in free markets:

> In the 1930s, a large part of the resources (of the economic system) were not being used for anything at all; Keynes diagnosed the cause as a deep-seated defect in the mechanism and thereby added an exception to the comfortable rule that every man in bettering himself was doing good to the commonwealth, so large as completely to disrupt the reconciliation of the pursuit of private profit with public beneficience
>
> (Robinson, 1964, p. 74).

This view added to the idea that government intervention in the system can help to effect a cure, has clear implications for the role of a democratic state in steering society in the general interest: 'Keynes . . . General Theory brought out into the open the problems of choice and judgement that the neo-classicals had managed to smother. The ideology to end all ideologies broke down'. (Robinson, 1964, p. 76). As a 'theoretical explanation of the possibility of under-employment equilibrium' and 'a group of doctrines in public policy about how to control the economy at the desired level of economic activity' (Klein, 1968, p. 191), it provides at once a justification and a recipe for government intervention.

The significance of Keynes for post-war social policy is argued by Beveridge, who made economic management to ensure full employment a foundation-stone of his recommendations for social security. In a book published in 1944, he points out that the idea that unemployment might be due to a chronic mismatch of supply and demand for labour was 'raised only to be dismissed' in earlier work on the subject. He goes on to give the 'gist' of the implications of Keynes's work as inaugurating 'a new era of economic theorizing about unemployment':

> employment depends on spending, which is of two kinds — for consumption and for investment; what people spend on consumption gives employment. What they save . . . gives employment only if it is invested, which means, not the buying of bonds or shares, but . . . adding to capital equipment, such as factories, machinery or ships . . . . There is not in the unplanned market economy

anything that automatically keeps the total of spending of both kinds at the point of full employment . . .

(1944, pp. 93–4)

The state must step in:

full employment means ensuring that outlay in total is sufficient. Only the state can ensure that . . . . The state cannot escape ultimate responsibility for the general direction of outlay by reference to social priorities

(1944, p. 187).

In a sense, the work of Beveridge and Keynes in social security and economic policy was complementary:

poverty and insecurity through the interruption of earnings had been the greatest hazard of twentieth-century industrial life. Now Keynes attacked the problem on one side, Beveridge on the other. Moreover . . . social services could be seen as an additional instrument of demand management, while Beveridge was persuaded . . . of the validity of Keynesian techniques for maintaining full employment on which the . . . viability of the insurance scheme rested

(Skidelsky, 1977a, p. 314))

These approaches constitute a foundation for large-scale state interventionism in economic management and in resolving the problems due to the shortcomings of the capitalist system. They suggest action to tackle the failure of the free market to serve human interests to be taken by the state: the independence of the state from the conflict of interests in the economic system is thus assumed. As Sweezy puts it, the state becomes a *'deus ex machina* to be invoked whenever human actors behaving according to the rules of the capitalist game, get themselves into a dilemma' (1947, p. 108). Thus Keynes appeals in his Open Letter of 1933 to President Roosevelt as rational supervisor: as 'the trustee for those in every country who seek to mend evils of our condition by reasoned experiment, within the framework of our existing social system' (quoted in George and Wilding, 1976, p. 42). Harris's comment, that Beveridge's insurance proposals 'were grounded in the belief that social insurance could synthesize and reconcile certain contradictory principles that seemed . . . inherent in modern industrial society', sets out a similar role for the state as independent coordinator of an anarchy of interests.

The idealism that divorces political and economic relations and thus provides a basis for rationally guided reform of the latter by the former, is also apparent in the stress on ideas as the motor of change. Robinson discusses Keynes's 'optimistic view that when theory was understood, reason would prevail' (1964, p. 97). Beveridge writes in a section headed 'social conscience as a driving force':

> we cure unemployment in war, because war gives us a common objective that is recognized by all . . . . The cure . . . in peace depends on finding a common objective that will be equally compelling . . . this . . . depends on the degree to which social conscience becomes the driving force in our national life
>
> (1944, p. 254).

The respect for change in consciousness as the root of reform is part of a view that does not regard the make-up of society as generating formidable obstacles to those changes that serve the common interest. Tawney and Titmuss provide an analysis of the ills and the reform of capitalism that parallels the critique of the market as an equilibrium system with a critique of its moral worth.

## Tawney and Titmuss: human interests and capitalism

Tawney's conception of normative order was based firmly on the christian ethic: his condemnation of capitalism was that:

> Religion has been converted from the keystone which holds together the social edifice into one department within it and the idea of a rule of right is replaced by economic expediency as the arbiter of policy and the criterion of conduct
>
> (1936, p. 279).

This position led to an archetypal and brilliantly expressed idealism. In his quest for 'the conditions for a right organization of industry' (1923, p. 6) he argued:

> The first condition . . . is . . . intellectual conversion . . . it is that emphasis should be transferred from the opportunities which it offers individuals to the social functions which it performs . . . . It is because the purpose of industry, which is the conquest of nature in the service of man, is neither adequately expressed in its organization nor present in the minds of those engaged in it . . . that the

economic life of modern societies is in a perpetual state of morbid irritation.

(1923, p. 223).

The result was what Tawney termed a functional theory of society: 'a society which aimed at making the acquisition of wealth contingent upon the discharge of social functions . . . might be called a Functional society' (1923, p. 31; see also 1929, ch. 6). This was to be sought through spiritual conviction and an effort of will. This in turn rests on the idea of the possibility of social consensus — a common interest which society may serve — justified by transcendent argument.

The critique of capitalism represents an idealist complement to some aspects of marxism. The 'acquisitive society' makes capital accumulation an end in itself which stultified free human development — a counterpart to the notion of alienation. The transformation required is to bring modern industry under the control of members of society so that it may be servant not master. The crucial difference is that since damage to people arises ultimately not from alienating material relations but from self-interest and the inability to follow correct ideas, the road to change is through direct change in ideas and motives and not primarily in objective economic relations.

> Marxian socialists are not revolutionary enough. They say that capitalist society is condemned because the worker does not get the equivalent of what he produces . . . . The real condemnation of the capitalist spirit is contained in the suggestion that men should get only what they produced . . . . A barbarous inhuman, sordid doctrine, that would weigh immortal souls and scale them down because they are not economically useful.
>
> (1972, p. 69).

The unacceptability, indeed the 'breakdown' of 'the existing order' results not from the development of material forces but 'through neglect of the truism that even quite common men have souls' and therefore 'no increase in material wealth will compensate them for arrangements which insult their self-respect and impair their freedom' (1936, p. 284).

The transcendent basis of Tawney's thought enables him to link together the ideas of power, freedom and equality. Capitalism stands guilty because 'the supreme evil of modern industrial civilization . . . is the absence of liberty i.e. of the opportunity for self-direction'

(1972, p. 34). 'The fundamental idea of liberty is power. Power to control the condition of one's own life' (pp. 22–3).

> When liberty is construed realistically, as implying not merely a minimum of civil and political rights, but securities that the economically weak will not be at the mercy of the economically strong and that the control of those aspects of economic life by which all are affected will be amenable . . . to the will of all, a large measure of equality so far from being inimical to liberty is essential to it.
>
> (1929, p. 244)

If people have equal souls they have equal potential. Thus they should have equal power over the conditions of their lives. The radical and practical social policy results of this argument are clearly illustrated for example in the Labour Party pamphlet on education produced by a group chaired by Tawney:

> The organization of education on lines of class has been at once a symptom, an effect and a cause of the control of the lives of the mass . . . by a privileged minority. The very assumption on which it is based, that all the child of the workers needs is 'elementary education' . . . is itself . . . nonsense . . . . Organized labour . . . if it is to liberate the lives of the rising generation . . . must also liberate their minds.
>
> (1922, introduction).

Equality therefore freedom. The notion of freedom expressed here differs from that of the individualists. A perspective on social action that started and finished with the individual led to an idea of freedom as the absence of deliberate coercion. Tawney's basis in the unattained potential of the human spirit, and his recognition that existing social and economic organization prevents its realization leads to the view that freedom requires positive action. Because society takes its character as a structure of ideas, conscious political regulation can achieve this goal.

Tawney's beautifully expressed and fervent idealism carries with it the stamp of conviction. A theory of human nature leads to a critique of oppressive social structures and a recipe for their transformation through intellectual change. The thought of Titmuss is far more complex. As Reisman points out, he was a leader (a 'pathbreaker' as Mishra constantly reminds us) in modern social policy studies: 'it is

no criticism . . . to say that he asked more questions than he answered'
(Reisman, 1977, p. 172).

The scope of Titmuss's work is breathtaking: from the political
economy of *Income Distribution and Social Change* (1962) to the social
and political history of *Problems of Social Policy* (1950); from the practical studies of developing countries (1961 and 1964) to the social
philosophy of *The Gift Relationship* (1973) and *The Irresponsible
Society* (1960). Reisman (1977) provides an excellent introduction.
Here we are concerned principally with those features of normative
thought that reveal an idealist orientation: to the attempt to produce
social consensus through intellectual and moral conviction and the
advancement of particular ideals for integration resting on a normative theory of human nature. We stress the elements in Titmuss's
thought that lead to a reformism, rather that the consideration of the
power of structures to create intractable problems beyond the control
and intention of their designers that was used as a bridge between
reformist and structuralist approaches in chapter 2.

The clearest statement of the idealist strand is perhaps contained in
the discussion of the academic subject he did most to mould, in the
keynote lecture to the inaugural meeting of the Social Administration
association:

> Social administration is . . . concerned . . . with different types of
> moral transactions, embodying notions of gift-exchange, of recip-
> rocal obligations, which have developed in modern societies in
> institutional forms to bring about and maintain social and com-
> munity relations.
>
> (1968, pp. 20–1)
>
> Its primary areas of unifying interest are centred in those social
> institutions that foster integration and discourage alienation
>
> (p. 22)

A concern with integration is revealed in the concern with, at the level
of detail, stigma significantly highlighted by Pinker (1971, p. 136);
and at the general level, the universality of welfare described by
Reisman as a 'key concept' (1977, p. 99). This stands at the head of a
tradition in social policy writing developed, for example, by
Townsend (1973) and Pinker (1979).

The theme is explored in detail in the complex part empirical, part
normative *Gift Relationship* (1973). Arrow points out that

> his blithe disregard of the usual epistemological strictures against

confusion of fact and value permits him to raise the largest descriptive and normative questions about the social order in a highly specific and richly factual context

(1971, p. 362).

Titmuss writes:

We suggest . . . that the ways in which society organizes and structures its social institutions . . . can encourage or discourage the altruistic in man; such systems can foster integration or alienation; . . . . This we suggest is an aspect of freedom in the twentieth century which, compared with the emphasis on consumer choice in material acquisitiveness, is insufficiently recognized

(1973, p. 255).

Here the authentic Tawney note rings through.

However, why should consensus be the goal of social organization? As Reisman points out (1977, p. 35) it is not necessarily a sign of social well-being 'when conformity and compromise replace diversity and pluralism'. This question appears to be posed directly and answered systematically nowhere in Titmuss's work. Perhaps the clearest statements are contained in chapters 13 and 14 of *The Gift Relationship.* Here Titmuss continuously asserts the idea of a foundation in human nature for social integration. 'If it is accepted that man has a social and a biological need to help, then to deny him opportunities to express this need is to deny him the freedom to enter into gift relationships' (pp. 273–4). This is linked to a normative concept of human interest: what unites social policy

with ethical considerations is its focus on integrative systems: on processes, transactions and institutions which promote an individual's sense of identity, participation and community and allow him more freedom of choice for the expression of altruism

(p. 253).

Integration is an ethical issue because people need integrative institutions.

## Crosland and Donnison

If Titmuss and Tawney are concerned to condemn market capitalism for its failure to minister to true human needs and seek to provide the social philosophy appropriate to a regeneration of that system, the tradition of revisionist socialism most ably articulated by Crosland (1974) seeks to found its critique in a political economic analysis of capitalist society. We shall attempt to show that this approach shares the sociological orientation of idealism.

For Crosland socialism embraces three aspirations: 'the cooperative ideal', 'concern with social welfare and the desire for an equal and classless society'. The first of these is vague and possibly unfeasible (1964, p. 76). Of the two others 'the belief in social equality, which has been the strongest ethical inspiration of virtually every socialist doctrine, still remains the most characteristic feature of socialist thought today'. (p. 77) Correspondingly, 'the promotion of welfare' receives one chapter and 'the search for equality' nine. In later writing, the case is more bluntly put: 'socialism, in our view, was basically about equality' (in Blowers and Thompson, 1976, p. 165).

For Crosland, the welfare state is as concerned to promote equality as it is to relieve material distress. On what grounds is action to relieve inequality justified? There are three arguments:

> . . . the ethical basis for the first argument for greater equality is that it will increase social contentment and diminish social resentment . . . . Such a statement . . . is justified first by the ethical premise that a contented society is better than a discontented one, and secondly by the judgement that the contentment of the community is an increasing function of the contentment of individuals
> (1964, p. 137).

The commendation of fellowship carries strong echoes of Titmuss. The second argument rests on the idea that inequality is unjust. This is advanced on three grounds: 'first . . . most liberal people would now allow that every child had a "natural" right as a citizen . . . to that position in the social scale to which his natural talents entitle him' (1964, p. 140). The second ground applies similar reasoning to the distribution of wealth and the third extends it to power. Unequal distribution is unfair because it offends against 'natural' ideas of right. (Incidentally, these arguments take Crosland's position beyond the commendation of mere 'equality of opportunity', a fact not always sufficiently acknowledged).

The third argument is to do with social waste: 'we are still not extracting the best from our population or making the most exhaustive use of scarce resources of human ability. This is a definite social waste, and one directly related to a stratified social system' (1964, p. 147).

The arguments against inequality are cased in a hard shell of practical reasoning: inequality is subversive, offensive and wasteful. However, they contain the prior assumption that equality is possible under capitalism, that subversion of and waste in that system are a bad thing and that the preferences of liberals in that form of society are viable. These claims rest ultimately on a dismissal of materialist approaches to socialism:

> Marxism has little or nothing to offer the contemporary socialist, either in respect of practical policy, or of the correct analysis of our society, or even of the right conceptual tools or framework.

> (1964, p. 2).

The argument for this statement (which is repeated in later work (Blowers and Thompson, 1976, pp. 171–80), rests on the idea that capitalism has changed its essential nature. To Crosland, capitalism may mean one of two things: in the narrow sense, private ownership of the means of production, or in the broad sense, a society characterized by six key features. These are: the autonomy of economic life; the effective control of decisions by a class of private owner-managers; the unequal distribution of wealth; an ideology of individualism, competition, private property and subservience to the dictates of the market; and sixthly class antagonism. On either definition, Crosland argues, capitalism is history.

In respect of the first:

> ownership of the means of production has ceased to be the key factor which imparts to a society its essential character. Either collective or private ownership is consistent with widely varying degrees of liberty, democracy, equality, exploitation, class-feeling, planning, workers control and economic prosperity

> (1964, p. 41).

In respect of the second, the lineaments of society have radically altered from those of the age of *laissez-faire*: 'the national shift of power to the left with all its implications for the balance of power may be accepted as permanent' (1964, p. 9). In particular the loss of power from the business class to the state, the spread of nationalization, the increased power of labour stemming from full-employment policies and the psychological changes in industry as ownership and management become increasingly divorced means that the system ceases to take its essential character from the most ruthless profit-maximization and exploitation. In essence the state and the labour movement provide alternative centres of power which may harness the beast of the free market. The pursuit of equality and welfare become viable projects within suitably managed capitalism.

Some of Crosland's empirical arguments may be open to question in the late 1970s when the effective power of the labour movement may well be on the wane; when the government of the day is at any rate committed to a reduction in nationalization and when full employment has ceased to be a viable policy option. Crosland recounts the story of 'the most traumatic incident of the 1930s' — the decision by private monopoly bodies to close down the Jarrow shipyards and the failure to provide any alternative source of jobs — as an illustration of the past power of private capital (1964, p. 6). It may be true that 'today the capitalist business class has lost this commanding position' (1964, p. 7). However, the subsidy decisions taken by government in 1979 are likely to compel a nationalized industry (British Steel) to deprive very considerable proportions of the population of Shotton and Corby of jobs. An increase in the power of the state is no guarantee that the disasters resulting from the barbarism of the market will not be repeated.

In any case it is not on such empirical evidence that Crosland's 'revisionist' thesis rests, but on an analysis of the nature of capitalist society, and as such it must be assessed. This analysis is idealist in the sense that the structure of power is understood to consist in people's ideas rather than in material economic forces. This approach tends to exaggerate the significance of parliamentary decision-taking — the power of conscious management of the economy — at the expense of those factors in the economy argued for example by Miliband (see chapter 2) that restrict the scope of action of governments. Similarly Crosland places a disproportionate emphasis on the psychological manifestations of changes in business structure — the fact that the individuals who make up management tend to assimilate the goals of their enterprise, to think of themselves as members of a team and so on — and to ignore the form in which they are set. The competitive nature of corporate enterprise, the imperative to growth, if not profit-maximization, the overriding necessity to control and exploit labour successfully remain constant.

The pragmatic form of Crosland's arguments against materialism and his defence of equality conceal their idealist origins. A distinct echo of Tawney's accommodation of freedom and equality may be heard in the declaration of the universal acceptability of the principle that equal opportunity to develop human potential is desirable — equality as a basis for freedom (cf Lukes in Blowers and Thompson,

1976, p. 67). The result of this position is a lucid — perhaps the most clearly argued — defence of democratic welfare capitalism. The political results of revisionism are well known. Two will be discussed.

First the contradiction between the capitalist goal of growth and the humanist goal of welfare. In his early analysis of the economic crises afflicting post-war Britain (1953), Crosland argued that: 'the doctrine of "fair shares" cannot be so rigidly interpreted that it jeopardizes national recovery' (1953, p. 217). Twenty years later, the obstacle to progress is the attack on inflation: 'for a Labour Government wishing to reallocate resources on a considerable scale, slow growth is an additional cause of inflation. We must, in order to finance our collective spending, reduce the share of consumption in total income. But this . . . can only be done without extra inflation if the *absolute* level of consumption is rising steadily; and that requires a rapid rate of growth' (Blowers and Thompson, 1976, p. 186: see also Crosland 1964, p. 145 where the obstacle to equality is the preservation of incentives and therefore of growth). The question of how growth is to be assured under parliamentary welfare socialism remains unresolved.

Secondly, Crosland is left with the problem of why his ideas are not more successful if there are no structural economic forces inherent in society opposing their execution. This leads in later writing to an emphasis on the metaphysical concept of will — we must try harder. 'Against the dogged resistance to change we should have pitted a stronger will to change' (Blowers and Thompson, 1976, p. 180) 'Only if we concentrate our effort shall we make a significant advance' (ibid, p. 186). This is the result of the assumption that the real obstacles are opposing wills.

Donnison puts forward a political philosophy that is similar in many respects to Crosland's, in a rare departure from the brilliant and incisive analysis of the problems that confront the particular services of the modern welfare state. The argument is that equality, freedom and economic growth go together. In a nutshell:

> eventually it should be possible to sustain the process by which policies for the equalization of income, wealth and living standards extend freedom and promote innovation and development which ensure the continuing economic growth that makes further progress towards equality possible
>
> (1976, p. 203).

The solution to problems is the destruction of class in Crosland's sense — a claustrophobic order of rigid status differences which numbs social creativity and progress and fosters resentment through its effect on people's consciousness. No problem in relating growth and welfare under capitalism is recognized. There is nothing about capitalism — in particular, no structural distribution of power, no objective constraint on human action, — that acts as an obstacle. Class is an anachronism, sustained by vested interests.

The idealism of the British socialist tradition leads at once to an exaltation of ideal goals and at the same time to the view that the social barriers to their attainment can be overcome by change originating in people's minds and expressed through the rational argument of a plural parliamentary political system. The fourth reformist view to be discussed is the political economy of Galbraith.

## Galbraith

Galbraith's dissection of modern industrial society is presented in three books: *The Affluent Society* (1977); *The New Industrial State* (1969); and *Economics and the Public Purpose* (1973). The second stands to the first 'as a house to a window. This is the structure; the earlier book allowed the first glimpse inside' (1969, p. 11). The third extends analysis to the non-corporate sector of the economy and to the international system (1973, pp. IX–X). We shall concentrate on the analysis of the modern politico-economic system in the second.

*The New Industrial State* contains an impressive statement of technological convergence theory. The projects of large corporations require the investment of colossal sums of money over considerable periods. For such enterprise, the entrepreneurial model of competitive risk-taking is inappropriate.

> In these circumstances, planning is both essential and difficult . . . one answer is to have the state absorb the major risks. It can provide or guarantee a market for the product. It can underwrite the costs of development so that if they increase beyond expectation, the firm will not have to carry them. Or it can pay for and make available the necessary technical knowledge . . . . Technology under all circumstances leads to planning . . . . Technological compulsions and not ideology or political wile, will require the firm to seek the help and protection of the state
>
> (1969, pp. 30–1).

And again 'size is the general servant of technology not the special servant of profits' (p. 42). '. . . the enemy of the market is not ideology but the engineer' (p. 43). Technological progress requires large-scale enterprise accommodated to state planning systems in all advanced economies. 'The modern large corporation and the modern apparatus of socialist planning are various accommodations to the same need' (p. 43).

Such technological determinism has been criticized elsewhere (see above, ch. 1 or Mishra, 1977, ch. 3). Nonetheless its capacity to summarize (as opposed to explain) the facts of international politico-economic development cannot be denied.

The modern industrial corporation differs in several respects, other than size, from the small-scale market-oriented firm. Its decision-making apparatus — its guiding intelligence — tends to include not only a board of directors, heads of departments and top executives but also 'all those who bring specialized knowledge, talent or experience to group decision-making' (p. 80). Galbraith terms this steering mechanism the Technostructure.

If an accommodation between state and business is a technological inevitability, the members of the technostructure tend to assimilate motives appropriate to the progress and expansion of the industrial giant. These include the general acceptance that social purpose is identical to corporate interest and subservience to the direction of a secure level of earnings and maximum growth for the corporation legitimated by the assimilation of managerial to corporate and both to national interest. This process is aided by the decline of confrontational labour politics and the further assimilation of the interests of the workforce into those of the enterprise. The overall tendency is to justify a situation in which the consumer sovereignty of the free market is increasingly supplanted by the monopolistic sovereignty of the giant corporation. In *The Affluent Society* the process of moulding of private need and want, principally through advertising, had already been detailed (1977, ch. 10 and 11). Here the analysis is extended to public expenditure by the observation that 'modern military and related procurement and policy are, in fact, extensively adapted to the needs of the industrial system' (1969, p. 237). 'Defence expenditures in their present magnitude are, in part, an accommodation to the needs of the industrial system and the technostructure' (p. 236). Both public and private demand are tailored to supply.

Since the coordination of state and corporation is the result of consistency of interests and motive no conspiracy is needed to explain it:

The state is strongly concerned with the stability of the economy.

And with its expansion, or growth, and with education and with technical and scientific advance. And most notably with the national defence. These are *the* national goals . . . . All have their counterpart in the needs and goals of the technostructure. It requires stability in demand for its planning. Growth brings promotion and prestige. It requires trained manpower. It needs government underwriting of research and development.

(1969, p. 313).

'It is the genius of the industrial system that it makes the goals that reflect its needs . . . coordinate with social virtue and human enlightenment.' (p. 347).

The industrial system is regarded as a system of constraint. The final chapters of the book discuss the possibility of emancipation. These concentrate on 'the dimensions of life, which the industrial system, by its nature, does not or cannot serve . . .' (p. 347). In later work these are more clearly brought out. The distortion of the public purpose achieved by the success of the planning system — the process of political-industrial management outlined above — produces the belief that 'the purposes of the planning system are those of the individual' (1973, p. 223).

Galbraith tends to be vague and eclectic in his assessment of the goals of human life. In *The New Industrial State* he asserts that 'aesthetic goals' should have pride of place (p. 399). In *The Affluent Society* the emphasis is on quality of life rather than quantity of goods. Significantly, he here refuses to define the goals of the good society:

The present argument has been directed to seeing how extensively present preoccupations, most of all that with the production of goods, are compelled by tradition and myth . . . . It will remain with the reader . . . and one hopes with democratic process to reconcile these opportunities with his own sense of what makes life better.

(1977, p. 269).

Elsewhere the public purpose is to be decided by an emancipated democracy resting on a political pluralism (1969, p. 372).

To describe such a trenchant critique of material economic arrangements as idealist may seem obtuse. Galbraith's idealism is most clearly apparent in his characterization of the contemporary alliance of technostructure and state, and in his recipe for change. In the former sphere it is ideas that have the predominant role in two aspects. First the motivations of technostructure and state personnel are of primary importance. It is a distortion at the level of motive that leads the system to fail to serve common interest. Yet no convincing explanation of the accommodation of motive that underlies the alliance of public and private Leviathan is given. It is simply observed fact. Secondly, in the process of technological innovation, the historical process whereby some invention is adopted and some not in a profit-oriented economy is scarcely discussed. Technology *per se* is the motor of social change — and it is a given. New ideas are the basis of social development, and the social structures in which they are set and through which they act, are conceived in terms of ideas.

In the latter area, change is achieved through conviction. 'The emancipation of belief is the most formidable of the tasks of reform and the one on which all else depends.' (1973, p. 223; cf 1969, p. 347). The obstacles are the vested interests of the planning system to be confronted with diligence and effort. Since the basis of these obstacles is identified at the psychological level (motive) the suggestion that reform is possible through rational argument is plausible.

## Idealism — a summary

The writers whose ideas are discussed in this chapter have a wide range of disciplinary orientations and of objectives and have written at periods when the problems facing western society differed radically in character: slump or affluence, unemployment or stigma. However, they share an idealist orientation that tends to a reformism. Because their approach to society is at the level of ideas, institutions are seen as independent rather than as aspects of an integrated structure. State intervention in the market to relieve the ills of unemployment, to rectify inegalitarian trends or to achieve the public purpose is regarded as a policy presenting no essential problems other than that of convincing people that it makes sense. Certainly Crosland and Tawney do not minimize the difficulty of converting present privilege. Political and economic systems relate externally.

The divorce of state and market is presented as less complete in the work of the socialist idealists than in that of the interventionists. All see the free market economic system as incapable of balancing people's interests. Keynes and Galbraith tend to see the problem essentially as a failure to serve a common interest defined in terms of resource utilization or public purpose; Tawney and Crosland go beyond this position to suggest that capitalism produces class inequalities. Class inequalities produce more pervasive structures of vested interests that tend to penetrate the political level. However, there is no essential reason why vigorous action at that level cannot overcome them. Thus the political economists tend to a consensus politics; the Fabians tend to acknowledge the existence of conflict, but not a conflict that fails to admit of resolution or at least containment within capitalism. Both groups stress the importance of rational argument within a democratic system as the way in which to advance correct ideas and thereby correct institutions.

Thus idealism finds its natural home in a reformist sociological approach to social problems. Problems, in general, are rooted in the unfettered operation of or in the inequalities and vested interests resulting from the capitalist system. Piecemeal tinkering (which perhaps Beveridge regarded as easier to achieve than Crosland does) can in principle reorganize existing services and create new ones to tackle them. Such adaptation can serve to further human interests, which are understood at the level of intellectual conviction independently of the social system. Idealists who tend to a class analysis of free markets see interests in terms of equal capacity for human flourishing; those who regard the uncorrected market as a system incapable of serving common human purposes interpret interests in terms of the wishes that would be articulated through the democratic system independently of economic distortion.

Idealism, necessarily, lacks a consistent notion of ideology as structures of ideas rooted in a form of society capable of exercising power. Thus the efficacy of rational argument, and the relative weakness of structure. Society as a whole does not generate ideas that prevent the achievement of the idealist's goals.

In the next chapter, we shall consider approaches that suggest that the character of the welfare state results from its structure taken as a whole. These theories tend to rest on a materialist approach that emphasizes the importance of social relations that people have no choice about entering into for the ideas they share about their society.

# 4

# Normative theories of the welfare state II — Structural accounts

A structural approach understands society as an integrated whole. In this chapter, we consider three variants: the historical materialism of marxism and critical theory, structuralism founded on normative consensus and structuralism centred on an immanent logic of societal convergence. First, however, we discuss Hirsch's work. This occupies an interesting transitional position. Reformist conclusions are drawn from a structural account, and solutions to problems of material origin sought at the level of ideas.

## Hirsch

Hirsch's elegantly written and forceful study (1977) argues an ineluctable disjunction between the expectations fostered by democratic welfare capitalism and the capacity of the economic process to meet them. The crisis of stunted aspiration produces social limits to growth more pressing and more subversive then 'the distant and uncertain physical limits' of resource constraint, population explosion, pollution, 'greenhouse effect' and so on, analysed, for example, by Meadows *et al.* (1972).

The approach tends to a materialism because it argues that economic circumstances produce dominant ideas. A 'structural characteristic' of modern economic growth 'is that as the level of average consumption rises, an increasing proportion of consumption takes on a social as well as a physical aspect' (p. 2). As goods come to satisfy a demand for the display of social status and relative privilege, rather than brute need, what we get out of having them is increasingly influenced by what others possess. This results in the development of a category of goods which Hirsch claims is neglected in neo-classical economics. These goods are subject to 'social scarcity'. For example, the pleasure of driving on uncongested roads by its very nature is only accessible to a privileged minority. As car ownership spreads, the satisfaction diminishes (to pass to the corresponding enjoyment of a private jet-plane?) Latecomers can never derive the same satisfaction from a standard of living that includes a motor-car as those who own when ownership is restricted to the minority. Similarly the enjoyment of peaceful country cottages, the advantages of suburban life on the fringe of both country and city, the command of the job market that results from possession of scarce qualifications, the snob appeal of exotic food and exclusive life-styles are intrinsically unshareable. Hirsch may exaggerate the extent to which the banishment of crude want has created a dominant role for socially scarce goods in our consumption, but the point remains. Some things cannot be redistributed.

A good illustration is provided by the recent explosion of educational qualifications. For the individual more qualifications often led to a higher income. This is not the case en masse. Between 1965–66 (when the certificate of secondary education was introduced) and 1976–77 the proportion of school-leavers with no qualifications fell from just over half to about 15 per cent (*Social Trends*, 1976, p. 76). This seems to have had little effect on the earning power of the group as a whole.

Hirsch's second point is that the intrinsic scarcity of social goods gives rise to frustration. This is an economic not a psychological process (p. 7). A market system is founded on self-interest — on the ideology that economic advance leads to more satisfaction. Otherwise, what's the point? In the sphere of social scarcity this ideology is falsified by the facts. The mass of the population is chasing the leaders in consumption up an escalator that is moving against everyone. Thus modern capitalism cannot sustain the structure of motives on which it depends and which is implicit in it.

Hirsch appears to have detailed an insoluble problem within the system — a problem of crucial significance to welfare states that, after all, claim to redistribute satisfactions. His solution is disappointing, depending on change in our 'culture of individualistic advance' (p. 9). By an effort of will we should abandon the principle of self-interest as a social organizing device, to construct a 'social morality' (p. 12), that would justify sharing economic goods and detach our satisfaction from the basis of the enjoyment of what is scarce. This is a return to the values of fellowship and equality embraced by the Fabians whose assumptions of the compatibility of growth and welfare are vigorously attacked earlier (Hirsch, 1977, p. 17). The idea that a constellation of ideas that have their origin in material relations may be altered by a fresh ideology constructed on a rational basis and imposed by an effort of will is an interesting conflation of a materialist and an idealist approach. The outcome is first, a view of the problems of democratic welfare capitalism that suggests they are insuperable, and then a solution pulled like a rabbit out of a hat, and resting on no basis other than armchair social analysis.

### Marxism

For a fully fledged materialist approach we must turn to marxist writers. Marxism contains a tradition of social thought at least as diverse, profound and sophisticated at the range of non-marxist thought, some of which is sampled in the preceding pages. An attempt to express main points in a small compass will inevitably result in omission and oversimplification. The only defence we can offer is that chapters 6 to 8 are concerned with the construction and chapter 9 with the application of a more developed model.

The materialist basis of Marx's thought as expressed in the 1859 Preface has already been quoted (chapter 1). The idea that economic relations determine all other social relations is at once powerful and simplistic. Powerful, because it provides a holistic account of social order and social change. Simplistic, because the basis of this account is open to challenge. A mono-causal explanation of society lays itself open to the criticism that since it provides a total account of everything, any evidence fits it by definition and it is therefore invulnerable to empirical refutation (see Popper's comments on 'reinforced dogmatism', 1969, p. 334; or Donnison *et al.*, 1975, p. 36). However, this view both misses the point that such criticism applies to any world view (including those implicit in alternative theory) and refuses to take seriously the development of the 'guiding thread' of materialism in Marx's work.

To argue that one level of human relationships determines in a material sense other levels is not to deny all causal efficacy to those levels: the material necessity of eating may constrain one to enter into a contract with an employer that restricts one's freedom during hours of work. This does not (in logic) refute the (unlikely) possibility that one might choose not to enter into it. To do so in a systematic way simply removes you from society. Interpretation of Marx simply in terms of an economic determinism ignores the complex structure of interdependent relationships he saw as constituting human society. In *The German Ideology*, the argument for materialism is that if you don't eat there won't be any history, and that the choice of a range of activities for satisfying brute need is conditioned by what happens to be available:

> Men can be distinguished from animals by consciousness, by religion or anything else you like. They themselves begin to distinguish themselves . . . as soon as they begin to produce their means of subsistence, a step which is conditioned by their physical organization . . . . The way in which men produce their means of subsistence depends first of all on the nature of the actual means of subsistence they find in existence and have to reproduce. . . . The nature of individuals . . . depends on the material conditions determining their production
>
> (Marx and Engels, 1970, p. 42).

This does not mean, of course, that a description of simple arrangements to satisfy brute need is an adequate description of society:

> The first historical act is . . . the production of the means to satisfy those needs, the production of material life itself . . . the satisfaction of the first need . . . leads to new needs.
>
> (pp. 48–9).

The process continues as a 'double relationship': on the one hand natural, on the other social, involving social cooperation in order to satisfy natural needs, in a way that leads to the social production of fresh needs.

Human history requires production — the application of labour to create goods to meet needs. In a practical (but not in an apriori) sense people have no choice about whether to enter into production relations. Moreover, in an established form of society these relations are themselves established and constitute an existing structure of society which exerts power:

> Men make their own history, but they do not make it just as they please: they do not make it under circumstances chosen by themselves, but under circumstances directly encountered given and transmitted from the past.
>
> (Marx and Engels, 1969, p. 360).

The necessity of production stamps a character on civilization which includes political, social and spiritual processes. However, since what is being sustained and reproduced is a form of society, a structure for satisfying material needs (for this is the defining characteristic of society) any approach which considers society as less than a totality is likely to be misleading. The separation of economic and other processes into (as it were) material production (essential) and superstructure (optional) in order to construct a determination of one by the other tells only part of the story. Marxism analyses society as an irreducible whole whose important feature lies in its continuing production of social life.

Lukacs argues that 'it is not the primacy of economic motives in historical explanation that constitutes the decisive difference between marxism and bourgeois thought, but the point of view of totality . . . . The primacy of the category of totality is the bearer of the principle of revolution in science.' (1971, p. 27). Marxist approaches that ignore this point tend to interpret societal development in terms of the interaction of classes narrowly conceived as economic interest groups. This diverts attention from the limitations which social structure imposes on class action, and from the understanding of these limits in terms that transcend the social actors' conception of interest. Holloway and Picciotto point out how the 'British empiricist' tradition in marxism (exemplified in the earlier work of Miliband (1973)) tends in this direction. (1978, p. 10). Ultimately, such a marxism reduces to a political conflict approach. The conception of society as totality offers a route between such a pluralism and determinism.

This approach leads to a theory that periodizes history by the production relations that tended to be dominant. Any society beyond the most primitive must produce a surplus in addition to the immediate consumption necessary to maintain life. Human labour is the basis of all production. From a political viewpoint the most important feature of history is the mechanism whereby this surplus is separated from those whose work produces it. In a slave society, the direct ownership of labour involves ownership of its product and thus of surplus above the maintenance of labour. In a feudal order the structure of obligations and responsibilities results in a system whereby unpaid labour is contributed to the aristocracy. Capitalism is distinguished by the fact that the expropriation of the surplus is carried out by a process that is not immediately obvious to all social actors. Wage-labour is hired through a free contract between legal equals. Marx's analysis of the process of extraction has since been challenged (Steedman, 1977) and need not concern us here. Suffice to say that the social order is understood as containing a system of extraction of surplus by the owners of the means of production (principally factories) in the form of realized profits, expanded capital for fresh investment and so on. The growth of a capitalist economy is founded on the extraction of a surplus from the labour of the working class.

The economic foundation of social relations leads to their second important characteristic — the division of society into classes. Since the immediate interests of capital and labour centre on the zero-sum conflict over expropriation of an economic surplus, the short-term interests of these two categories inevitably conflict. This is true irrespective of the view taken on whether the relation of workers to the ownership of that which is necessary to the employment of labour to meet human need is in the long-term interest of both parties or not. In an objective sense capitalism, which relies on a strong ideology of private ownership, identifies self-interest with acquisition. The ownership system, when applied to industrial production, prevents most people owning what they contribute to make, and thus works against their interest as defined in this form of society.

This clash of class interest sets the scene for class struggle — the effort by the workers to wrest a greater proportion of the social product from the expropriators. Class struggle can take a bewildering variety of forms. One distinction is between the unintended collective results of the process whereby individuals with rare skills acting out of self-interest may bid up the price of their labour when the market is favourable, and conscious coordinated action. This distinction parallels that drawn by Weber between 'societal' and 'communal' collective action (Weber, 1948, p. 185). Thus, sportspeople, musicians or divers may get large rewards without mutual organization. In the latter area, collective struggle is increasingly likely as individuals organize to enhance their power in the market. Thus professional associations and trade unions. Here conflicts of interest between different groups may exist. Collective action has been of great importance in maintaining the living standards of the working class.

A second distinction lies between action directed at redressing the balance in the industrial sphere (what Lenin termed 'mere Trade Union consciousness') and action based on the recognition that industrial exploitation is simply a facet of social relations in a particular form of society: this embraces the whole range of political action both through the formal democratic process and outside it (the Labour party and the labour movement).

The third essential feature of modern society is the production of particular structures of ideas. That value should be attached to private property or to the performance of adequate labour contributes to a structure of motives that help to render the system stable. Marxists attach importance to the perpetuation of such legitimating ideologies and to the material processes in society which engender and sustain them.

The stage has now been set for the emergence of the modern state as a rapidly developing entity playing a key role in the accumulation of capital and in the management of the relations of classes. O'Connor (1973, introduction) categorizes the two main roles of the modern state as the securing of conditions suitable for the continued accumulation of capital and the legitimation of the social system. Under the first head came the provision of infrastructure — principally communications and assistance in maintaining a suitably trained, healthy and reasonably content labour force. Similar considerations led Galbraith to regard the New Industrial State as working hand in glove with the modern corporation. Under the second lie those social processes that serve to justify existing relations as right and proper. These are principally the provision of a structure of law and order that acts as a bastion to private property, and the construction of welfare services that maintain a balance between subversion of the will to satisfy needs through work and the creation of a caring society.

Cockburn (1977, p. 53) argues that both these heads may be seen as aspects of the guarantee of continued expansion of capital. Both the securing of conditions contributing to capitalist production and the maintenance of the essential features of the capitalist form of society are necessary to this process. The latter falls into two parts: the continued reproduction of the necessary labour force secured through the interaction of family and welfare systems and the reproduction of the relations of production secured, on the one hand, through the direct repression of dissent (the police kicking pickets at Grunwick) and on the other through the maintenance of an appropriate structure of motives and ideas (private property, work, pluralist consensus and so on). These ideas exist in social structures beyond the state: their relation to the state is through that part of socialization carried out by formal education and through the principles reinforced by law and contained in welfare and other regulations.

The state's welfare role is part and parcel of its total role in society. To give an abstract account of its function however is not to explain its origins and development. Under present circumstances a particular form of the state may be an important support of capitalism. The story of how those circumstances arose and the part played by various interests in constructing the modern state is a tale that cannot be entered into here. Saville points to the pre-eminent role of working-class struggle in this story:

The welfare state has come about as a result of the interaction of three main factors:
1   The struggle of the working class against their exploitation;
2   The requirements of industrial capitalism (a convenient abstraction) for a more efficient environment in which to operate, and in particular, the need for a highly productive labour force;
3   Recognition by the property owners of the price that has to be paid for political security . . .
the pace and tempo of social reform has been determined by the struggle of working-class groups and organizations . . .
(Butterworth and Holman (eds.), 1975, pp. 57–8).

This aspect saves the marxist account of the state from being simply an account of a conspiracy by industrialists to establish a social structure that suits them. The part played by industry (both in immediate interest and as a response to pressure in the workplace) and by the propertied classes in the story must not be ignored. A useful survey is provided by Hay who demonstrates that shifting alliances of various interests lay behind the establishment of various welfare measures. In particular he stressed that 'employers have an interest in welfare both within the firm and as developed by the state', (1979, p. 4) and traces the varying balance of 'the motives of social control and economic efficiency in the area of labour discipline'.

Given the varying costs and benefits of welfare to employers, it is hardly surprising that employer attitudes to welfare have changed and developed according to economic and social circumstances . . . . From the late nineteenth century to around 1920, as foreign competition and labour unrest intensified, many influential employers began to argue for state welfare as a means of social control and as a contribution to economic efficiency . . . . When mass unemployment took the edge off labour militancy and guaranteed a supply of labour, employers became more sensitive to the costs of welfare

(1979, p. 6).

The situation after the second world war is more complex as the development of large industrial units and the growing importance of skill puts a premium on loyalty to the firm and encourages the growth of occupational welfare 'now supported by tax concessions, rather than a corresponding increase in institutional welfare provided by the state'. The prognosis for employer attitudes to state welfare in the heyday of unemployment of the 1980s is clear.

The view of the state as the product of social relations that may ultimately be traced back to their roots in material relations suggests limitations on the state's capacity to resolve the problems that confront it. Two kinds of obstacles lie in the way to the mitigation of social problems: first, powerful social interests may struggle against the resolution of the problems that afflict many members of society. The accumulation of profit does not necessarily coincide with welfare aims. Secondly, the capitalist system of production continually produces and reinforces problems, both in terms of the social conflicts engendered (of which class struggle is the most obvious example), and through the tendency to a continued expansion of the scope of need.

The argument of a recent memo from the Department of Industry to the Ministry of Social Security provides a good example of the first issue. It claims that state welfare benefits enable strikers to avoid real hardship, and proposes measures to redress this 'fundamental imbalance in industrial relations'. 'It is contrary to all reason that the Government should add to industrial difficulties . . . we are tilting the balance against employers and allowing strikes to be held on the cheap'. (*Guardian*, 6 September 79) In other words, the relief of poverty must take second place to the ascendancy of the power of capital in class struggle.

As an example of the first kind of issue, let us consider the structure of motivations appropriate to capitalism. These include a strong impulse to acquire property and respect for work. (MacPherson, 1973, part 3). The state in a capitalist society must walk a tightrope between popular pressure for welfare and support for these widely held principles. Welfare in kind must be organized so that any tendency to distribute access to or control over property is severely restricted. Cash welfare payments must be hedged about with restrictions to avoid the subversion of the primary work-income link (see the concluding chapter of Kincaid, 1975). The task is made easier by the fact that the state is not an external imposition on society, but an integral development. Its policies are expressions of dominant values, supported by a reservoir of popular culture and aided by the cultural sanctions of stigma, work ethic and so on. Thus Holman reports on research into a negative-income tax scheme in America that 'the desire to work was so strongly entrenched that the poor chose to do so even if offered an income for not working'. Similarly a study in the UK revealed the 'striking' persistence of the will to work, even among men 'badly treated by employers and employment', (1978, pp. 126).

In other areas, the ideological obstacles to change are still formidable but less powerful. The principle that it is good to live in families is, in practice, incorporated into support for the existing order. Family — the sphere of private consumption — provides a focus and a justification for acquisition through work. It also serves to socialize children and as a convenient location of part of the reserve army of labour. Some women can be absorbed into domestic work in times of slump. However, alternative mechanisms could carry out these roles. The historic accident of the family could, in principle, be dispensed with in a market society without damaging the principle of capitalist social relations. The existing role of the family provides an obstacle to change and generates a barrier of vested interests. This barrier is not insuperable as the recent expansion of compulsory education into the sphere of socialization and legislation introducing formal equality between men and women in some areas of social security and employment rights indicates.

These examples illustrate the power and limitations of restrictions on state action. The conflicts that are contained within the practice of state welfare between work and need as criteria for income or between ability to pay and need as criteria for distribution of welfare goods result from a more basic contradiction: that between pressure for more welfare in their own obvious interest by the working-class majority in a democratic society and the widespread respect for the anti-welfare principles intrinsic to capitalism. Such contradictions also form part of the second aspect of the problems of welfare-capitalism: the production of new needs which are hard to resolve. There are two aspects to this.

First, class struggle is only the most obvious of the contradictions of the capitalist system. In an oft quoted passage (1976, ch. 32) Marx discusses the future development of society:

> Hand in hand with this centralization (of capital) develop on an ever-extending scale, the cooperative form of the labour-process the conscious technical application of science . . . the transformation of the instruments of labour into instruments of labour only usable in common . . . the entanglement of all peoples in the net of the world-market . . . . Along with the constantly diminishing number of magnates of capital, who usurp and monopolize all advantages of this process of transformation, grows the mass of misery, oppression, slavery, degradation, exploitation, but with

this too grows the revolt of the working class, a class . . . disciplined, united, organized by the very mechanism of the process of capitalist production itself.

The outcome of the contradiction between the concentration of capital and the exploitation of labour grouped together and forced to organize by the system of exploitation is the dissolution of capitalism. Thus the instability of the system results from its production of pressing problems for its members, and creates further problems. The series of depressions culminating in the great slump of the inter-war period is an obvious example. The response to that crisis was enhanced interventionism in the management of the economy. Yet steps required to achieve this end themselves conflict with welfare goals. A recent White Paper setting out cuts in intended expenditure across the range of state services concludes:

> public services . . . are prerequisites of efficiency, as well as of welfare and personal freedom. However, at this juncture, further improvements must depend on the prior achievement of our economic and industrial objectives
>
> (HMSO, 1977, p. 14).

The second aspect of the expansion of need has already been mentioned in Titmuss's observation that industrial growth imposes costs on some people (chapter 3). If we expand our awareness of such costs to include not only the pollution that attracts Friedman's attention and the stultifying effects of inequality that Crosland discusses, but also the expansion of 'positional goods' stressed by Hirsch, the scope of this process becomes impressive. It is possible to argue that, so long as we understand poverty in a relative way, as referring to the individual's position in relation to others in society, instead of an absolute measure of the goods she can buy, growth may well increase poverty. Townsend points out (1971 ch. 1) that a relative approach is the only one that can make sense of the fact that westerners commonly call people poor whose standard of living is ten times that of the better-off Indian peasants or medieval serfs. As standards rise, the potential for the creation of new needs — the gap which calls out for extra welfare spending — may expand. For example the value of supplementary benefit long-term rates for a married couple has risen from about half to about 60 per cent of the net pay of a male manual worker between 1967 and 1977 (SBC Annual Report for 1977, p. 18). Over the same period the number of cases recognized by SB staff as requiring discretionary lump-sum grants has risen from less than a sixth to over a third (calculated from information on p. 62 of the report and p. 115 of *Social Trends*, 1979). As living standards rise so does the pressure for higher benefits.

As standards rise, the potential for the creation of new needs — the gap which calls out for welfare services — may expand.

In other areas, technical advance imposes fresh demands. A clear example is that of medicine, where the application of science creates the possibility of unfulfilled demand for renal dialysis or screening women for breast cancer. As the recent Royal Commission on the NHS comments 'while some scientific advances reduce costs, most tend to increase them', (Royal Commission on the NHS, 1979, p. 380). Thus as time goes on a process founded on the accumulation of profit, may produce unsatisfied need as a by-product to the detriment of its own legitimacy.

Marxism provides both a powerful account of the obstacles to the resolution of some social problems and an explanation of the way in which new problems develop to face society. In contrast to the idealism that formed the basis of reformism, a materialist approach stresses both the strength of obstacles and the processes leading to destruction of those obstacles and the form of society they constitute. Its approach to human interests is immanent in the idea of human labour as the foundation of social relations. The ideal is that of a free association of producers, unoppressed by class relations, which constitutes a socialist order. Emancipation and coercion are linked in a thoroughgoing manner to social relations.

Two kinds of problems with marxist approaches may be outlined. First, a materialist historical analysis claims to provide an objective account of human society. If this is so, all it seems we can say about each epoch is 'so it goes: next please'! Wood points out (1972a, p. 244) that Marx avoids the passing of normative judgements on social relations. Yet the reader is left feeling that Marx's work adds up to 'a passionate attack on our type of society', which is 'at bottom, a moral condemnation of it' (Plamenatz, 1975, p. 472). How to reconcile materialism and value-judgements? To claim that marxism implicitly relates contemporary affairs to a shadowy and undeveloped ideal of a socialism to come seems utopian and unsatisfactory.

The second problem is linked to this. Marxism's success in accounting for human social appropriation of outer nature is paralleled by a lack of concern for inner nature — for psychology (see Corrigan and Leonard, 1978, ch. 10). Habermas puts the point well:

Marx was convinced that at one time the human species elevated itself above animal conditions of existence by transcending the limits of animal intelligence and being to transform adaptive behaviour into instrumental action. Thus what interests him as the natural basis of history, is the physical organization specific to the human species under the category of possible labour: the tool-making animal. Freud . . . in contrast . . . made the assumption that men distinguished themselves from animals when they succeeded in inventing an agency of socialization for their biologically endangered offspring, subject to extended childhood dependency . . . . Thus what interests him as the natural basis of history is the physical organization specific to the human species under the category of surplus impulses and their canalization: the drive-inhibited and at the same time fantasizing animal

(Habermas, 1978, p. 282).

The psychoanalytic approach throws emphasis on the family. It also provides a basis for theories of undistorted, uninhibited and unfantastic human nature, as a basis for social judgement, and for a materialist psychological theory of illusion and ideology. This is developed by the critical theorists of the Frankfurt School.

## Critical theory and materialism

The conception of critique is of great significance in marxist thought: indeed *Capital* is subtitled 'A Critique of Political Economy'. The argument is founded on an analysis of the major concepts of bourgeois political economy (commodity, exchange, profit, labour, value) that points to structural conflict lying behind the surface appearance of individual competition. The understanding of the market as free and fair exchange between legal equals overlies and conceals that aspect of it which is the exploitation of one class by another. The former viewpoint is that of the individual within the system; that latter is a historical materialist perspective that sees society as a whole in its place in history.

Slater shows how critical theory developed this approach into a 'critique of ideology in its broadest sense' (1977, p. 31). This involves the interpretation of concepts in their historical context and in their relation to the reality of the society they describe and the social life in which they inhere. In an essay of 1937, Horkheimer, setting out the distinctive features of the approach, opposes Traditional and Critical theory: the latter term is used 'not so much in the sense of the idealist critique of pure reason, as in the sense of the dialectical critique of political economy' (quoted in Slater, 1977, p. 26). Kant's *Critique of Pure Reason* attempts to give an account of how people come to have the picture of the world that we share. Understanding is a given. The categories which must exist in human minds to produce that common understanding are deduced from it.

Marx's critique follows an opposite process. The starting point is a holistic analysis of capitalist society. Theory is directed at understanding how social life produces a different and limited interpretation in the minds of members of society and renders that perspective dominant so as to direct social action. The categories in question are not timeless structures of consciousness, but social constructions that form part of a particular form of life. The essence of the method is not the deduction of the roots of consciousness-taken-as-reality, but the reinterpretation of the dominant currents in consciousness-treated-as-ideology.

In different contexts, other writers use interpretational critique. Freud's analysis of psychic life postulates a process of the production of categories of mind (ego, id), through the mechanisms of repression, sublimation and so on in the adaptation of brute instincts to the demands of social relationships. Psychic phenomena: mundane, as in *The Psychopathology of Everyday Life* — the freudian slip —, mystifying, as in *The Interpretation of Dreams* — wish fulfillment, or bizarre as in pathological behaviour, are manifestations of the inner, to be interpreted. Interpretation operates practically: in the process of psychoanalysis, worrying mental events are reinterpreted to the patient in Freudian categories. A truer understanding of self leads to relief from the burden of the problem — the psychoanalytic cure. Similarly, marxism suggests that the understanding of a correct analysis of capitalism leads to change: 'the proletarians have nothing to lose but their chains. They have a world to win.' (Marx and Engels, 1972, p. 76). Ideology forms a powerful part of the chains.

Critical theory posits a conflation of theory and practice. If ideology is the outcome of material conditions, truth demands a society in which material circumstances do not militate against rational discourse — a society without an individualization of interest in the market and a reduction of social relations to relations with things through the interposition of commodities between buyer and seller. Production and distribution is a collective enterprise: capitalism obscures the apprehension of the system as a whole.

Thus, critical theory 'shot through with an interest in reasonable conditions', Horkheimer claims. Marcuse puts it more forcibly:

> free and equal discussion can fulfill the function attributed to it only if it is rational — expression and development of independent thinking free from indoctrination, manipulation, extraneous authority . . . such a construction badly fits a society in which powers are and remain unequal . . . a free society is indeed unrealistically and indefinably different from existing ones.
>
> (1976, p. 309)

The interpretive approach of critical theory suggests a way of tackling the problem of linking materialism with a critique of values. Values are socially produced and form part of the totality of a society. Yet different social systems offer different possibilities for citizens to pass correct judgements on them. At once the problem and the condemnation inherent in a normative approach to capitalism is its mystification. Judgement on the system must be clouded and this is grounds for judgement. Truth, freedom and justice are inseparable. If critical analysis can construct an 'Archimedean point' from which to reinterpret the appearance of social relations, correctly grounded judgement can be sustained, and emancipated action in the interests of human welfare is possible. But where to found judgement?

A useful introduction to the issue of changing materialism so that it does justice to inner nature is provided by Fromm, who attempts to found a critique of capitalism on the union of marxist political economy and psychoanalytic theory: this rests on the development of the notion that people who participate in capitalist relations become estranged from themselves and from their true needs. Man is 'estranged from the world. He does not experience himself as the centre of the world, as the creator of his own acts, but his acts and their consequences have become his masters . . .' (1963, p. 120). Capital accumulation takes precedence over human creativity, market relations motivated by alienated self-interest over relationships informed by concern to meet each other's needs. The critique of capitalism is transmuted from marxist scientific analysis of the internal conflicts that render it unstable to a normative condemnation, on the grounds that it contradicts an ideal of mental health.

Fromm's goal is 'a sane society . . . in which qualities like greed, exploitation, possessiveness, narcissism have no chance to be used for greater material gain . . .' (p. 276). The present system of exploitation fosters such qualities which in turn reproduce the system: no nourishment for relationships that express true human nature is available.

The problem with this approach, as Plant points out (1974, pp. 83–4) is that construction of any transcendent ideal of sanity or normality would appear to rest on judgements that are themselves unfounded. How can the human ideal that is to serve as yardstick against its corruption by capitalism be justified? Marcuse develops the approach in relation to the idea of basic instinctual drives discovered by psychoanalysis: while all human society involves repression of such drives, the problem of capitalism is that it requires a surplus repression in order to produce an unhealthy compulsion toward accumulation and acquisitiveness (1956, p. 37). Present society may be condemned because it involves more distortion of people than previous forms.

This distortion extends throughout human relationships to the production of a one-dimensional society in which critical discourse is contained and redirected to serve the needs of the existing system. Under such a radical unfreedom, concepts are remoulded: the 'desublimation' of libidinous drives associated with greater social tolerance becomes repressive rather than liberating because it is confined to contexts where it fails to engage with the major exploitative structures. Similarly the tolerance associated with bourgeois political democracy becomes repressive when it extends to the permission of all strands of opinion and action: 'expressed in . . . impartiality, it serves to minimize or even absolve prevailing intolerance and suppression' (1976, p. 312).

The introduction of an approach which moves away from a focus on political economy to the attempt to integrate it with the study of social relations and discourse is opposed by many marxists: Sidgewick comments sourly on Marcuse: 'the expulsion of the metaphysical, and even the theological, from the rational tradition of marxism, has become a task requiring conscious, perhaps painful, effort' (1966, p. 186). Perhaps the most impressive attempt to introduce the study of normative discourse in this area is provided by Habermas.

Habermas's approach is founded on an attempt to identify human interests; general analysis of the form of interests enables us to discover the conditions under which they may be attained. He points to three realms of interest (1978): the economic sphere of production to meet material need; the sphere of inner nature in which people strive to come to terms with their psychic life; and the sphere of social action in which people wish to understand each other's needs and motives and to act collectively in the advancement of interest. In the first two areas marxism and psychoanalytical theory provide appropriate interpretive schema: our interest in social welfare directs us to the arena of social life. It is in consideration of this area that Habermas moves beyond Fromm and Marcuse. He argues that the starting point for judgement is the extent to which sociopolitical arrangements provide the possibility for people to control society. The method of enquiry rests on the hermeneutic tradition associated with the German philosopher of history and critic, Dilthey.

Our concern is with the possibility of members of modern society interpreting its reality for themselves. Dilthey points out that in the reading of literature, interpretation operates within a circle:

> The whole of a work must be understood from the individual words and their combinations, and yet the full comprehension of the detail presupposes the understanding of the whole
>
> (1976, p. 115).

Culture also rests on shared meanings and meaning is meaning in a context. For example understanding of means-test stigma presupposes participation in a whole range of meanings — the tradition of the workhouse, the work ethic, paying one's way, the status of the pauper — which are interdependent and which rest on appropriate social institutions. (Imagine trying to explain one by itself to a Martian on an asteroid: snow and Hottentots!)

The analogy between being able to grasp a text — whole and part — simultaneously, and being a citizen who can use and understand language in relation to a society is now complete. The problem of the legitimacy of modern social forms becomes one of the extent to which contemporary culture contains intersubjective meanings that enable us to discuss satisfactorily the fairness of those forms. Habermas furnishes the possibility of 'reading the text' of modern sociopolitical culture to argue that this is not the case.

Communication may be 'systematically distorted'. Yet language also contains in its very structure the possibility of rational discourse about normative issues:

> what raises us out of nature is the only thing whose nature we can know: language. Through its structure, autonomy and responsibility are posited for us. Our first sentence expresses unequivocally the intention of universal and unconstrained consensus.
>
> (1965).

The fact that we can talk about norms presupposes the possibility of our passing judgements on social arrangements: however, this is only possible in an 'ideal speech situation' where the fragmented interests of capitalist society do not distort communication. In present culture, the discourse appropriate to a free, democratic citizen is simply not available. Both the possibility and the unrealization of a normative critique of contemporary society exist.

Habermas's approach puts ideology at the centre of the stage. The displacement of social contradictions at other levels to this area is well illustrated in his theory of crisis.

A social system faces a crisis when it generates problems it cannot solve without fundamental change. Habermas suggests that the concept may be deployed in relation to economic, political and cultural systems. Each level is in theory vulnerable to a crisis of input or output: it may fail to get what it needs or to meet the demands placed on it. However in practice catastrophic deficit in input at the economic level (factors of production) or the cultural level (human social interaction) is unlikely at present. The other four categories of crisis are real possibilities.

The *laissez-faire* stage of capitalism generated a structural separation of state and market. An ideology of private property and free exchange underpinned free market and minimal state. The peculiarity of advanced capitalism is the progressive 'repoliticization' of economic relations.

The recurrence of economic crisis (a failure in output of sufficient goods/profits/employment to measure up to expectations) results in increased state intervention. Such intervention can only be justified as an output of technically successful rational administration in the common interest: the government must be seen to

> collect the necessary sum in taxes by skimming off profits and income, and put it to such rational use critical disturbances in growth can be avoided
>
> (1976, p. 377).

If growth falters, rationality crisis results. Intervention is not measuring up to expectations.

Political action also demands an input of mass loyalty. If 'the selective raising of taxes, the recognizable scale of priorities according to which they are employed and the administrative procedure' fails to measure up to popular criteria of what is fair, legitimation crisis occurs. Values (such as fairness) are outputs of the cultural system.

The point of Habermas's analysis is that the meanings, the shared attitudes and values that make up social life, are resistant to change by the political level. If political actions fail to measure up to dominant ideologies a crisis of legitimacy results. The political system is dependent on the meanings created by the totality of society (including economic and political levels) and inherited from the past. At root the crisis of legitimacy is a crisis of motivation at a cultural level (1976, p. 380).

Here the critique of culture re-enters. The technical success of state intervention in curbing economic crisis is associated with the dominion of modes of thought that operate in technocratic terms — the capacity of systems to achieve given goals. The normative element in the specification of goals is driven out of consideration by this process. Advanced capitalism demands new roles for the state. It destroys the possibility of playing the language game appropriate to the consensual justification of relevant norms. The state is compelled to intervene in the economy to ensure growth. Intervention becomes intervention against the minimalist norms of the market and increasingly for one side or another in industrial conflict. The theory that displaces crisis to the level of ideology and suggests its peculiar intractability is developed in detail in chapter nine.

Habermas suggests that human welfare is bound up with the creation of a social form in which communication unclouded by ideology is possible: the limitations of the welfare state are structurally linked to those of developed capitalism. The importance of the critical perspective for marxism is twofold: it shows the intimate interconnection of ideology with material relations. It also posits structural limits to satisfactory normative discourse in contemporary social forms, providing an immanent basis for judgement. The paradox of the approach is that the limits themselves suggest that the judgement cannot be uncontested.

## Functionalism

Functionalism provides an approach radically different to that of marxism. The latter suggests that irreconcilable contradictions are the motive force of history, the former stresses structural integration of various elements in society. A focus on integration leads in two directions: The conception of society as consisting of sub-systems that either are, or can be, organically related; and the tendency to analyse social elements in terms of contribution to the whole.

Before discussing the dominant modern approaches — the normative functionalism of Talcott Parsons and the technological determinism of convergence theory — we shall mention three strands that contribute to the perspective. These are the 'social darwinist' tradition of writers such as Spencer, the social organicism of the Durkheim school, and the neo-Hegelianism of the English Idealists.

Spencer stressed the interdependence of human and societal evolution. Pressure of population provides a stimulus to the increased production of necessities, and places a corresponding premium on advances in human skill, intelligence and self-control. These qualities lead to the development of higher forms of society: 'every improvement is at once the product of a higher form of humanity and demands the higher form of humanity to carry it into practice' (1852, p. 468) The resulting strictures against state intervention in industrial society, on the grounds that it damaged societal progress by favouring the least successful human types are well known (see Pinker, 1971, ch. 1, for a clear review of Spencer's polemic). The strand of human interest as, in the short run subordinate to, and in the long run advanced by societal progress is a theme that recurs in later structural functionalism.

Durkheim's central concern in his discussion of industrial society is the decline in social solidarity and the tendency to 'anomie' — the absence of a moral force sufficiently strong to direct and control individual action and justify the individual's place in an unequal social order to him. This results from the loosening of feudal bonds and the atomization of collective interest in the market. The legitimacy of society is a paramount consideration:

> a society is not a collection of individuals which an enormous and monstrous machine keeps united and compressed against each other by the use of force. No, solidarity comes from the inside . . . the affinity which [people] hold for each other . . . is no less natural to man than egoism . . . . This solidarity is expressed externally by an appropriate structure. The state is one of these structures.
>
> (Giddens (ed.) 1972, p. 56).

The state expresses rather than imposes moral order. Thus, the problems that arise from inequality will be resolved not by government legislating appropriate differential rewards, but by the completion of the division of labour: the attainment of a situation in which 'social inequalities exactly express natural inequalities' (Giddens (ed.) p. 182). The problem of order that results from the need to reconcile the motives of individual action with the requirements of society is a central issue of later functionalism. However, Durkheim's perspective is dynamic, demanding social change to achieve an ideal. Structural functionalism has tended to transpose concern with normative stability in itself to concern for the normative stability of existing institutions. The distance between ideal and the status quo dissolves and the approach becomes apology.

A concern with the goal of normative consensus has surfaced in recent discussion of social policy. In a major cross-national study, Pinker builds on earlier work (1971, chapters 3 and 4) in an attempt to 'characterize moral sentiments which citizens hold about welfare in terms of their notions of felt obligations and entitlement' (1979, p. 66).

The ideal of redistribution in the interest of social welfare is 'most likely to be achieved in a society with some overriding sense of a collective purpose and pride in its common productive endeavours' (p. 249).

The English idealists developed the theory of action implicit in Hegel's metaphysics. Rational action is action which can be justified. Technical action can be judged by its efficiency: no comparable criterion is available for moral action. The only object of action available to a free individual is self: the decision as to which plan of life is worthwhile must be made then 'with reference to the best self he can realize in the circumstances' (Milne, 1962, p. 79).

However, the moral self is also a social self. Thus, moral life consists in the integration of competing needs and plans of life in an organic social unity:

> we have found self-realization, duty and happiness in one, yes, we have found ourselves when we have found our station and its duties, our function as an organ in the social organism
>
> (F.H. Bradley — quoted in Milne, 1962, p. 61).

Green develops this idea to suggest that moral rights are dependent on consensus:

> no one can have a right except (a) as a member of society and (b) of a society in which some common good is recognized by the members as their ideal . . . . There can be rights . . . only in a society where there is fundamental agreement
>
> (Quoted in Milne, 1962, p. 128).

The organic society, and the recognition by the individual of his place in the overall order is a prerequisite of any justification of action. The link between consensus and stability in society is normative as well as empirical.

## Structural functionalism: normative consensus

The themes of the subordination of individual to social organism, of the consequent limits to state action and of the importance of normative consensus are united in Parson's work, but with a crucial difference. If Durkheim and Neo-Hegelians were concerned with the quest for social order, Parsons made it his central assumption. His theory defines society as a totality founded on that principle.

In *The Social System* sociological theory is defined by its 'concern with the phenomena of the institutionalization of patterns of value-orientation in the social system' (1951, p. 552). The author argues if a social system 'is to constitute a persistent order or to undergo an orderly process of . . . change, certain functional prerequisites must be met' (1951, p. 27). These include meeting biological needs, existence of language as a prerequisite for culture, a minimal command of 'technical lore' and so on. Focus on function is a matter of definition:

> a social system which meets all the essential functional prerequisites of long-term persistence from within its own resources will be called a society
>
> (1951, p. 19).

The definitional prerequisites of society are elsewhere summarized in terms of the successful completion of four essential tasks: adaptation, goal attainment, integration and pattern-maintenance (Parsons and Smelser, 1956, pp. 18–19). The power of the theory is such that it may apply to any organization of life from the simplest organism to the most complex society. Society must adapt to its physical environment. The economic system must appropriate, process and distribute outer nature satisfactorily. Secondly, a system for defining and attaining objectives must exist. Thirdly, a degree of solidarity is essential to prevent disintegration. Fourthly a process to ensure integrity is required: in the organism, the cohesion and mutual service of interacting organs: in society shared values that direct and coordinate human actors.

This analysis bears close similarity to Habermas's identification of economic, political and cultural realms — the first, adaptation; the second, goal attainment and legitimacy, united in a democratic state; the third, shared meanings. However, Habermas situates the relation of the categories in a particular politico-economic form. His concern with the possibility of irresolvable crisis and stress on the significance of the material level give the analysis a dynamic potential denied to Parson's timeless focus on integration and pattern-maintenance.

The problems a Parsonian approach, operating in the dominant category of order, encounters in conceptualizing social tensions are often argued. For example:

> the propensity to social change arising from the functional incompatability between an institutional order and its material base has been ignored by normative functionalists, because of their concentration on the moral aspects of social integration
>
> (Lockwood, 1964, p. 256).

Moreover, discussion of social welfare stemming from this perspective has been heavily criticized (see George and Wilding, 1971; Wilson, 1977, p. 36). Parsons himself set out the limitations of his approach as 'a second-best type of theory'. Justification for it starts from the idea that science is concerned with 'the analysis of elements of uniformity in empirical processes' (1951, p. 20). Structural functionalism provides a system of descriptive categories applicable to 'all relevant parts . . . of a concrete system in a coherent way'. Secondly, the approach integrates social processes through its stress on normative order. Values lead people to act in ways that fit in with the structural theoretic.

The justification is only presented as adequate in the present 'highly fragmented' state of sociological knowledge. It is simply a heuristic tool stressing uniformity as convenient to a certain type of scientific approach. The assumption of order makes a general explanation easier.

Elements which might contribute to social tension drop out of view. Thus power (1961, p. 41) and anomie (1954, p. 125) become properties of the system as a whole rather than of individuals or groups within it. Similarly human interests become secondary to social order:

> from the point of view of the functioning of the social system, it is not the needs of all the participant actors which must be met . . . but only a sufficient proportion for a sufficient fraction of the population . . . social forces are directly responsible for injury to or destruction of some individuals, and of some of the wants and needs of all individuals
>
> (Parsons, 1951, p. 28).

Structural functionalist analysis of the welfare state is mainly concerned with the integration and the maintenance of order. The clearest account is perhaps Smelser (1959). The development of modern society does not alter the four basic tasks; simply the institutions which are called on to tackle them. The differentiation of institutions in industrial society leads to new forms of integration. For example, the separation of production from kinship structure in the supplanting of household by factory industry creates a host of problems: the provision of appropriate labour-supply to the workplace, the protection of families from market fluctuations, and so on:

> Development gives birth to dozens of institutions . . . geared to these new integrative problems — labour recruitment agencies and exchanges, labour unions, government regulation of labour allocation, welfare . . ., cooperative societies and savings institutions (Smelser, 1964, p. 268 quoted in Mishra, 1977 p. 49).

Functional prerequisites remain constant.

The autonomy of the political level is firmly confined by the requirements of normative order. This holistic structuralism also leads to an immanent consensualism. The status quo is by definition ordered and order is the goal and reality of the social system. The capacity of present institutions to resolve social conflict is thus posited.

## Convergence theory — technological determinism

Convergence theory mirrors the structural functionalist subordination of individual interest to that of the social whole. It differs in including a dynamic element and in according less central significance to normative consensus. The contribution of this approach is the emphasis on trends to uniformity and diversity in modern industrial society, particularly in the role of the state. Convergent trends are readily documented. Wilensky's massive cross-national study of welfare expenditure has already been mentioned (chapter 1). Gough (1975, pp. 58–61) reviews data from all OECD countries since the second world war and draws comparable conclusions. In an earlier work, Wilensky and Lebeaux point out that in general, 'the more industrialized the nation, the larger the slice of its national income spent on welfare services' (1965, p. x).

Within the broad tendency of overall expenditure is the tendency for national policies to grow markedly similar. Gough (1978, p. 20) gives the example of social security. The European countries which initiated social insurance for specific occupational groups are tending to move towards more universal coverage, more unified administration, towards pay-as-you-go financing and towards the establishment of a national minimum standard. Conversely countries that incorporated a unified national minimum early on are tending to add earnings-related elements, which reflect the pattern of coverage of the first group.

Within such convergence, the evidence for diversity also remains powerful. The observed trends exist in countries of different ideologies, different political systems, different military involvement, different labour organization and so on (Wilensky, 1975 p. xiv). For example, in the field of welfare, the relative 'backwardness' of US social provision and the pioneering inception of comprehensive schemes in New Zealand are often remarked.

Convergence theory argues that of unity and diversity, unity is the dominant theme, and that the origins of the tendency are to be found in the ubiquitous development of industrial society. Two major strands within the approach may be identified, one assertive, the other more cautious. The *locus classicus* of the former is the work of Kerr and his associates:

> the place the society starts from and the route it follows are likely to affect its industrial features for many years, but all industrializing societies respond to the inherent 'logic of industrialism' itself. The empire of industrialism will embrace the whole world; and such similarities as it decrees will penetrate the outermost points of its sphere of influence and its sphere come to be universal
>
> (1960, p. 46).

The logic of industrialism, the motor of change, is simply the impact of a 'new and vastly superior technique of production' which compels a trend to uniformity by demanding certain social changes. These include the provision of a trained, healthy, geographically mobile workforce, the organization and coordination of a large-scale society, and the development of a consensus on appropriate values. Such changes incorporate the development of similar state welfare systems (pp. 179–81).

If the achievements of industry tend to force out inappropriate social forms, diversity is to be explained by the response to industrialization and by context.

we identify the universal with 'the logic of industrialism'; the related with the strategies of the 'industrializing elites' and the unique with specific cultures and environments

(p. 11).

The new system is introduced by varying dominant groups. Different sponsors tend to develop systems corresponding to their particular values and interests; the middle class favour a free market and a minimal state (the UK, the USA); dynastic industrializers (Germany, Japan) a paternalistic authority; revolutionaries, state control of society and universal care (USSR, China) and so on. However, the demands of industrial success themselves force elites towards a common goal. Political factors are secondary to the structuralism centred on growth. Nevertheless 'a clear ideology held by a distinct ruling class' together with particular cultural patterns are the most forceful patterns making for diversity. The result is that the ideal type is a common but unrealized objective: industrial society 'varies around a general central theme' (p. 290).

A more cautious treatment of the convergence thesis is provided in the development of Wilensky's position. His early work, originally published in 1958, contained an account of convergent trends in social welfare:

all industrial societies face similar problems, and the solutions are prescribed more by industry than by other cultural elements
(Wilensky and Lebeaux, 1965, p. 47).

The book also includes a postscript that contains a Parsonian functionalist account of the constitutive tasks of society (pp. 337–48); yet here the authors warn against the kind of technological determinism that characterized Kerr's approach. The possibility of a relation of reciprocity rather than of dependence between technological and ideological change is entertained and with it the potential partial autonomy of the political level.

In a preface to the second edition, the assertion that more growth means more welfare is tempered by caution about future developments. In later work, inherent and destabilizing conflict between the expansion of industry and the attainment of human interests is posited. (1975, ch. 5). However, although the links between technological change and political action may be weaker than in Kerr's model, ultimately it is industrial growth that is the 'root cause' of the welfare state throughout (see 1975, pp. 47 and 86; 1976, p. 13).

Convergence theory tends to link human interest to observed trends. Kerr:

> industrialization is technically so superior . . . that it tends . . . to raise living standards, as measured by life expectancy, health and education . . . . The prospects are for increased well-being rather than for increased misery

> (1960, p. 29).

Wilensky refers to the 'humanizing' and 'civilizing' effects of the global expansion of state welfare (1975, p. 119). However, his sympathy is for the underprivileged (p. xv) and he is equally concerned to chart the shortcomings of modern welfare states in providing for such groups (pp. 87–104).

In pure form, the approach is a functionalism, based on the prerequisites of economic growth, rather than normative order. It tends to the conservative leaning of Parsons's work. However, as Wilensky's work shows, judgement on modern forms can be independent of a more or less determinist assessment of their development. In this sense, convergence theory hovers uneasily between the structural materialism of Kerr, who unites judgement and explanation in observation, and the idealism that we earlier detected in Galbraith. The detachment of the observer from social trends in an independent standpoint of 'public purpose' or (in Wilensky's case) 'equality' prefigures the possibility of a detachment of political action from economic imperative. This returns the approach to the category of reformist idealism reviewed in chapter three.

In Wilensky, the idealist trait is far weaker. The dominant tendency is for all political forms to converge on the most practically successful solutions to the problems the industrial system generates (1976, p. 8). This leads to an unresolved ambiguity, in which the ideology guiding political action is 'both a dependent variable . . . explained by . . . attributes of structures, and a weaker independent variable' (1975, p. 50). Structural determinism ultimately overcomes idealism.

The strengths of the convergence variant of functionalism are obvious: it has an immense capacity to handle the considerable evidence of worldwide structural uniformity in social welfare. Its weaknesses derive from its account of political action: how far does the approach imply a technological determinism that writes the human actor out of history? The dilemma is that any move towards an independence of the political level tends to dilute the strength of the accounts of historical development. If human decisions, rather than brute growth enter into an account of contemporary affairs, the force of the technological emphasis is vitiated.

## Problems of functionalism

There are perhaps two main strands to the critique of functionalism conveniently available within social administration. The first is that of Goldthorpe, who is concerned to analyse the responses of left-wing historians such as Polyani, Carr and Beale to the interpretations of the rise of the modern state offered by anti-collectivists working in a Spencerian tradition. These writers concentrate on the explanation of social action in terms of the functional role it fulfils, and do not elaborate through the Parsonian concept of a value-system an account of the way people find certain changes acceptable. Thus Goldthorpe defines functionalism as the view that the explanation of the growth of social provision is to be given ultimately 'not in terms of great men, nor of group interests, or pressure, but rather in terms of the objective demands of certain social situations, which are seen as virtually imposing certain courses of action' (1962, pp. 50–1). He criticizes this approach on two main grounds: that it does not enable us to explain why the response to broadly similar objective social circumstances (e.g. industrialization) in different welfare states differed in some respects, and that it is in any case logically impossible to show that a particular policy was functionally necessary, since we cannot study history minus that event.

Such criticisms of the functionalist claim that may be summed up in the tag 'social environment determines social policy' are repeated by Webb, Heisler and others in social administration (Hall *et al.*, 1975, pp. 9–11; Heisler, 1977, p. 19). Interestingly, it is still possible to advance such arguments and maintain an analysis of social policy that is very close to functionalism in its stress on society as a closed, stable, essentially consensual system. This underlies Webb's 'bounded pluralism' and Heisler's 'integrative' approach.

Goldthorpe stresses that functionalism represents an advance over the approach to history that bases analysis on the influence of dominant individuals, an approach that finds its classic statement in the work of Dicey. A second and far more powerful critique of functionalism is however available. This tackles the more sophisticated development of the approach in the work of Parsons and others that attempts to account for the grip of the social environment on social man in terms of the central value-system. This critique is found in social administration in the work of such writers as George and Wilding, and Carrier and Kendall, and we may trace it elsewhere to the work of Gouldner, Giddens, Lukes, Rex and others.

Giddens claims that the Parsonian notion of a social system is a misleading oversimplification — in effect a mystification: 'it is impossible to make satisfactory conceptual recognition of the diversification of interests in society which intervenes between the actions of its members and the overall structure of the global community' (1976, p. 98). Gouldner elaborates:

> when the Parsonian conception of a system is brought to bear on the relation between individuals and the group as a whole, what is emphasized is the individual's plastic potential for conformity. Emphasis is placed on the conformity of individuals with the social position in which they find themselves or with the needs of the group. Thus tensions between the individuals and the group are seen as fortuitous . . .
>
> (1971, p. 218).

It is this deterministic emphasis in functionalism on the limitless potential for the social moulding of people that Carrier and Kendall seize on when they define functionalism as a variety of positivism (1973, pp. 215–20). Thus they write of the 'puppet-theatre' model of society in which the actors are seen as 'cultural dupes', compelled to act as they do by the forces of the social environment. George and Wilding take a similar line of argument further. They stress the inability of functionalism to accommodate class-conflict and focus not on the differences between individual human subjects but the differences between class-interests in capitalist society in their critique (1971, p. 238).

## Conclusion

In chapters 3 and 4 we have reviewed three approaches to the welfare state. We have attempted to emphasize the way in which overall perspectives influence the way in which people tackle the task of giving an account of this form of society. Individualism equates personal autonomy with non-interference. This corresponds to the conception of the self-regulating free individual in pursuit of the *summum bonum* — self-conception of self-interest.

In its denial of any role to social structures and institutions in shaping people's ideas and action, it effectively denies any place to social science as a sphere of study. The root of problems lies in individual failure and inadequacy or in misguided governmental action for there is no other possible source.

Reformist and structuralist approaches differ on whether human welfare can be achieved within a suitably modified capitalism. The former tends to be associated with an idealism that bases social institutions in ideas and sees them as susceptible to piecemeal rational improvement in spite of whatever obstacles may be offered by the operation of the social system: the latter tends to a materialism that sees the social whole as the generator of recognized problems. Marxist perspectives see capitalism as the producer of thoroughgoing conflicts of interests that cannot be resolved within existing structures. Convergence theorists regard the necessity to solve the problems produced by modern industry as the motor of change. Structural functionalists on the other hand, using order as their central category, define society in terms of its capacity to resolve social conflicts.

In analysis of free market economic systems, individualists understand them as capable of achieving a self-regulating balance of interests, idealists claim that equilibrium demands a measure of political intervention, and structuralists see the system in terms of the whole of society. Marxists claim that tendencies to imbalance and crisis are inherent, structural functionalists subordinate the economic level to the demands of social values, convergence theorists see it developing in response to the progress of modern industry. Similarly, at the political level, individualists see consensus as readily established, idealists occupy a middle position ranging from the view that consensus on common interest is readily established, to the view that conflicts can only be resolved with difficulty. Structuralism interprets political relations as part of a social whole.

Individualism implies a complete divorce of political and economic realms; idealism brings them into closer, but none the less contingent, relationship; materialism suggests complete interpenetration. The capacity for the political system to control the operation of society becomes steadily weaker as one moves from individualist to materialist perspective.

This completes our review of normative theories of the welfare state. In the next chapter we tackle the problem of choosing between the various approaches.

# 5

## Cutting the knot

### Choice and the problem of relativism

Chapters 3 and 4 review a range of theories that suggest conflicting interpretations of the welfare state. How to choose between them? The first hurdle is the problem of relativism. Understanding must start somewhere. If the first link in a chain of explanation is not susceptible to foundation, it is hard to see what makes a particular approach preferable to another, other than merely personal judgement. This radical reduction of truth is reinforced by the influence of two traditions in philosophy: logical positivism which suggests that all judgements are similarly mystical — one's orientation to slum housing is on the same level as one's orientation to flower-arrangement, and there's little more to be said, and the more cautious idea that many social concepts are by their nature contestable — their correct use is dispute (Gallie, 1956).

Social policy studies could avoid such issues so long as they remained within an unexamined tradition that provided an accepted foundation for judgement. More recently, under the influence of phenomenological approaches, this consensus has tended to be questioned. Carrier and Kendal, for example, reduce all accounts to a basis in normative judgements and suggest 'our aim in . . . welfare studies must be to expose more clearly the value-choices, and to indicate the widest possible range . . .' (1977, p. 290). Choice is the prerogative of the chooser, and falls outside the domain of rational discussion.

Any social science that takes seriously the idea that people as rational actors collectively produce society must avoid the arbitrariness of this approach in order to produce an account of the rationality — the meaning — of their actions. This is doubly true of social policy studies which also wish to produce a founded normative critique of social arrangements to meet needs that are consciously produced by a democratic process. We wish not only to arrive at a defensible understanding of why the welfare state is as it is, we also wish to make judgements on it as a social form. How do we provide a basis for our account that is not susceptible to relativist reduction?

Rein argues that the value-loading of theory is a fact of life 'since the meaning of social events is inextricably bound up with the values we attach to them' (1977, p. 72). At minimum, the choice of features to be included in description of a social situation involves judgements of priority. However, the fate of the policy researcher is not to flounder in a morass of possible accounts: rather her role is akin to that of the story-teller. The point is to be aware of the normative loading of descriptions and to present a picture of the world *persuasively*. Acknowledgement of the social scientist's own value-commitment leads to a sophisticated relativism, which recognizes its roots in the fact that people's judgements differ and counsels the most sensible course of action in the face of the problem.

This is an accurate description of what many writers on the welfare state do. A description of unemployment as the product of an 'economic system that throws away communities with little less compunction than it throws away old cars or non-return bottles' (Batley CDP, 1974, p. 49) is also a condemnation of the system. Crossman writes that the National Health Service runs a 'two-class system': 'we, the healthy, who go [to hospital] for a short time, and come out after our operation, are magnificently looked after. They, who may spend the rest of their lives in these places, are treated in an infinitely inferior way' (1972, p. 14). This is a correct account: for example the average cost per bed for the mentally ill and for short-stay maternity wards differed by a factor of three in 1973 (Parker, 1975, p. 82), a gap that cannot be wholly explained by the difference in cost of the services needed, but must to some extent reflect a difference in standards of diet, staffing and so on. However Crossman's juxtaposition of 'magnificent' and 'inferior' also contains an implicit demand for change. Abel-Smith and Townsend conclude their classic study of poverty statistics:

> the evidence of substantial numbers of the population living below
> national assistance level . . . calls for a radical review of the whole
> social security scheme . . . the fact that nearly a third of the poor
> were children suggests the need for a readjustment of priorities
>
> (1965, p. 67).

The sober language of 'calls for' and 'the fact that . . . suggests the need' embody judgements about what ought to be done.

Rein's approach takes account of the fact that the understanding of social policy issues is part and parcel of social action. However, the problem of choice between perspectives remains, translated to the level of a competition of persuasive accounts. In an acknowledged tradition of values — Batley CDP's radicalism, Crosland's egalitarian Fabianism, Abel-Smith and Townsend's reformism — persuasion draws on this heritage. In discussion of the full range of accounts outside a consensual value-framework this does not help. The problem is given an added twist by the consideration that from particular viewpoints particular perspectives are seen as serving social interests. For example, structuralists will not only argue that, in general, an individualist approach to social problems is wrongheaded, misleading and runs the risk of blaming the victim: they will also suggest that, on their view, the adoption of such interpretations and the policies that flow from them serve particular interests.

Piven and Cloward point out how a moral interpretation of unemployment produces a will to work that serves employer interests: it justifies the humiliating treatment of paupers that is essential

> so long as there are workers who are so poorly paid that they must be coerced into staying at their jobs by the spectacle of degraded paupers
>
> (1974, p. 346).

Similarly, Cockburn claims that the values bound up in the use of the idea 'community action' in a class society tend to obscure social relations and confuse class struggle in the interests of capital:

> the phrase that has come to be used to describe almost any collective action going on outside the workplace is 'community action'. It rings with implausibility. Why? . . . First, to think in terms of community action places struggle on ground prepared, over a long historical period by the state . . . . The second related argument . . . is that what has been called community action has been rationalized as something that arises NOT from capitalism itself, but from some of the more unfortunate, but curable effects of the current stage of technological development . . . . Third, community action is all too often described as classless . . . . The function of such community action is the maintenance of membership in a capitalist social formation, class positions firmly held though culturally muted
>
> (1977, p. 159–61).

This viewpoint assumes the correctness of a theory that can then only be tested in practice: thus, the authors of Coventry Community

Development Project's final report acknowledge the problem of relativism:

> Our conclusions are controversial and . . . they cannot be 'proved' from the work we have done. Their correctness, or otherwise, has to be judged by the cogency of the analysis and its capacity to explain observed contradictions; the consistency in practice of the strategies which flow from the analysis; and the effectiveness in practice of the lines of action suggested . . .
>
> (1975, Preface, vol. 1).

In a more forceful vein, Castells points to the explanatory limitations of research:

> The last word on this issue . . . does not lie with us. For the urban social movements are not simply a subject for research. They have their birth and development in everyday facts, posing new problems and issuing new challenges, in a cry of life and conflict that drowns the technocratic myths of urban rationality
>
> (1977, p. 378).

The view that the proof of the pudding is in the eating: that 'the conclusion lies in the streets' (Castells, 1977, p. 376) is in one way convincing. If prediction is a criterion of scientificity (and it is at least a good guide to the utility of theory), falsification by practice seems appropriate. Does Coventry CDP's analysis correspond uniquely to the development of the circumstances of that city? The only problem is that one is left with prediction after the event, which again does not help us. The issue of choice of theory returns in the understanding of the present.

Value judgements are bound up with the theory that directs explanations and can be seen as serving social interests, again interpreted through theory. The relationship between values and theory is circular: particular judgements found a particular approach which identifies the structure of interests such that the judgements based on the approach are justified. Individualism locates interests at the level of the freely acting individual and condemns interventions which disrupt them and so on. The issue of relativism means that choice of theory becomes choice of approach, of method. While nothing carrying the conviction of a logical proof is available, considerations that tend to make one or another of the approaches set out in the preceding chapters convincing may be found. It is our (cautiously advanced) contention that materialist methods offer the most useful theories of the welfare state advanced to date. Before the basis for this argument is set out, the theoretical positions that have been discussed must be considered.

## The three approaches

Normative approaches to issues recognized as social problems within the structure of the welfare state and to welfare states as a form of society have been loosely clustered under three heads: individualist, reformist and structuralist. Individualist perspectives start their analysis from the member of society. In dealing with social problems this leads to the assumption that problems are properties of those who suffer them and to a focus on the characteristics of such individuals in an attempt to explain them. Solutions are typically seen in terms of interventions that affect individuals directly and tackle their problematic characteristics at root. Since individuals are separated from society and the structure of expectations and institutions is taken as given, this tends to involve changing the individuals so that they fit into the structure better. For example, one could (in principle) suggest solving the poverty of the poor by giving them more money. However, this would involve interventions throughout the social order in terms of redistribution; it would alter the balance of rich and poor with profound repercussions for economic organization; and since the cause of poverty in the individual presupposed by this perspective might remain, it would not necessarily prevent the reproduction of that circumstance in given individuals. Thus, the emphasis tends to be on the identified individual feature, be it indolence, fecundity, lack of saleable skills, lack of budgeting capacity or whatever.

In general, such approaches have failed to identify a convincing link between problem and characteristic. It is hard to point to a feature of poor individuals (for example) that uniquely corresponds to poverty and is not shared by some of the well-off. This fact tends to make individualist theories of social problems less convincing, though it does not make it impossible that either some explanation of the patchiness of correspondence or some further personal characteristic that relates well to poverty might be constructed.

At the level of the welfare state as a social form, an individualist approach tends to conceive society as consisting simply in separate people who may relate as they choose, and to diminish or deny the importance of social structures in influencing their relations. Thus it is argued that a free market can articulate the maximum of individual freedom. The goal of social organization is seen to be the untrammelled action of people in such a setting. State welfare with the object of meeting need is either irrelevant or counterproductive.

The foundations of an individual perspective on social problems, and an individualist exaltation of unconstrained economic relations can thus be found in the general orientation of this approach — in particular the denial that human interactions tend to create social structures that limit people irrespective of intention. If the approach to problems is weakly supported, its perspective on the welfare state seems (simply) boring. We have argued that such approaches involve a more or less rigorous individualism of method which limits the capacity of the theory to give an account of society. This is most clearly elaborated in Hayek's work. It amounts to a denial of structural social processes and thus of social science, by fiat rather than by argument.

We now move on to the realm of sociological theories where we are faced with a division between reformist and structural approaches. At the level of social problems, reformism suggests that piecemeal action within the existing social structure may resolve problems. At that of the welfare state, the approach commends the capacity of that system to achieve desirable ends within the structure of democratic welfare capitalism. Structuralism interprets social problems as products of the operation of the social system as a whole. The nature of the system imposes powerful constraints on the capacity of the welfare state to act autonomously at the political level. Its activity is moulded by forces operating at a deeper level in society.

These labels cover a wide range of approaches. Reformism is often exemplified by the uncritical empiricism so brilliantly articulated in the social administration tradition. However, the more sophisticated variants of this approach, that make the goals of social action explicit rather than taking for granted the perspective of the state, fall into an idealist mould. This is for two kinds of reasons: first, abstract, conscious ideals of welfare are set up, conceived as independent of and untarnished by existing social relations. Secondly the capacity of rational action to achieve these goals is stressed and the obstacles that form part of present society underplayed. The exhibition of an ideal, and the pursuit of rational action to achieve it link together in a perspective that regards society as the product of coordinated ideas. Such obstacles as are recognized — vested interests, bureaucratic tangles and administrative failures — may be overcome with patience, effort and hard work.

Structural approaches constitute the category of materialism because they conceive society as a totality. Here too there are disputed positions. Marxism claims that capitalist society is founded on a conflict of interests that both tends continually to produce recognized problems and to stultify the efforts of the state to tackle them. Structural functionalism points to the role of a normative consensus in maintaining order, defining problems in relation to the requirements of order, and directing policy to resolve them. Convergence approaches see the common constraint of underlying trends in the development of modern industry as giving impetus and direction to the growth of welfare. The conception that all three approaches share is the understanding of society as a whole. The freedom of political action is limited, by mode of production, central value system or the dictates of technology.

We have reviewed these approaches at the most general level — as methods of analysis of modern state welfare. The presuppositions inherent in the theories tend to lead them in particular directions. We shall attempt to list the positive and negative features of the approaches and to devise a criterion for making a choice between them.

**The criterion**

Individualism places the member of society at the centre of the stage. It does this, however, by eliminating from consideration any aspect of societal process.

Idealism also respects humanism: social events can be judged by an independent and humanly constructed criterion; moreover social change as a result of human will is possible since political, ideological and economic aspects of society are loosely linked. However, the possibility that different criteria are provided by different theorists leads directly to the problem of relativism. If norms are not in some way related to society, how is any particular judgement to be founded except in its appeal to the judge? Moreover, an approach that stresses the possibility of social change (given the political will) must run into problems in explaining uniformities in and between societies.

Materialism questions the pre-eminence of the will of the human actor. In doing so it provides the possibility of giving accounts of social uniformity, persistence and ordered development, whether through the marxist notion of a mode of production, the structural functionalist idea of an adaptive value system or the convergence theory conception of technological development. However this explanatory power is purchased at considerable cost: such accounts must run the risk of falling into a determinism that writes the human actor out of history.

A useful criterion for choice is provided in the notion that society is to be understood as having two aspects, objective and subjective, and that theory must take account of both. Simmel puts it neatly:

> the nexus by which each . . . individual is interwoven with the life and activities of every other and by which the external framework of society is produced, is a causal nexus. But . . . they feel themselves to be egos, whose behaviour grows out of self-determined personalities. The objective totality yields to the individuals that confront it from without, as it were; it offers a place to their subjectively determined life-processes
>
> (1971, ch. 1).

On the one hand social theory must do justice to the recognition that people experience their life as self-determined; the failure to do so would deprive social theory of any possibility of being true, false or worth thinking about. If all social events are determined, communication is determined. One might as well ask whether a statement is right or wrong as ask whether the grass growing is right or wrong. It just happens.

On the other hand constraining social forces exist. People do not act independently, but their social life is coordinated within a culture. Without this aspect communication would again collapse; symbols uttered would cease to be shared symbols and would lose meaning. Society depends on the maintenance of an intersubjective reality, beyond the individual.

Berger and Luckman put a similar point aphoristically:

> Society is a human product.
> Society is an objective reality. Man is a social product . . . an analysis of the social world that leaves out any one of these three moments will be distortive
>
> (1971, p. 79).

Most major social theorists acknowledge the dual perspective of people acting in and being acted upon by their society. Weber distinguishes between the 'level of meaning' or motive and the 'level of causal adequacy' or 'statistical uniformity' within the social structure in his account of action (1964, p. 101). Marx and Engels stress that 'the production of life . . . appears at once as a double relationship, on the one hand as a natural, on the other hand as a social relationship' (1970, p. 50). People labour in response to needs which are subjectively experienced. One result of collective labour through history is the development of society which is experienced as external constraining force. Smith points to the 'invisible hand' of the market coordinating self-regarding action (1930, Bk 1V, p. 421). Giddens argues that society is 'constituted by the active doings of subjects'. At the same time 'the realm of human agency is bounded. Men produce society . . . but not under conditions of their own choosing' (1976, p. 160).

Any theoretical approach must be capable of doing justice to both areas: the objective and the subjective. In relation to social welfare, the double bond between the action frame of reference and the structural approach must be incorporated in any account. On the one hand the objective development of the welfare state as a social form, particularly regarding the evidence of overall similarity so powerfully pointed out by convergence theorists. On the other hand, the story of how citizens as free subjects have collectively willed such development.

Armed with this criterion, we may tackle the range of approaches. Individualism and convergence theory may immediately be eliminated. The former stresses self-motivated human action and does not acknowledge social structure either at the level of the production of social problems, or at that of the development of welfare states: the latter posits a structural determinism that lacks any account of the autonomy of human action. The choice that remains is between idealism with its tendency to relativism, and materialism with its determinist bias.

The idealist approaches offer no possibility of escape from the problems of relativism; theorists that posit fraternity, equality, altruism, a public purpose, or the taming of the market as a societal goal to be consciously recognized and achieved by political action can have no way of founding their particular perspective in opposition to the others. Society is separated from the human actor to provide the scope for normative judgement: it is also analysed as consisting of loose-linked political and economical spheres to provide an arena for reformism. The first divorce leads to the second. The political independence of people is essential to the free exercise of their political reason. However it is hard to see how their judgements once made can be grounded. Normative theory is irremediably fragmented.

Whose ideal is right?

Functionalism is determinist. Giddens identifies in Parsons's *Structure of Social Action* the thesis that 'voluntarism can be incorporated into social theory through the axiom that values form both the motivational components of action and the core elements of the "consensus universel" which is the condition of social stability' (1976, p 95). The problem is that in his prior assumption of stability Parsons subordinates voluntary human action to the requirements of consensus. The order of understanding is reversed: the nature of society becomes the presupposition on which argument is founded rather than the outcome. In this sense, the theory is not an explanation at all.

Marxism appears to us to offer the most fruitful approach because it makes it possible to unite an account of social structure resting on the notion of mode of production with an account of human action resting on a theory of ideology. However, the problems of determinism and an associated functionalism remain powerful obstacles. We shall attempt to sketch out the contribution of marxism in both areas.

The account will fall into two parts. First the general level of the historical development of modern social forms. Secondly the specific level of the activity of the welfare state.

## The strengths of historicism

Determinism may be seen as pre-defining the structure of events — as viewing the future as history. The vulnerability of marxism in this direction is closely allied to its strength, which is to emphasize the roots of the present in the past, in the historical development of a given form of society based on particular relations of production. This relates to the explanatory capacity of marxism in relation to history: Hobsbawm claims that 'Marx's approach is still the only one which enables us to explain the entire span of human history' (in Blackburn, 1972, p. 282). His argument is that 'the immense strength of Marx has always lain in his insistence on both the existence of social structure and its historicity . . . its internal dynamic of change' (p. 274). Social structure is understood in relation to a mode of production: change is understood in relation to crises, in relation to the problems that that mode throws up for itself and its capacity to surmount them. This is allied to a 'directional' theory of history. 'The growing emancipation of man from nature and his growing capacity to control it . . . makes history as a whole (though not every area and period within it) "oriented and irreversible", to quote Lévi-Strauss . . .'

(p. 279). The utility of such direction is that it provides a criterion for the comparison of social formations. 'To compare societies in respect of their system of internal relations between members is inevitably to compare like with like. It is when we compare them in respect of their capacity to control outside nature that the differences leap to the eye' (p. 276).

Whether or not this theory of the directionality of history implies a historical target (as Popper suggests — 1962, vol. II, ch. 18) is doubtful. To say that in the twentieth century the human race appropriated more of the material resources of the planet than they did in the thirteenth or that a link can be drawn between the sequence of human relations required for such appropriation does not however commit us to the view that Utopia awaits at any stage.

The significance of the capacity of marxism to supply holistic historical explanation for our studies is that a marxist approach enables us to apprehend the welfare state in its historical setting as a stage in the evolution of modern industrial society. This provides a basis both for its international ubiquity and its historical fragility noted in chapter 1 — the former the result of the spread of similar relations of production, the latter the outcome of the crises immanent in those relations. These crises face us at both the specific level of social welfare within a society and the general level of the welfare state. At the former level, a continual stream of social problems is produced (see chapter 2); at the latter, the question of whether state welfare can actually fulfil the role it takes on presses (see chapter 9).

As Gough points out (1978), the major alternative attempt to provide an account of historical development is contained in convergence theory. However, this approach, if it is to be anything more than description, seems to produce a determinism more rigorous than historical materialism. Since it does not contain an account of human action to correspond to the theory of class, it is forced to suggest that the dynamic of development itself is the motor of history: which writes human actors out of the story (except as inventors).

## Consciousness and human action

The capacity of marxist thought to give a structural account of historical persistence and change in terms of the stability of modes of production punctuated by crises is perhaps unsurprising. It is as a deterministic historicism that the approach has often been criticized. However this objective reality also has a subjective dimension. In *The*

*Communist Manifesto* Marx and Engels write 'The history of all hitherto existing society is the history of class struggles. Freeman and slave, patrician and plebeian, lord and serf, guild-master and journeyman . . . stood in constant opposition to one another' (1972, pp. 30–1). An account of the mainspring of class antagonism is provided by the idea that production relations involve exploitation — the appropriation by one group of a surplus produced by another. The problem of the subjective dimension is now reversed. If society is in fact a continual conflict of interest, how does it come about that people do not notice, and reduce the ordered progress of history to turmoil?

The social processes which produce a legitimating ideology help sustain the dominant class. These processes have two main aspects. First the production of ideas by the powerholders in their own interest. Such production may be a deliberate conspiracy on their part or may simply result from an uncritical perspective on the social order from their point of view, interpreting existing circumstances as natural order, and justifying the status quo. Either way

> the ideas of the ruling class are in every epoch the ruling ideas, i.e. the class which is the ruling material force of society is at the same time its ruling intellectual force. The class which has the means of material production at its disposal, has control at the same time over the means of mental production so that thereby, generally speaking, the ideas of those who lack the means of mental production are subject to it
>
> (Marx and Engels, 1970, p. 64).

The importance of the production of legitimating culture by a dominant class must not be ignored. However, the second aspect of stabilizing ideology is of even greater significance. This is the tendency of particular relations of production to give rise to self-justifying ideas. We have already noted Marx's reluctance to set up a normative criterion to condemn the effects of capitalism (chapter 4). Indeed he points out that such norms are socially relative:

> The justice of the transactions between agents of production rests on the fact that these arise as natural consequences out of the production relationships . . . . This content [of juristic forms] is just when it corresponds to the mode of production . . . . Slavery on the basis of capitalist production is unjust
>
> (1972a, Bk.III, p. 340).

Exploitation, so long as it is based on the free market purchase of labour-power, is not.

Production relationships tend to produce appropriate ideas as well as goods. In a very obvious sense, people have no choice about entering into these relations. Thus society contains a general tendency to legitimate its dominant mode, which is its defining characteristic irrespective of the activities of the ruling class. Taken together, class production of ideology and the social tendency to generate appropriate legitimation provide constraints operating on a subjective level: 'Men make their own history, but they do not make it just as they please; they do not make it under circumstances chosen by themselves . . . .' Society contains a value-slope which tends to mould free human action to fit in with the framework of development described on the objective level. We now move on to consider the more specific area of the activity of the welfare state.

## Constraints on state activity

From a marxist perspective the problem of the modern state consists in reconciling its role as a public and more or less democratic, political arena with its relation to the class system. The notion of capitalist society suggests the dominance of a capitalist class. How does this account of power relate to the alternative reality of state power? Capitalism is founded on private profit, political democracy on the government of society in common or majority interest. Wolfe summarizes the problem:

> Liberal democracy . . . neatly symbolizes a contradiction at the heart of western politics, . . . an inherent . . . tension between the needs of accumulation and legitimation. The demands of a private system of accumulation gave rise to a liberal ideology that structured public conceptions about the state: the desire for popular acceptance and obedience gave rise to democratic notions about political life quite at odds with the earlier liberal ones
>
> (1979, p. 247).

An objective approach to the problem of how the modern state relates to the capitalist class is exemplified by Miliband. He argues that there are three factors explaining the nature of the state 'the character of its leading personnel, the pressures exerted by the dominant class, and the structural constraints imposed by the capitalist mode of production' (1977, p. 73). These factors are explored in greater detail in chapter 7. Here we may point out that the first two — the fact that top civil servants, judges, politicians share the education, values and often family background of leading business people, and the fact that the major industrial organizations are in a position to act as an extremely influential pressure group — would not necessarily conflict with idealist approaches. Crosland, for example, sees such factors as the vested interests against which Fabian socialism must struggle. The distinctively marxist aspect of the approach is the reference to the insertion of the state in capitalism. This has both objective and subjective aspects. These two areas must be combined in any account of the limits to reform by the capitalist welfare state.

On the objective side 'the commitment which governments in advanced capitalist countries have to the private enterprise system and to its economic rationality enormously limits their freedom of action in relation to a multitude of issues and problems' (Miliband, 1973, p. 71). The subjective dimension includes the dominance of a particular ideology of citizenship which tends to direct the citizen activity in a particular direction. Miliband has placed little emphasis on the materialist account of structural constraints on the welfare state, especially on their importance for understanding ideology, on the grounds that this approach runs the risk of setting up 'arbitrary limits to the possible'. It is our contention that only by introducing the idea of a 'value-slope', tending to direct ideology in a certain direction and rooted in material relations, into our analysis of capitalism is it possible to produce a coherent account.

The development of Miliband's theory is instructive. His approach stresses the 'relative autonomy' of the state — the fact that it is structurally separate from any class and therefore in principle, capable of responding to pressure from any direction. Such a state is not arbitrarily confined. However difficulties arise in explaining how it comes about that state action has tended to follow the interests of the capitalist class. Here functionalism re-enters: four functions of the capitalist state are listed (1977, p. 90). The significance of its 'relative independence' is that it 'makes it *possible* for the state to play its class role in an appropriately flexible manner' (1977, p. 87). It is hard to see how the state could be linked to capital from this viewpoint without some such assumption of a pre-defined class role.

Materialist theory of the structural constraints on the capitalist state sometimes tends in an opposite direction. A good example is Altvater, who derives the form of the capitalist state from the structural necessities of capitalist production: 'capital cannot itself produce through the actions of the many individual capitals the inherent social nature of its existence' (in Holloway and Picciotto (eds), 1978, p. 41). The individual pursuit of profit degenerates into anarchy. Capital requires a state to represent its general interest in the reproduction of labour, law and order, international relations, and so on. It is not in the interest of any individual capitalist to do this.

This approach sheds considerable light on the relation between state and capital. However, as Holloway and his co-author point out (1978, p. 21) it fails as an account of how the relation arose and is sustained. It lapses into a functionalism that assumes the human actor will act to follow the needs of capital.

From opposite starting points, the one emphasizing the relative autonomy of the state from capital, the other its functional necessity to it, both Miliband and Altvater arrive at a functionalism in their accounts of the modern state. It is necessary to attempt to steer a middle course between these positions. We suggest that this can best be done through consideration of the subjective dimension of social action. Can a materialist account of a general ideological tendency in capitalist society, such that people will tend to will the state to act in the interest of capital, be constructed? This will unite accounts of the state acting as an instrument of class domination, and human tolerance of it.

### Ideology of citizenship

To arrive at an understanding of how capitalism tends to foster particular ideas about the proper role of the state we need to consider two aspects of marxist thought: the notion of critique discussed in chapter 4 and the notion of the ideology that rests on commodity relations (chapter 2).

A central feature of marxist thought is the attempt to grasp the social relations that lie behind the categories immediately presented. Social relations are to be understood in terms of a particular stage in history, a mode of production. Non-marxist thought, on the other hand, continually runs the risk of taking the superficial for granted, abstracted from the historical context: as Marx observes in the first chapter of *Capital*, Bk. I:

> man's reflections on the forms of social life, and consequently his scientific analysis of those forms, take a course directly opposite to their actual historical development. He begins, *post festum*, with the finished results of the process of development.

The result is that the historical particular is overwhelmed by the ideal universal. Present circumstances are treated as eternal because they can be subsumed under abstract categories. The underlying distinctive features of the capitalist mode drop out of sight. The tendency then is to legitimate the status quo as embodying an ideal. Marx gives the example of the justification of relations by contemporary economists who point out that all production requires instruments of production and the accumulation of the fruits of past labour. Capital falls into these categories: 'therefore capital is an eternal relation of nature; that is if I leave out just the specific quality which makes "instrument of production" and "stored-up labour" into capital' (1973, pp. 85–7). This element is, of course, the principle of private property which concentrates capital in the hands of a particular social group and makes exploitation possible.

Similarly Marx criticizes Proudhon who 'holding things upside down like a true philosopher, sees in actual relations nothing but the incarnation of these principles' (quoted by Coletti in the introduction to Marx, 1975, p. 24). In *Capital* Bk. 1, ch. 1: 'if I say Roman Law and German Law are both systems of law, that is obvious. But if I say, Law, this abstraction, is realized in Roman and German Law, . . . then the relationship is mystical.'

The emphasis on historical development presents a powerful critique of abstracted categories. Coletti traces this theme to Marx's original analysis of Hegel's 'double error'. Hegelian metaphysics postulates a spiritual basis to reality and interprets history as the self-development of the spiritual Idea according to an internal principle. Marx's point is that such idealism incorporates both an 'uncritical positivism' and an 'equally uncritical idealism' when applied to historical development. The idealism is contained in the abstraction of reality to a spiritual level. The positivism results 'because Hegel cannot help in the end restoring the empirical object-world originally denied — the Idea has no other possible Earthly incarnation or meaning.' (1975, p. 20) How else can the approach gain a foothold in contemporary affairs to demonstrate its relevance, except by justifying the status quo, as corresponding to the development of the Idea?

This point lies behind Marx's examination of Hegel's defence of the Prussian state. He comments on Hegel's analysis of the chain of historical development:

the family and civil society [the market system] make themselves into the state . . . . According to Hegel, however, they are produced by the real Idea; it is not the course of their own life that joins them together to comprise the state, but the life of the Idea, which has distinguished them from itself

(Marx, 1975, p. 63).

Marx argues that the development of the modern state as an abstracted political level in society is the result of the growth of the market and the breakdown of feudalism. To abstract a timeless political principle and see it as the dominant force in society is to assume the legitimacy of the state. To relate this principle to the anarchy of the market as a guiding body is to assume its capacity to resolve the conflict of private interests by pursuing a common interest.

Here Marx's methodological critique takes a further and crucial twist. The idea that capitalist society presents a limited impression of itself re-enters. Hegel's interpretation of that society inverts it by imposing an abstract ideal onto real relations. In another sense, however, it reflects the truth of a reality which *contains* inversions. It takes for granted the superficial. The state is itself an abstraction produced by the processes of the market system. As we argued at the end of chapter 2, this system gives people the status of free individuals and their interests that of the private command of property. The political aspects incorporated in the social roles of previous societies become separate and independent: people as free, equal citizens in the political realm as the counterpart to free equal competitors in the economic realm. From the point of view of the individual, political relations are designed to secure a common interest over and against the anarchy of the market. However, such an abstract interest can only be successfully put into practice in terms of the concrete reality of civil society — in terms of respect for private property. The fact that the state's democratic role must be seen in relation to this principle means that members of society will tend to follow a dominant ideology that reduces the capacity of the state to interfere with property-holdings:

. . . just because the 'general interest' has been reached by neglecting or transcending genuine interests, the latter are bound to persist as its true content — as the unequal economic reality now sanctioned or legitimized by the state. The political idealism of the hypostatized state serves only to secure and fix the crass materialism of civil society

(Coletti, Introduction to Marx, 1975, p. 36).

The general value-slope of capitalist society tends in a direction that favours political action in the interests of capital. This must be united with the objective accounts of the power of the capitalist class to produce an account of the capitalist state. The tendency is no more than that: a pervasive and influential presupposition. Thus the questions of the capacity of working-class action to affect state policy and of whether the union of state and capital is necessary remain open. An understanding of the role of ideology and its origins in social relations is crucial to the presentation of state activity as the result of willed human action as well as of overwhelming social forces.

> If in all ideology men and their circumstances appear upside-down as in a camera obscura, this phenomenon arises just as much from their historical life-processes as the inversion of objects on the retina does from their physical life-processes
>
> (Marx and Engels, 1970, p. 47).

The interweaving of accounts of the subjective realm of human action and the objective realm of constraining social forces is thus a central feature of marxist thought: history is the story of the succession of modes of production, reflected in their corresponding ideology; the modern state relates to the contemporary mode both through the power of constraining social forces and through the 'value-slope' of capitalist ideology.

## The ideology of the welfare state

This approach has implications for some of the more specific problems of social policy studies. The careful analyses of the empirical tradition show that social welfare has failed to achieve the objectives of its originators. These shortcomings form part of the common sense of the subject. We have argued in chapter 2 that social security has failed to eradicate poverty. Halsey's recent monumental study shows that the massive changes in the educational system between the 1920s and the 1960s made little impact on the chances of working-class children entering the most advantageous state secondary schools — the selective sector. (Halsey's summary of findings, *Times Higher Educational Supplement*, 11 January 80). Miliband charts the regularity of Ministerial pronouncements of programmes designed to remove slum housing since the end of the first World War against the evidence of the continued existence of the problem (in Wedderburn (ed.) 1974, pp. 185–6). Townsend demonstrates that 'the right of the sick to free access to health care, irrespective of class or income, remains firmly to be established'. (1974, p. 1189). Overall the privilege of the upper classes remains little challenged. Why does democratic social policy not result in more redistribution of opportunities in life?

George and Wilding tackle the problem of why the welfare state has failed to live up to expectations of its originators and advocates. They argue that explanations in terms of ad hoc factors — shortage of resources in trained staff, finance or buildings, administrative weakness, central/local government relations and so on — are inadequate.

> They might explain causal, occasional and limited failures but when used as explanations for fundamental failure to achieve central objectives they lack basic credibility . . . we can see other and . . . mo.². fundamental reasons for the failure of welfare policies
>
> (1976, p. 118).

Their solution is in terms of a clash of values. The ethic of self-help, freedom, individualism, competition and achievement 'which is required for the successful operation of a capitalist economy is in clear opposition to the values needed to underpin a successful public welfare system' (p. 118). In one sense this approach is convincing. Respect for individual achievement and for the outcome of competition between individuals with different qualities and possessions legitimates stratification and inequality of opportunity. Private property operates both as the reward of achievement and acquisitive talent and as the fuel for inequalities in starting position. A notion of freedom which focuses on the individual and tends to exclude consideration of those social factors which structure the life-chances of people is dominant over a perspective which stresses state involvement in mitigating inequalities and barriers to mobility.

The problem that faces this approach is to explain where values come from — and where they're going. One is left with a Manichean struggle — the conflict of liberalism and welfarism as unanchored ideals, with no end in sight. An advantage of materialism is that it provides an opportunity to give an account of such values. This account also includes a theory of the changing material factors that mould their present and their future.

The relevant ideologies may be seen as rooted in capitalist social relations. These presuppose and incorporate the ideas of property, freedom and individual self-interest that give society its tone and provide the barriers to welfarism. Thus Marx pointed out that, with the development of capitalism, man 'was not freed from property — he received the freedom of property. He was not freed from the egoism of trade — he received the freedom to engage in trade' (Marx, 1975, p. 233). In this sense, private interest becomes identified with private property. The state is inserted in and becomes part and parcel of social relations that presuppose this basic idea. Political relations represent the struggle of groups of people organized to advance their interests as they see them, assuming this principle. Any collective interest that government may pursue can only be the enhancement of the sum of private interest writ large.

Social services tend to follow the lines of majority interest, covering the main elements of insecurity of the mass of the population: health care, social security for periods when one does not work, education to ensure employability and so on. Shackled to this notion, as part of this ideological whole, state welfare stands little chance of advance except through accommodation with the principle of individual private property. This leads to respect for the private sector in occupational, financial, health and education services. It also vitiates an approach based on pressure for redistribution of that property in the majority interest. Welfare is provided in a way that leads to horizontal rather than vertical redistribution, and the benefits of the better-off groups go generally unchallenged. The superior benefits from health care and education to a minority are the price that a majority that regards that privilege as legitimate pays, as the outcome of willing services that (more or less) meet its own needs. The overall failure to redistribute is simply the general reflection of this tendency. A capitalist 'welfare' state contradicts itself.

## Conclusion

In this chapter we have reviewed the various methodological approaches. Any satisfactory approach to a form of society must do justice to the twin components of social reality: society is experienced by its members as an over-arching framework of constraining factors. At the same time human action is experienced as (at least potentially) free, and society consists in the sum total of actions of its members. The situation is reflected at a theoretical level in the determinism of an approach which explains in terms of constraint and the relativism of perspectives which rest on free human choice of social goals. Both determinism and relativism destroy the capacity of theory to give a satisfactory account of social life by on the one hand denying the possibility of alternatives, and on the other eroding the basis of intellectual choice. We suggest that marxist perspectives offer the most fruitful approach: the objective element derives from the stress on the absolute necessity of production giving the overall character to society and setting the stage for historical development. The subjective element is provided by an account of how ideology influences but does not determine social action.

It is now possible to situate other approaches in relation to marxism. Goldmann argues that, all things being equal, an elementary criterion for social theory is its capacity to give an account of the social location of other theories:

> Some value judgements permit a better understanding of reality than others. When it is a question of determining which of two conflicting sociologies has the greater scientific value, the first step is to ask which of them permits the understanding of the other as a social and human phenomenon, reveals its infrastructure, and clarifies, by means of an immanent critical principle, its inconsistencies and its limitations
>
> (1969, p. 52).

From a marxist perspective, the other approaches considered represent partial accounts of society. Individualism inhabits the superficial realm of

> Freedom Equality Property and Bentham. Freedom, because both buyer and seller of a commodity, . . . are constrained only by their free will . . . . Equality because . . . they exchange equivalent for equivalent. Property because each disposes only of what is his own. And Bentham, because each looks only to himself.
>
> (Marx, 1976, p. 280).

The task of critical analysis is to look behind these categories to discover the relations of class.

Idealism is concerned with the reform of society, but fails to acknowledge the link between contemporary circumstances and underlying processes. The lack of a perspective of totality is lampooned in *the Communist Manifesto*:

> A part of the bourgeoisie is desirous of redressing social grievances, in order to secure the continued existence of bourgeois society . . . .
> The Socialistic bourgeois want all the advantages of modern social

conditions without the struggle and dangers necessarily resulting therefrom. They desire the existing state of society, minus its revolutionary and disintegrating elements . . . a bourgeoisie without a proletariat

(1972, p. 68).

The problem of non-marxist materialism is that it fails to link a theory of human practice to an account of objective constraining social forces. These become unquestionable determinations:

the chief defect of all hitherto existing materialism . . . is that the thing, reality . . . is conceived only in the form of the object . . . but not as human sensuous activity, practice, not subjectively.

(First Thesis on Feuerbach, Marx, 1975, p. 420).

# Part II

## A Marxist Perspective

In chapter 1 we suggested that the term 'welfare state' referred to the many different ways in which modern states in capitalist society use their political and administrative power to intervene in the market — providing social services, regulating the actions of employers, the family and so on. These actions involve among other things the definition of what are to be regarded as 'social needs' and how, and to what extent, such needs will be met. We then went on to consider competing perspectives on how the welfare state and social problems should be understood. Our initial formulation of the welfare state as state intervention in the market was thus shown to be very loose, and largely empty of content because the concepts involved are contested. Nevertheless, it was useful in directing us towards certain key concepts: state, market and need. In this second half we shall examine these concepts in more detail. Chapters 6 to 8 will look in turn at the market, the state and needs. The first half of each chapter will review different approaches to be found in social science literature, while in the second half we shall move from more abstract considerations to exploring the issues raised by concrete application of the materialist approach advocated in Part I to the analysis of the British welfare state. Chapter 9 asks whether Britain is in a state of crisis, and reviews theories of the causes of such a crisis, and how such theories are reflected in trends in the contemporary welfare state.

# 6

## The market and the welfare state.

### Introduction

The fact that we begin by considering the economic level of society, rather than the state or needs, and that we single out the state and the market for separate discussion immediately reveals two theoretical biases. In the first place, we start with the economic system because we believe that it is fundamental to understanding other aspects of society. This is not to say that it *determines* what happens elsewhere (we shall return to this problem of determinism later), but that it sets certain basic limits and thus helps us to predict likely tendencies.

In the second place, we deal with the economic and political/administrative systems in different chapters, because in capitalist society they assume different forms and enjoy some degree of separation. The *degree* of separation is a matter of considerable controversy: in part I we have already indicated that a materialist approach presupposes much less separation than individualist or idealist theories, which see the state as autonomous from the economy, in which it is seen as meddling unnecessarily (by the individualists), or which it is capable of controlling (the reformists). Within a materialist framework there exist considerable differences along a continuum between those who believe we can understand the political system as a response to impulses from the economic system, in which case the two can hardly be said to enjoy any degree of separation, and those who see systematic biases in the actions of the state but argue that these cannot be reduced to statements about economic imperatives. This debate is considered in chapter 7: here we need only look ahead to the point of saying that we shall end up adopting the latter perspective.

### The market system of production and distribution

The economic system refers to the system of organizing people into units for the production of goods and services. Even in capitalist societies not all production takes place within the market — in many capitalist countries subsistence family farms remain as a remnant of the pre-capitalist peasantry. More significantly, in all capitalist countries a form of non-market domestic production takes place within the family. The housewife provides services for her husband and children and transforms goods purchased on the market into final consumption goods through activities such as cooking, sewing and creating a home. Thus domestic production interacts with the market, but it is not itself subject to market forces: social custom and ties of affection and/or dependence largely condition what is produced in the home, and how it is produced. Production is geared to satisfying immediate needs, not to exchange in the market.

What, then, are the characteristics of the capitalist market? Three appear particularly crucial both to distinguish capitalist market from non-capitalist economies, and to highlight the difference between the economic and political systems. In the first place, the economic system consists of units of production which are *privately* owned. Thus, despite nationalizations especially of certain basic industries such as energy and transport, all advanced capitalist economies remain largely in private hands.

In the second place, the capitalist market is characterized by the way in which all inputs and outputs of the process of production become commodities to be bought and sold. Production is for exchange and not use; land and labour power, whose role in the pre-capitalist production process was governed by custom, and the notion of reciprocal duties backed up by the force at the disposal of the dominant class, is replaced by the cash nexus. Land can now be disposed of at will, and the labourer is freed from legal restrictions to exchange labour power with a capitalist in order to gain a livelihood.

In the third place, the market involves a particular steering mechanism namely the quest for profits. In a competitive market individual producers and consumers come together in the market place, and the price mechanism, over which no individual has control, coordinates their activities, signalling to producers where the highest profits can be made, and hence where to invest, and to consumers how they can maximize their purchases of desired commodities. The market mechanism is often referred to as 'anonymous' ('of unknown origin': *Concise Oxford Dictionary*) to highlight the manner in which economic changes, cumulatively of great significance, result from individual decisions about marginal changes undertaken by a large number of private units coordinated through the price mechanism. Responsibility for the overall direction of change cannot therefore be attributed to any particular agency.

Modern advanced capitalist economies do not, however, conform to this competitive model. We live in an era of giant monopolies and multinational corporations which form what Holland calls a 'meso-economic' sector (Holland, 1975). These firms attempt to control markets and set prices, such that Galbraith argues that advanced capitalist economies are in fact planned economies, albeit planned by the large corporations (Galbraith, 1969).

It is fundamentally misleading however to equate state planned economies with those of advanced monopoly capitalism. The basic steering mechanism under capitalism remains the profit motive, and as Habermas points out:

> . . . political planning does not occur as long as the priorities of the society as a whole develop in an unplanned, nature-like manner — that is, as the secondary effects of the strategies of private enterprise
> (Habermas, 1976, p. 34).

In contrast social priorities in a planned economy can be decided collectively in the political system. So long as such an economy participates in an international capitalist economy, it will obviously be subject to the pressures of international capitalist competition: but this does not invalidate the distinction we have drawn.

Whilst we may agree on what constitutes the market system of production and distribution, there is considerable disagreement on how we should understand the relation between this and society as a whole.

## Economy and society: competing perspectives

Probably the majority of writers within social administration and both orthodox schools of economics and more radical political economy would adopt the position that the economic system forms the most fundamental constraint on the manner in which any welfare state develops. Understanding of the nature of this constraint depends, however, on wider perspectives adopted.

The most important theoretical cleavage concerns whether the market system is seen as functioning satisfactorily as a system of production. Those who argue that it does either see little reason for state intervention (the neo-classical school) or wish to confine state intervention to the regulation of demand (Keynes) or the modification of distribution (social administration). Within this perspective the market system is usually seen as conforming to a competitive model. It forms a constraint, because state intervention must not destroy the price mechanism, but the constraint is largely self-imposed. We do not move beyond the market because we believe it to be the best system of production which maximizes the interests of members of society.

As against this is a school we shall refer to as political economy. It has a heterogeneous membership — we would include both marxists and non-marxists such as Galbraith particularly in his later writings — who nevertheless share certain assumptions about capitalism as a system of production: that it tends to cumulative disequilibrium because of certain structural features which cannot be put right by simple action on the demand side, and that the system of private control of the means of production confers power. This is accentuated in the present period, where monopoly firms can gain control over markets, and have an important influence on state policies. Thus the market system forms a constraint, not because we all agree that it best maximizes the social interest, but because of power — the power of capital in the view of marxists, or the power of the technostructure of the giant corporations according to Galbraith.

We shall explore more deeply later the very considerable cleavage between marxist and non-marxist political economy, particularly in the analysis of power. Nevertheless the basic distinction between neo-classical economics and political economy is a useful starting point, and we shall now consider the different strands within the two schools in more detail.

## The market as a self-imposed restraint

### Orthodox neo-classical economics

The predilection for market systems of production and distribution among orthodox economists has led to a relative neglect of welfare state studies. We shall examine here the approach adopted by authors such as Culyer (1973 in particular) and Sleeman (1973 and 1979) who attempt to apply the basic concepts of neo-classical economics to an understanding of the welfare state.

Both Culyer and Sleeman understand the market as a competitive system in which individual choices, based on individual utility maximization are transmitted via the price mechanism to producers. The market system is taken as the norm, and economic analysis is then brought to bear on the problem of why the social services are provided outside the market. The method adopted involves identifying particular characteristics of the goods in question which justifies their provision by the state. Thus the approach is as much normative as explanatory, and more attention is usually directed towards arguing what the state should do than to explaining why it does what it does.

Neo-classical theory argues that the regulation of production and distribution is best left to the market except in certain defined circumstances: first, where the good is a 'public good' whose provision is indivisible, so that people cannot be excluded from enjoying any benefits of provision. The only universally recognized public goods are defence and law and order. In the second place there may be externalities — benefits or penalties from economic actions falling on people who are not party to the particular actions — which justify state intervention. On this basis environmental controls are generally accepted as necessary. In the case of social services, the external benefits may accrue to the whole of society. Thus, Sleeman refers to the social services as 'merit goods' where:

> though . . . their private provision is perfectly possible, yet they are felt to be in some way particularly desirable, so that the socially optimum provision of them and distribution of their consumption would not be achieved through the market
>
> (Sleeman, 1979, p. 3).

Thus Sleeman argues that provision of social services creates benefits to society above and beyond the sum of benefits accruing to individual consumers. Such a concept is fraught with difficulties — as Judge points out, it contradicts the basic neo-classical belief in consumer sovereignty and is rejected by the Institute of Economic Affairs, the main protagonists of a neo-classical approach to social policy (Judge, 1979).

There are thus differences within the school, and these are apparent when it is viewed as normative theory. The concept of externalities can be used to justify almost any level of state intervention. The limits are set in practice by three basic tenets: first, the belief that the market is more efficient than other systems of distribution; secondly, the centrality of an individualist interpretation of the concepts of liberty and choice (see chapter 3); and finally, a scepticism of what governments can achieve based on the recognition that any action is likely to have unintended consequences elsewhere, such that the results of any action cannot be predicted. In social policy this leads to critiques of, for example, rent control which it is argued has harmed the interests of those who were intended to benefit because of the unintended result that the supply of privately rented housing has dried up.

This sensitivity to the unintended consequences of state action links in with the individualist view that society as a whole cannot be known. (See chapter 3). Whilst in some cases it accurately describes what has happened, opponents argue that the real source of the problem is the ultimate reliance on the market mechanism whereby final decisions about investment remain with private individuals. An alternative answer then is to replace the market mechanism: in other words more not less state intervention.

This analysis of the economy does not provide any direct route to understanding what the state does. Rather it locates the limits consistent with a flourishing free market to be set to the state's actions. Nevertheless economists have attempted to apply the same basic concepts of individual choice and utility maximization to the explanation of political behaviour. We shall consider this approach further in the next chapter which deals with the state and political theories. Here we need only reiterate the point that the economic system can be theorized as a constraint only because people choose it to be so. The concept of power does not appear in the analysis.

### Keynes — a revolt assimilated

In the 1930s the advanced capitalist world was hit by a deep recession. The misery of the dole queues led some economists to reassess the basic neo-classical assumption that the economy was self-regulating and could be left to itself to find an equilibrium level of activity. Keynes's answer was that the market could reach equilibrium at many possible points and that, if the resources of an economy were to be fully utilized and full employment achieved, some system of regulating aggregate demand was necessary.

At the time this was seen as a dramatic break from orthodoxy: Galbraith points out that until then, whether one agreed with Say's Law that output would always find buyers was the means of distinguishing an economist from a crackpot! (Galbraith, 1973). Whereas the orthodox approach to recovery from the slump was couched in terms of reduced government expenditure and wage cuts, Keynes called for increased expenditure and the maintenance of aggregate demand.

Nevertheless the Keynesian 'revolution' was easily absorbed. Keynes believed that once the state had created a framework of monetary and fiscal policies which would maintain demand, the economy could once again be left to become self-regulating. Thus Keynes fundamentally accepted the neo-classical idea of the competitive market and was in sympathy with the individualist theories of Hayek discussed in chapter 3. (See George and Wilding, 1976). The stage was set for Keynes's ideas to be absorbed into the corpus of knowledge of neo-classical economics: the traditional emphasis on interaction between individual producers and consumers became 'micro-economics', complemented by the study of 'macro-economics', or economic aggregates.

In conclusion we can see that Keynes's contribution was to provide a superior analysis of the real world to the abstractions of neo-classical orthodoxy, and thus a firmer basis for policy guidelines. These included greater state intervention, limited to the overall direction of demand, so that beyond the argument that social security payments should be maintained during a depression to raise demand, they offer no guidelines as to what the state should do in the field of welfare. Similarly, the theory has little explanatory power. Like the authors considered in the previous section, Keynes had a basically consensus view of society: the state should maintain market relations in everyone's best interest. The market is seen as subordinate to the state, which as Skidelsky points out, Keynes saw as completely autonomous, and best run by a group of enlightened Treasury mandarins. (Skidelsky, 1977b).

## Social administration and the fetish of economic growth

Social administration is often seen as hostile to markets — in chapter 8 we shall consider the tension that exists between the subject and orthodox economics. Nevertheless, like Keynesian economics, the state intervention it favours is directed almost exclusively towards distribution rather than relations of production. This leads to an emphasis on resources — the welfare state is constrained by the level of output which the market can produce. This approach is exemplified by Klein (1975).

Klein sees the market as producing a certain output, at which point the political system comes into play to modify the distributional impact which the market would otherwise produce. If the production of resources slows down, then there is a gap between expectations and possibilities:

> To discuss social policy without any sense of crisis — a sharp awareness that the combination of rapid inflation and non-growth

has created an entirely new setting for the debate — is therefore not simply realistic. It is also calculated to make the eventual confrontation between what is desirable . . . and what is possible . . . even more painful.

(1975, p. 4).

The policy prescription thus becomes one of 'enlarging the cake'. In other words, policies to increase the rate of growth must be emphasized such that political decisions to devote a larger absolute share of resources to welfare can be taken painlessly and without increasing their *relative* share.

This argument creates a Catch 22 situation. Policies to increase economic growth often create 'diswelfares'. These affect us all, but they fall disproportionately on the most economically vulnerable sections of society: the unskilled, or older worker, women and blacks. We can see this when we look at the effects of technical changes on employment. Economic growth involves raising the productivity of labour in the economy through increasing technological investment. In a highly developed economy such as Britain's this involves restructuring the capitalist sector of industry — in less developed economies the existence of pre-capitalist sectors such as peasant agriculture may leave scope for raising overall productivity through absorbing labour from these into the capitalist sector.

The restructuring process, involving the elimination of small firms, the concentration of industry into larger units and investment in labour-saving technology has happened both spontaneously and as a result of state encouragement: between 1966 and 1970, for example, the Industrial Reorganization Corporation encouraged mergers through giving financial support to companies which agreed to undertake managerial reform, and favouring particular companies in their bids for state contracts. It was recognized that this process would create redundancies: the 1965 Redundancy Payments Act introduced payments for workers whose jobs were axed on the grounds that they would have:

an important and necessary part to play in allaying fears of redundancy and resistance to new methods and economic change.
(Ray Gunter, Minister of Labour,
quoted in George, 1968, p. 111).

Whether this process of rationalization leads to greater profitability, and if so, whether this generates sufficient new investment to absorb

housing, where the public sector accounts for only about a third of dwellings in England and Wales. The encouragement of owner occupation as the ideal, exerts a downward pressure on the standard of local authority housing, and intensifies allocation problems in a situation where a whole series of priority groups are competing for a limited stock of good quality public housing. Whilst the private sectors in health and education are very small, they nevertheless have a distorting effect: for example, opportunities for private practice encourage consultants to concentrate in the wealthier, over-doctored southeast, whilst the public school system continues to play a role in the perpetuation of privilege and access to powerful positions in society.

Thus despite the fact that the state actually replaces market forces in some cases, particularly in the distribution of certain goods and services, and thus harms the interests of particular capitalists, the provision of social services cannot be extricated from the effects of market forces. We should not, however, see this as the only source of the inadequacy of the social services — we shall be looking at the problems of the bureaucratic administration of social services in chapter 7, and the perpetuation of dominant values in chapter 8. In this chapter we shall continue our theme of the economic interests of capital by looking at the effects of the growth of the welfare state on capital accumulation.

### The growth of social expenditure

So far we have discussed the question of *how* the state intervenes, our focus being on the manner and extent of displacement of market forces. We now turn to the issue of resources. The state not only reduces the sphere of capital accumulation by removing certain goods and services from commodity production, it also pre-empts resources in the form of money, (tax revenue and borrowing), labour (those whom it employs) and commodities (its purchase of goods and services from the private sector). Whether these activities depress the overall rate of capital accumulation in the economy is a matter of considerable debate amongst economists.

Before we can consider the arguments we must first clarify, briefly, the evidence as to the growth of public expenditure and resource appropriation. A fuller discussion and analysis of this area is provided in Gough (1979). Overall public-expenditure statistics provide a global figure for the income received by the government in the form of tax revenue and borrowing, and for its expenditure on resources (labour and commodities), and transfer payments (items such as pensions and subsidies where purchasing power is merely transferred from one private individual or body to another). To compare the magnitude of government expenditure both over time and between one country and another, it is generally related to size of overall national income, measured in terms of gross national product (GNP). For a discussion of the calculation of GNP see Sleeman (1979).

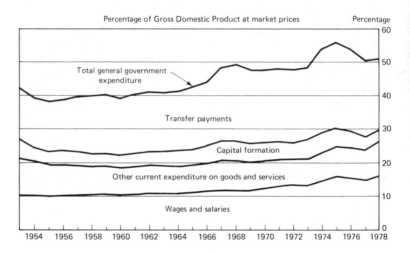

Fig. 6.3 *Government expenditure by economic category as a percentage of GNP.*

Source: CSO *Social Trends*, HMSO 1979. Reproduced by permission of the Controller, HMSO.

The three categories capital formation, current expenditure on goods and services and expenditure on wages and salaries all constitute resource expenditure.

State expenditure in the UK has risen from around 13 per cent of GNP in 1910 to more than 50 per cent in the 1970s (Gough 1979). This increase has not been smooth — in particular spectacular periods of growth were associated with the two world wars, after which expenditure fell, but to a level well above that obtaining before the wars. The years of the 1960s and early 1970s constituted a third period of major expansion. Before we go on to consider whether or not this constitutes a rising *burden* on accumulation we need, however, to distinguish between different types of expenditure and different types of government income since they do not all have the same economic impact.

On the expenditure side we return to the distinction made earlier between 'real' or resource expenditure (on labour, goods and services), and transfer payments. In the former case resources consumed by the state are not available to the private sector. In the latter case, shifting purchasing power around from one individual to another does not leave the private sector with fewer resources, it merely alters the structure of consumer demand according to whether individuals are net contributors or net receivers, or the relative profitability of different firms. Thus, for example, the consumption of pensioners is raised at the expense of childless families on average or above incomes; the financial position of British Leyland is improved at the expense of profitable industries and childless families. Figure 6.3 shows the balance between different types of expenditure.

On the income side, government spending is financed by taxation charges and borrowing. The bulk of revenues are raised from households in the form of income tax, property taxes, expenditure taxes, and council-house rents. In 1978, for example, income tax, expenditure taxes, social security contributions and rates accounted for 83 per cent of government income (National Income and Expenditure, 1979). Rising taxation is obviously politically disadvantageous for any government, although its economic impact is less clear. The most familiar economic argument against high personal taxation is its effects on incentives. Sleeman points out, however, that the evidence as to whether taxation leads to people working less or more is by no means clear (Sleeman, 1973). Government borrowing — the public sector borrowing requirement — has its most direct effect on the company sector. Increased competition for funds reduces their availability to companies and pushes up interest rates. If, however, increased government borrowing is associated with an expansion of the money supply there is a general inflationary effect which is felt both by companies and households.

## Is the welfare state an unproductive burden?

During the past decade the British economy has been characterized by:

rising inflation, stagnation in industrial output, growing unemployment and a lack of investment in the expansion and modernization of the productive equipment of the economy

(Sleeman, 1979, p. 84).

To what extent can this failure of the capitalist economy to live up to its promise to expand the productive forces be explained by the encroachment of the state and its appropriation of resources? This issue is a matter of considerable debate amongst economists, and we shall consider some divergent views below. The question involves two issues. In the first place, do the social services make any contribution to capital accumulation? In other words are the social services purely a gain for the working class at the expense of capital, or does capital in any way benefit economically from their provision? Secondly, and related to this, who finally bears the cost of the expansion of the welfare state, capital or labour?

Those who see the welfare state as a burden generally base their case on some kind of distinction between productive and unproductive labour. This distinction is used to indicate that state expenditures are unproductive and hence make no contribution to the creation of surplus value, and that the full cost falls on capital and not labour. Yaffe, for example, takes this view. State expenditures, he argues, are required to maintain employment, and ease the *sale* of commodities. Thus, although they contribute to the *realization* of surplus value, they do this at the expense of the *production* of surplus value, viz:

The point about state expenditures is that they are financed and paid out of taxes or by budget deficit financing and government borrowings . . . . In both cases, present or 'future' suplus value is appropriated from private capital by the state in the form of taxes or loans . . . . This represents a decline in surplus value available for private accumulation. This is so because state-induced production is 'unproductive'.

(Yaffe, 1973, p. 51).

Yaffe's argument thus rests on the distinction between productive and unproductive workers. The former labour for capitalists, producing commodities for sale. They produce surplus value which is appropriated by a capitalist to expand the productive forces. The latter group do not produce surplus value, and they are paid out of the mass of surplus value produced by other workers.[3]

Two objections have been raised against this argument. First, can we automatically assume that state workers' wages are paid out of surplus value? The question can perhaps best be approached using the diagram below.

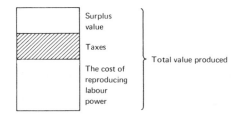

We have seen above that most taxes are paid by households. If we want to argue that all taxes ultimately fall on surplus value then it must be taken as given that all taxes on wages and workers' expenditure will be recouped in the form of higher wages. Whilst there will obviously be a tendency in class society for this to occur there seems no *apriori* reason to assume that workers will *always* be successful in achieving this. A second objection to Yaffe's argument concerns whether all state-induced production is unproductive. Since no capitalist is involved, expenditure cannot be *directly* productive. But it may be indirectly so.

Before we move on to examine this possibility we shall look at a non-marxist study which adopts a similar viewpoint to Yaffe's on the issue of the unproductive character of the welfare state.

Bacon and Eltis in an influential study of the British economy published in 1978 argue that the economy should be seen as comprising two sectors: marketed and non-marketed. This has certain similarities with Marx's productive/unproductive distinction, but also certain crucial differences. The marketed sector consists of goods and services which are sold (i.e. private-sector output, apart from loss-making ventures, and public-sector output where prices cover the costs of production); the non-marketed consists of goods and services which are not sold (free social services and loss-making private and public activities). The marketed sector is crucial to economic growth since it

3. Not only state workers are seen as unproductive. Capitalists involved in the circulation (process of buying and selling) of commodities are also seen as having their costs and profits met from surplus value produced by productive workers.

provides all exports, investment goods and marketed consumer goods. The growth of the non-marketed sector has meant that the size of the marketed sector in terms of labour force has declined whilst the claims made upon it have increased, since the new army of state employees put forward demands both for investment goods in the shape of schools and hospitals, and consumption goods to buy from their wages. Inflation and economic stagnation are thus seen as explicable in terms of three consequences of the growth of the non-marketed sector: the shortage of labour in the marketed sector, and the shift into services (de-industrialization), the inflated claims being placed on the marketed sector, and the wage demands of marketed-sector workers which are a direct result of rising taxation to finance the employment of non-market workers and the benefits paid to non-producers such as pensioners. Thus indirectly taxes have fallen on profits as suggested by Yaffe.

These arguments, often referred to as the 'de-industrialization thesis', have considerable influence not only amongst academic circles, but also on policy. The Labour Government of 1974 to 1979 began a policy of cutting expenditure from 1976 onwards, justifying their actions in terms of the need to release capacity for private-sector expansion.

The change of government in May 1979, brought into power a Conservative Party already converted to the principles of public expenditure cuts. Their case is mainly based on monetarist principles — the need to restrain the money supply as an indirect means of holding back pay and price increases — and also on arguments of incentives. In addition, arguments about public sector resources are brought in:

> Lower public spending and a progressive reduction in government borrowing will leave a growing share of the nation's resources for the private sector
>
> (Treasury, June 1979, p. 1).

Given their influence, it is worth considering in some detail whether Bacon and Eltis provide a conclusive case that the welfare state is a burden which capitalism cannot afford. Their arguments have been subjected to a wide-ranging critique, although not all their detractors challenge their basic premise, that the welfare state is a burden. First, their explanation for the growth of the public sector labour force — which they regard as the result of government policies to mop up unemployment — lacks plausibility. Second, their argument that the marketed sector is starved of workers due to the growth of the social services only holds in a period of full employment. This is hardly true of the recent period and in any case, the expansion of the public service labour force has largely been achieved by drawing on new sources of labour such as married women. Thirdly, the failure of investment to pick up since 1976 in the context of cuts in public expenditure suggests that the growth of the welfare state cannot be regarded as the sole cause of Britain's decline. This point is reinforced when we look at the international context: Britain does not enjoy a uniquely high level of social expenditure, yet her rate of de-industrialization has been rather faster than her international counterparts (Singh, 1977).

Nevertheless, whilst this may lead one to question whether the expansion of the welfare state is the *sole* cause of the ills of capitalism, it does not refute the basic premise that the welfare state is unproductive. This central premise has been challenged from several sides: from a social democratic standpoint by Glennerster and a marxist standpoint by Gough.

Glennerster argues in effect that we should be less concerned with whether the British economy is growing in terms of size of GNP, and more with whether we are producing the goods and services which people need.

> The manufacture of objects by industry has no value in itself. It is only if people wish to buy them that they add to the country's wealth. That proposition is not altered if we prefer services to goods or if we seek to buy a commodity, like education or health care, as a community rather than as individuals.
> The larger the share of final expenditure that is accounted for by public services, the less relevance GNP growth has to any increase in individual welfare
>
> (Glennerster, 1976, p. 7).

This argument brings us to philosophical questions rather far removed from those raised by Bacon and Eltis. The latter, in effect, simply question whether the expansion of the welfare state hinders capital accumulation. They leave aside the wider issue of whether economic growth should be regarded as leading to enhanced welfare. Glennerster broaches this question, but shies away from its radical implications, merely putting forward the plea for a more open debate on the issues involved.

Gough returns to the same ground as Bacon and Eltis — does the welfare state hinder accumulation and growth — and offers a marxist critique (Gough, 1979, ch. 6). He begins by noting that the costs of the welfare state are not a loss to the personal sector, but that, on the contrary, the bulk of tax resources taken return to the personal sector in the form of a 'social wage' (cash benefits) and 'collective consumption' items (collectively provided housing, health and other services). Insofar as these items are necessary parts of workers' consumption they can be considered as elements of the reproduction of labour power, and need not necessarily be seen as a cost falling on surplus value. Thus, for example, the absence of a National Health Service would lead to workers having to pay health service premiums. State expenditure on social services may, then, merely represent a different way in which the worker meets the same needs. We can illustrate this by returning to our diagram:

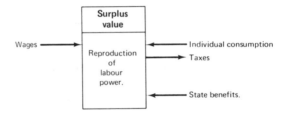

In this example, the production of surplus value has been unaffected for the majority of capitalists. Only those directly nationalized have suffered. If state health care is cheaper than private care then this benefit will be appropriated either by capital, if wages are reduced on a pro rata basis, or workers in the form of a higher standard of living.

As Gough points out, however, the situation is not as simple as this, because in the real world social services are not wholly elements in the reproduction of labour power: in particular, those providing for the non-working population and those concerned with social control fall into O'Connor's category of social expense.

Whether or not, then, the welfare state acts as a burden on accumulation depends on a number of factors: first the balance between the reproductive and unreproductive elements of expenditure; second the efficiency and rate of exploitation in the social services; and finally the extent to which the benefits of a cheap service will be appropriated by the working class in the form of a higher standard of living, or capital in the form of lower wages. Once again we are brought back to consider the role of class struggle and the balance of class forces rather than any *apriori* reasoning.

## Conclusion

In this chapter we have examined the manner in which the state intervenes in the market and the possible implications for the capitalist economy. We have been at pains to avoid *apriori* reasoning in many cases. In particular we have rejected a fundamentalist marxist approach which inevitably lapses into a determinist view of the relation between economy and society. We are left with an analysis which is structuralist, since the working of the capitalist system is seen to place definite limits on what people do, but which places considerable emphasis on the role of class struggle and hence human action in shaping social policy. The welfare state is not, however, simply the product of the class struggle. It is the creation of the *state* — the political sphere of society. We now face the task of showing how the state acts to create a welfare state which modifies but does not challenge capitalist relations and represents benefits to the working class, but also long-term benefits to the dominant class.

# 7

## The state

### Introduction

The welfare state refers to certain elements of the output of the state, in the form of legislation, administrative regulation, public expenditures and the production and distribution of certain goods and services. To study social administration is to study the state. The danger this presents of adopting a perspective of the state *as subject* has been drawn out in chapter 1. In this chapter we attempt to show the manner in which welfare state studies can enrich our understanding of the political level of society and its relation to the economic system once we cease to take the state for granted. We are concerned with explaining how and why the state acts in particular ways. The central issue which any such theory must confront is whether there are any consistent biases in the way in which states in capitalist society behave. If so, can they be systematically explained, and can such explanation be found by looking at the political system alone? Finally, if we can incorporate an explanation of common trends in capitalist states, can we also account for continuing diversities?

### Theories of the state: some basic concepts

Before moving on to compare different approaches to this question, some points about what we are looking at need to be clarified. We often talk about 'economic policy', 'social' or 'welfare policy', 'foreign policy' etc. The concern to know what we are talking about has led some writers to attempt to define each area. Boulding, for example, defines 'social policy' in contrast to economic policy in terms of 'the thread of what has elsewhere been called the "integrative system" ' (Boulding, 1967, p. 192). This may lead to the temptation of imagining that the state's welfare role can be separately analysed. That somehow the state which sends troops to Northern Ireland and thus identifies itself as 'armed bodies of men' is not the same — has a different motive force — from the state which provides meals on wheels for the elderly. This temptation is reinforced by the very use of the term 'welfare state', a point noted by Gough when he argues that: 'the very term "the welfare state" reveals the ideological nature of most writing about it' (Gough, 1979, p. 3).

The temptation must however be resisted — *the* state must indeed be analysed as such. If any overall theory can be advanced, it must be able to incorporate within it a coherent and consistent explanation of the multifarious interventions of the modern state in the social formation.

In order to compare theories of the welfare state we need to clarify three concepts: the state, the political system and politics. Miliband describes the state as a set of interrelated institutions, comprising the government, the administration, the coercive apparatuses (the military and the police), the judiciary, sub-central government (local and regional government) and representative assemblies (Miliband, 1973). This view of the state rests on a distinction between the state on one hand and 'civil society' on the other. This distinction is challenged by some marxists who adopt a structuralist quasi-functionalist approach to the state. Poulantzas regards this distinction as rendering 'impossible' any scientific examination of the capitalist state (Poulantzas, 1973). This leads to a situation however where the definition of the state is extended to embrace 'the Church, the political parties, the unions . . . the schools, the mass media . . . and, from a certain point of view, the family' (Poulantzas, 1969, p. 75). This view prevents us from distinguishing between dictatorships where for example every journalist is employed by and directly accountable to the state, transmitting only the official communiqués of the Home Office, and the media under bourgeois democracy. This view has been adequately criticized elsewhere (Miliband 1977). While civil society comprises all forms of social intercourse, the peculiarity of the state is that its dictates are backed up by publicly sanctioned force. The political system refers both to certain elements of the state system — the government, the administration, and representative institutions at both central and sub-central level — together with organizations which are the product of civil society but which are actors in the political realm — political parties, pressure groups, trade unions when they enter into negotiations with the government. Finally politics refers to collective action directed towards structures of power and authority. Political activity is concerned with replacing those occupying positions of authority, influencing their decisions or challenging the very structure of power and authority.

The theories which we shall consider differ fundamentally on whether the actions of the state are explicable in terms of the political system alone. On the one hand are individualist theories which see the state as merely responding to demands emanating from the political system, demands which are taken as given. On the other hand are theories which argue that the political process takes place within a context of unequal power relations set by the social relations of the economic system. In general neo-classical economic theories and pluralist political science fall into the first category, and political economy into the second. Nevertheless, developments in the social sciences are giving these categories fuzzy edges: in particular some of the attempts by pluralists to take account of the disproportionate power of particular interests are moving them away from individualism towards a structuralist approach. We shall examine these theories in more detail.

### Individualist approaches: neo-classical economics

In the last chapter we considered first neo-classical theories of the economic system. In this framework, economics is seen as to do with how individuals make choices between alternative ends, and how the market system translates consumer preferences into investment decisions by producers. This approach has also been applied to the activities of governments. (Individualist theories stress the role of the legislature rather than the state.) Society is seen as comprised of individuals seeking to maximize their wealth. Individual consumers have preferences for particular bundles of publicly provided goods and services, depending on their income, taste and the 'tax-price' of the goods in question. Decisions as to which collective goods are provided are arrived at through a kind of political market place: demands are expressed through political participation (voting and pressure group activity) whilst supply depends on the degree of competition between political parties and the respective strengths of bureaucrats and politicians. (See for example Breton, 1974.)

Thus the actions of the state are explicable in terms of the desire of politicians to maximize the votes they receive, intersecting with the political demands emanating from voters and pressure groups, analysed in terms of individual self-interest.

Whilst it has been argued that this has produced some accurate predictions about political behaviour and government policies (Levi, 1979), the approach is defective. First, just as in the analysis of economic markets, 'tastes' or political demands are taken as the starting point: no explanation is given for their source. Secondly, to build a theory *entirely* on an assumption of immediate individual self-interest does not square with the facts, either of voting behaviour or the actions of political parties: ideology cannot be written off the agenda in this way. In any case the question of how to identify people's interests is not so unproblematic as the theory, with its use of the utility maximizing approach, implies (see Lukes, 1974a). Finally, the theory suggests that the policies of the state can be understood entirely in terms of the level of participation in the political system.

In this last point, neo-classical economics finds common ground with the earlier formulations of pluralist political science. We can best illustrate the problems inherent in this analysis by showing how in political science it has been subject to an internal critique which has moved it further away from individualism and closer to a structuralist approach.

## Varieties of pluralism

Pluralism like neo-classical economic theory seeks to explain government activity in terms of the pressures emanating from the political system. Its distinctive characteristic is its stress on the formation of pressure groups and the manner in which policies are formed as the outcome of a lobbying process. In common with neo-classical economic theory, it takes people's motives and interests as unproblematic, and revealed in their activities. Early formulations of the theory implied that all pressure groups could gain a hearing in the political process, with the result that there could be no systematic bias in policy and no general theory of policy making.

More recently however, pluralism has been subject to both an internal and external critique on two grounds: its failure to provide an account of observable biases in policy which other approaches, notably marxism, were able to explain, and its individualist methodology.

The point that pressure groups enjoy unequal access to power has been noted by writers within social administration: for example, Glennerster (1975) notes the imbalance between producer and consumer groups in the social services. However the main challenge to pluralism has been how to account for the disproportionate power of business interests in the political process. Bachrach and Baratz (1970) argue that to understand this we have to discover which issues are *not* discussed, rather than concentrating on observable behaviour only. Powerful groups can manipulate the political agenda, thus preventing issues being raised. This has moved us a long way from the original position, but as Lukes (1974a) points out, the focus is still on power as an attribute of individuals, without an adequate analysis of the relationship between social structure and power.

A study by Hall, Land, Parker and Webb (1975) of particular initiatives in social policy seems to promise in its introductory chapters to fill this gap. They begin by adopting a straightforward pluralist paradigm, focusing on the demands directed towards the authorities in the political system, and the support these demands receive. They are aware, however, that:

> The danger of the pluralist picture . . . . is that the political process can easily become confused with political power (p. 130).

> They move on to consider the possibility that policy making takes place within an unequal distribution of power. They conclude that this is so, and put forward a 'bounded pluralist' approach which argues that the policy making process operates within a distinctly pluralist *process* but that the *limits* of policy-making are set by élites which for many purposes are indistinguishable from what Miliband calls a ruling class (p. 151).

This approach appears promising — the pluralist process alerts us to the fact that policy making involves bargaining between specific interest groups, but a broader theory of power is needed to indicate why certain groups get a hearing and their relative influence varies. The analysis of power is not, however, structuralist. It is couched in terms of ruling élites who as individuals regulate demands within the political system. We have not therefore proceeded further than Bachrach and Baratz. Furthermore, the substantive part of the authors' book takes the form of a series of case studies where no attempt is made to indicate how this process of regulation and selection occurs. We are left with pluralism in the eclectic mould familiar in social administration.

The political science approach which seems to move us furthest in the direction of a structuralist approach is that provided by Lindblom (1977). He refers to democratic institutions such as free elections, the right to form political parties, free speech, as 'polyarchy' (rule by many) and argues that in market societies major public decisions are taken in two areas: in the market sphere by businessmen, and in the sphere of polyarchy by elected governments. Because any government must be concerned with the performance of the market, it will inevitably pay especial attention to the views of business:

businessmen do not appear simply as the representatives of a special interest, as representatives of interest groups do. They appear as functionaries performing functions that government officials regard as indispensable

(p. 175).

Labour does not enjoy an equivalent position, because whilst businessmen can choose whether or not to invest and therefore have to be induced to conform with government proposals, workers to all intents and purposes, have no choice as to whether to work.

Thus effectively there are three systems of decision making: in the market, decision making by businessmen; in the political sphere, decision making determined by the privileged position of business; or by polyarchy.

This analysis moves Lindblom in the direction of a structuralist analysis: the power of business in the political sphere is not vested in individual businessmen but in the private ownership of the means of production which delegates decisions over, for example investment, to businessmen. Returning to our enumeration of key questions earlier in this chapter we can see that Lindblom provides a structuralist account of the systematic bias of government policies towards business which accounts for common trends over time and between capitalist countries, but at the same time his observation that there is a dual system of control over decision making with polyarchy existing alongside the privileged position of business, enables the theory to encompass as well the divergences between polyarchic-market states.

Where the theory seems inadequate is, first its failure to provide an analysis of the dynamics of the economic system which would enable us to specify more precisely 'business interests' and the changing character of what the state does; secondly, its lack of any consideration of the consequences for human interests in general of the disproportionate power of business; and thirdly an analysis of polyarchy which remains largely individualist. Polyarchy is seen as a *rival* arena of decision making to that of business privilege. Thus the structural explanation of the latter does not apply. At the same time the very limited political agenda of polyarchy is noted, and explained in terms of the activities of business, through advertising for example, in moulding opinions in favour of a status quo which people are already conditioned to accept. This seems weak in explaining similarities and divergences in the political debate and social change both over time and between countries.

## Marxist analyses of structured class conflict

Marxism involves a structural analysis of power which takes us beyond Lindblom by providing, first an analysis of the capitalist economy in terms of the changing dynamics of capitalist accumulation, which enables us to understand the changing form of the interests of capital, thus supplying greater precision than the rather bland notion of 'business interests'; secondly a class analysis of society, which enables us to analyse the structurally determined interests of all members of society rather than simply those of business; thirdly a theory of values which provides an understanding of the limits of debate in the political process.

In marxist theory, the state is seen as one aspect of class society. We have already seen how classes are defined in the economic sphere — one class through its ownership/control of the means of production extracting and expropriating the surplus produced by the subordinate class. The state forms one of the mechanisms whereby a particular mode of production is furthered and sustained. Thus the state serves the interests of the dominant class within any mode of production. The analyses of the state which we shall examine all refer only to capitalist society. The societies of the USSR and Eastern Europe are not based on the capitalist mode of production (this does not imply that they are socialist) and are therefore excluded from consideration.

Is the state then a *necessary* aspect of class rule? To answer this question in relation to capitalist society, we may begin by examining some of the functions which states perform in the course of defending and furthering the capitalist mode of production. We should be aware of the limitations of this approach in providing a full *explanation* of the questions of how states have come into being and how the capitalist class manages to ensure that its interests are implanted in the actions of the state. The first requires a historical analysis of the development of capitalism and the unfolding of class struggle in different geopolitical arenas. We shall make some further remarks on the second one below. The need then to avoid a functionalist explanation alerts us to the more general point that even though performance of these functions is characteristic of capitalist states, the form in which they appear varies considerably.

Despite the many intense debates among marxists on the theory of the state certain areas of common agreement can be discerned. In particular the general need for a state in capitalist society is derived from the peculiarity of the capitalist mode of production that the economic and political spheres assume different forms. Exploitation takes place in the economic sphere without direct coercion but simply through the operation of the market: the labourer faces the choice of working for a capitalist, or being without the means to keep body and soul alive rather than the choice between labouring for a feudal land-owner or facing branding or flogging. This, however, gives capitalist society a fragmentary character: both because of the lack of unity between the economic and political levels of society and because capital is divided into competing capitals with conflicting short term interests. The role of the capitalist state is thus characterized as playing a unifying role in society on behalf of the capitalist class *as a whole.*

This involves the state in carrying out various functions, described by Miliband (1973) as repressive, ideological, economic and international (i.e. *vis-à-vis* other nation states). These correspond to its tasks of maintaining law and order (suppressing class conflict), fostering consensus, maintaining capitalist accumulation, and advancing the specific interests of the nation state.

It would be foolish to attempt to place any particular activity of the state solely in one of these categories. When the government decides to subsidize British shipbuilders producing ships for Poland, is this economic (maintaining accumulation in the shipbuilding industry), fostering consensus (reassuring workers that they will not be made redundant), advancing British interests (ensuring the survival of the British shipbuilding industry in an era of fierce international competition)? Perhaps only repression is unambiguous — being hit by a rubber bullet doesn't leave one confused as to the ideological or economic intentions of the state!

Nevertheless, what are loosely described as welfare functions, generally fall into the economic, ideological and repressive compartments. An alternative formulation, which amounts to the same thing, is to describe these functions as accumulation and legitimation (O'Connor, 1973). In other words, welfare state activities are an appeasement to working-class struggles against the vagaries of the capitalist system, whilst at the same time contributing to capitalist production by raising workers' productivity and ensuring that they are adequately housed, fed and kept healthy, ready to labour afresh each day.

Thus far we have looked at areas of agreement amongst marxists. There are however immense disagreements, centring on the issue of how these functions should be understood, and how far such an approach takes us in understanding the question posed at the beginning of this chapter of the common trends exhibited in advanced capitalist societies, but also their wide diversity.

We begin by looking at the different ways in which the general functions of the state have been understood, in particular at the 'politicist' versus 'economist' interpretations. The first approach is represented by Poulantzas (1973) who places major stress on the role of the state in pursuing the political interest of the dominant class whilst undermining the ability of the dominated class to present an overall challenge to the existing social order.

Such an approach has been criticized from an 'economist' perspective by those who argue that it divorces analysis of the state from capital accumulation, (for example Holloway and Picciotto, 1977). This leads to an emphasis on changes occurring in the economic system and how these require the state to adopt different modes of intervention in order to maintain the overall interests of capital in general. Such an approach is applied to the development of the welfare state by Ginsburg, who argues that 'the state expresses the average interest of capital in general' (Ginsburg, 1979, p. 27).

This approach provides a useful corrective to those who assign too great an autonomy to the political level of society: if the role of the state is to defend and further a particular mode of production, then there will be a tendency for its role to change as the changing dynamics of that mode of production lead to new crisis points and tendencies. The problem with such analyses however is that they go beyond identifying certain limits and potential tendencies: they seek to explain state intervention in terms of the changing form of the interests of capital. Whilst this gives the approach a historical dimension, it makes it difficult to say very much about the differences between capitalist societies. Major differences, for example in the degree of centralization of the state apparatus between France and the USA, and in the scope of welfare activities between Britain and the USA, cannot be reduced to differences in the capitalist mode of production.

This raises broader questions about the status of discussion of functions. We have already suggested that the identification of social functions does not constitute an explanation of what human actors actually do. To suppose otherwise is to lapse into a functionalist methodology which writes human action off the social agenda. Turning to our present problem, we must be able to show concretely why the state apparatus will intervene in the struggle between classes in such a way as to further the interests of the capitalist class. We shall begin by looking at the treatment of the class struggle and then look at explanations of how the interests of the capitalist class become implanted in the state.

## Class struggle and the capitalist state

Capitalism involves forms of domination and subjection. We have already referred in chapter 6 to the class cleavages associated with the capitalist mode of production, and when we speak of class struggle we are generally referring to the myriads of ways in which the exploited class struggles against the power of those who own/control the means of production. In capitalist society other forms of oppression are superimposed on this basic class system, in particular oppression along the lines of sex, race and nationality. Such forms of oppression may pre-date capitalism and there may be no *necessary* reason why they should be perpetuated under the capitalist mode of production. Nevertheless they have generally been integrated into the power structure of capitalist society. We may therefore say that the successful struggle of the working class ultimately requires it to take up the oppression of other groups, whose own liberation in turn depends on their struggle taking an anti-capitalist dynamic. Thus when we speak of class struggles we refer to the challenge to forms of capitalist oppression posed by the working class and other oppressed groups.

Class struggles under capitalism may be viewed as falling into different categories — we may single out four in particular: trade unionism, community action, movements around specific oppressions (racial, sexual, national) and party political. These different forms of class struggle represent either responses to different aspects of oppression (the first three), or different ways of organizing (the political party). They are generally associated with a degree both of organizational and political separation. Such a separation is not of course *necessarily* the case. Whilst a degree of organizational separation may persist, any mass social upheaval would certainly be associated with a much greater *political* coming together of movements and demands than is the norm in capitalist society. In particular any revolutionary challenge to the existing social order must be able to unite the working class in a movement which espouses the interests and grievances of all the oppressed. Our purpose is, however, to understand the phenomenon of the welfare state, which represents the ability of the dominant class to maintain the essential structure of capitalism. One of the bases of the success of the dominant class is indeed its ability to prevent the working class from achieving the kind of political unity alluded to above. Thus, for example, the ideology that trade unionism should only concern itself with 'trade union matters' leaving 'politics' to others — an ideology supported by both the Conservative Party and social democracy in Britain — leaves most workers as passive spectators of the political process.

Returning to our four categories, trade unionism represents workers organizing at the point of production, challenging the rate of exploitation and capitalist control over the labour process. Community action is a loose term used to describe a myriad of different types of struggle outside the point of production. In particular, it encompasses struggles based on place of residence which are responses to inadequate collective urban facilities — housing, transport, social centres, parks — or to the state's bureaucratic attempts to control the spatial organization of the city through planning legislation. Community action may also be broadened to include struggles of the non-working population around social security. In this broad sense, the label 'struggles in the sphere of reproduction' used by Cockburn (1977) may be more useful than 'community action' with its implied limitation to residential area. Thirdly, struggles of groups suffering specific oppression include the women's movement, movements against racial oppression, such as black people in Britain, and those suffering national oppression — the nationalist (Catholic) population in Northern Ireland for instance.

These then are the main forms which class struggle takes. Some demands and actions are directed against individual capitalists, others at the state. In either case, capitalists rely on the framework of laws upholding private property and the repressive apparatus of the state to contain struggles. In some cases capital cannot rely on repression: the state must intervene to organize reform. It is this aspect of state intervention with which we are concerned.

Does a marxist analysis imply that the capitalist state intervenes in the class struggle to ensure that the outcome is wholly favourable to capital? To adopt such a position would entail the view either that the state stands outside the class struggle, or that it is totally in the pocket of the capitalist class. Neither seems satisfactory. Gough in fact identifies three ways in which class interests are expressed in state policies: first working-class pressure leads to concessions from the state especially in liberal democracies; secondly the state formulates and prosecutes the long-term interests of capital, either by initiating policies, or adapting the concessions it has granted under the pressure of class struggle to the needs of capital; thirdly the working class and the capitalist class may both see certain reforms as in their interests — for example the introduction of many of the social services were supported both by capital and labour, although for different reasons (Gough, 1979). This consensus is evident in the fairly narrow range of disagreement around for example the key welfare reforms of 1944–48: social security legislation was based on the recommendations of the Liberal, Beveridge; Butler's Education Act was passed by the Conservative-dominated wartime coalition; and the form of the NHS, hailed by many as a pillar of socialism, was the outcome of negotiations between the Labour government and the medical profession, in which the goal of a fully state-controlled free service was compromised.

Thus, it must be conceded that state policies may embody at least some short term interests of the working class. The state's accommodation to short-term interests may however be seen as compromising the long-term interest of the working class in socialism. Even this is not, however, self-evident. Concessions by the state may legitimate the existing social order and facilitate social control: but they may also become the basis for further struggle by the working class as it gains a sense of its own power.

In conclusion we can see that the state may introduce policies either because these are seen as directly aiding accumulation or social control, or in order to appease working-class struggle. In either case such policies can be seen as responding to the interest of capital in social stability. The long-term effects of such reforms on the class struggle however cannot ever be fully predicted. The state will do all it can to adapt concessions it has made to the interests of capital, but this may fail such that concessions fuel further class struggle. For this very reason the political representatives of capital often engage in furious debate on strategy. At the time of writing, for example, the Thatcher government is divided between factions characterized by the media as the 'hawks' and the 'wets', who argue the merits of stern monetarism, protecting profits but risking social turmoil, versus a more gradualist and reformist approach.

## The capitalist class and the state

What explanations do we have for the capitalists' ability to get the state to pursue its interests in the name of the general interest? An early answer to this question was given by Miliband (1973). He put forward three explanations: the class background of the top echelons of the capitalist state; the power of 'business' as a pressure group; and the requirements of the mode of production. This approach has been heavily criticized and indeed the first point is a description rather than a theory — why should the top civil servants come from one particular class, and would it make any difference if they shared a different social origin? The second point could be construed as implying that the capitalist state acts in response to pressures from business, whereas in fact it has already been pointed out that the state represents the interests of the class *as a whole* rather than acting at the behest of pressure groups. The third 'structural' explanation sets rather imprecise limits to the possibilities for change.

In a more recent book Miliband (1977) criticizes the inadequacies of his earlier approach, and attempts to develop a theory of politics which explains why the working class has failed to present a revolutionary challenge. He places considerable emphasis on the manner in which dominant ideologies are produced and reproduced, ideologies which thwart the dominated class from perceiving their true interests. This stress on ideology is important, and both Gough and Ginsburg point to the way in which the welfare state itself is part of the material base of the dominant ideology that antagonistic classes do not exist. Nevertheless, it is not a substitute to pursuing the enquiry as to how the state operates to further particular interests.

Drawing on the work of writers such as Gough, Offe (1974), Olin Wright (1978) and Therborn (1978) we would see class power as replicated in the state in the following ways. First certain economic imperatives do have to be fulfilled if the dynamism of the capitalist mode of production is to be sustained. Capitalist society is based on the continued expansion of the productive forces — a halt to this expansion leads to social crisis. The state generally attempts to promote the fullest development of the productive forces — to create material prosperity and social harmony, which in turn depends on the economic system producing an output sufficient to finance the welfare state. In this way we can see how the functions of the state discussed earlier lead to a tendency for it to respond to the changing requirements of capital. We shall examine this concretely in the next section.

Of course, those holding state power may choose the alternative route of socializing the means of production — such an aim is proclaimed in clause four of the Labour Party's constitution. Two reasons can be given to explain why such a challenge has not materialized in the most advanced capitalist country, the USA, and has been too weak to succeed in other highly developed economies. In the first place, the dominance of bourgeois ideology and the fact that none of the planned economies has achieved the level of material well-being or democratic rights enjoyed by the majority of workers in advanced capitalist countries inhibits the development of class consciousness. Secondly, the state is not merely constrained by external factors: its character is also stamped in its apparatus. Whilst then a radical anti-capitalist political party may gain power in the *legislature* the state apparatus as a whole is not an instrument that can be used to transform society.

The role of the state apparatus has been widely discussed and there is general agreement that the state serves the interests of capital most closely when the executive enjoys strength relative to the legislature, and is itself centralized in a way that insulates it from the full vagaries of pressure-group politics. Offe (1974) argues that the class character of the state is revealed in the way in which political institutions systematically exclude anti-capitalist influences and distill class interest from the external pressures to which they are subjected. These 'selection mechanisms' operate at a number of levels: in the structural limitations on what the state is permitted to do; the ideology of political institutions; the formal systems of rule and procedures which they follow; and in the final analysis the instruments of repression at their command.

In conclusion what the capitalist state does is explicable in terms of a number of factors: the necessity for continued capital accumulation, which may depend on the intervention of the state when impediments to accumulation are encountered; private ownership of the means of production, which limits the area of political decision making, and the dependence of the state on the output of private capital; the character of the state apparatus; and finally the balance of class forces and the perspicacity of the political representatives of the working class and its allies on the one hand and capital on the other.

## The changing role of the state

In this section we shall not concern ourselves with the global role of the capitalist state, but with its changing intervention in the economic sphere. This will be done briefly to provide a context within which to situate the welfare state. We shall take 1800 as a convenient starting point: although the emergence of capitalist commodity relations can be traced back to the Middle Ages, and the English civil war of the seventeenth century marks the break with a feudal state and the establishment of bourgeois forms, it is with modern *industrial* capitalism as it developed from the end of the eighteenth century that we are concerned.

We begin with the changing dynamics of capital accumulation since, as we have indicated above, these enable us to identify periods of crisis, arising when accumulation is halted or slowed down, when the state has had to develop new forms of intervention. Following Ginsburg (1979), we distinguish three phases: competitive capitalism, classical imperialism (from the 1870s to the end of the 1920s), and advanced monopoly capitalism. In the first period the economic system comprises many small capitals, and growth is largely achieved through the extension of the factory system, bringing more workers into the sphere of capitalist production and extracting more surplus value out of them through lengthening the working day. This was the period when Britain established herself as the first industrial nation and enjoyed a prominent position in the world economy. From the 1880s however, Britain began to be overtaken by newer developing economies such as Germany and the USA. This was a period of fierce international rivalry to which capital responded by introducing labour-saving technology to boost profits, and using colonial countries both as markets for domestically produced goods and investment outlets. This was particularly true of Britain with her export-oriented economy and high levels of overseas investment. This world was destroyed by the first world war and its economic aftermath, and from the 1930s to the present day we have seen the pressure of international competition and the drive for higher labour productivity reflected in the concentration and rationalization of industry into larger units using more advanced technology. This final period is divided by Olin Wright (1978) into the periods of the rise of monopoly capitalism, advanced monopoly capitalism and state-directed monopoly capitalism. Each period sees greater concentration of capital and intervention by the state to alleviate barriers to capitalist accumulation.

There is not a one to one correlation between changes in the economic system and state intervention. During the early nineteenth century the state was mainly concerned with establishing the general framework within which free competition could flourish. There was a virtually complete separation between the economic and political spheres. This does not mean that the state was not important, but many of its tasks involved the dismantling of controls and restrictions (such as the Corn Laws) inherited from the pre-capitalist era.

By the late nineteenth century Britain had entered a period of relative decline in international terms. Britain's initial pre-eminence now became a handicap: obsolete capital equipment needed replacing and industrial organization rationalized. The market mechanism did not provide the stimulus to bring about such changes, especially since low rates of return at home could be compensated for through investment overseas. The long-term needs of the British economy required the state to step in to promote such necessary restructuring, but the shift in attitudes and state intervention did not occur until the 1930s.

Since the 1930s government intervention in the economy has taken three forms: micro-economic intervention in relation to particular industries; macro-economic intervention, attempting to balance aggregate demand and supply using fiscal and monetary policies; and finally, production of the inputs for accumulation by nationalized industries. During the 1930s there was considerable micro-economic intervention as the state sponsored concentration and rationalization in many industries. After the second world war reliance was placed on Keynesian macro-economic policy and nationalization of some basic industries in fields such as energy and transport, whilst since the 1960s all three aspects of intervention have been expanded and brought together in an attempt to bring about a measure of capitalist planning. The result is an ever greater politicization of market relationships, which has created further problems for capital. We shall consider this further in chapter 9.

## The emergence of the welfare state

So far we have discussed the role of the state in relation to production. We now turn to welfare, using Gough's definition of the welfare state as intervention in the reproduction of labour power and the maintenance of the non-working population. The development of the welfare state can be seen as having three sources: the desire to modify the quality of labour power in order to facilitate accumulation; the attempt to integrate the working class; and the need to grant concessions in response to the demands of the labour movement.

Our periodization of the development of the welfare state is shown in Table 7.1. During the liberal period of state-economy relations the notion that capital could accommodate a system of state welfare was foreign to both capital and labour. Most histories of the welfare state begin with the 1834 Poor Law Amendment Act which remained the central plank of state maintenance of the non-working population until the Edwardian period, and was not finally abolished until 1948. Nevertheless, the Poor Law represented not an extension of state welfare, but an attempt to fashion the most minimal system of state support consistent with the then principles of political economy that people must be subject to the unfettered discipline of the market for the greater good of all. Relief was restricted to the workhouses, where conditions were to be 'less eligible' than those of the lowest class of independent labourer. In this way only the truly destitute would come within the orbit of relief policy, and in the process they would be removed from the labour market, and indeed from society.

It is untrue to say that *no* other social policy developments occurred; but they were either very minor and tentative — the decision to begin making grants to religious bodies providing schools; or had a chequered career in the face of strong public antipathy — the 1848 Public Health Act, about which the *Morning Chronicle* commented, 'Even in Constantinople or Grand Cairo where plague and cholera are decimating the population it is doubtful whether such a Bill would be desirable' (quoted in Finer, 1952, p. 320).

During the final quarter of the nineteenth century changes began to occur. These were in part a response to the emergence of a broad, well organized labour movement: trade unionism was now transcending narrow craft boundaries to embrace the unskilled. At the same time it was beginning to be appreciated that concessions to workers would not bring the system crashing down but might play an integrative or controlling role: capitalism had, in other words, reached a greater economic and political maturity. The liberal bourgeoisie began to argue for a less repressive attitude to unemployment and poverty, arguments which reached fruition after 1906. Meanwhile, public health and education became established areas of state responsibility and changes in legislation and administration lessened some of the penal aspects of the Poor Law as regards certain groups, in particular children and those who had been in receipt only of medical relief: in the latter case, an Act of 1885 ended the situation where receipt of medical aid led to deprivation of civil rights.

An interesting aspect of this period is that a full picture cannot be gleaned by looking only at the national level. The turn of the century was a flourishing period of municipal activity — 'gas and water socialism' as it was often called — and radical innovations in the field of municipal enterprise, public works and other services were the hallmark of certain major cities such as London, Birmingham and Glasgow.

In economic policy the watershed which represented a clear break in the state's role came in the 1930s and was extended through the post-

Table 7.1

Stages in the emergence of the British welfare state

| | Period | Characteristics of state intervention | Major social legislation | |
|---|---|---|---|---|
| (1) | *Laissez-faire* 1800–1870 | Minimal: either repressive or aimed purely at physical reproduction of the labour force | 1834 1848 | Poor Law Public Health Act Factory Acts |
| (2) | Interregnum 1870–1905 | Modification of the most repressive aspects of the Poor Law and consolidation of public health Acts. Interest in quality of reproduction of labour power, especially in connection with education | 1870 1875 1885 | Education Act Public Health Act Local government reorganization Medical Relief Disqualification Act |
| (3) | Embryonic welfare state 1905–1939 | Major departures from the Poor Law. Setting up of services to meet individual need. Development of national insurance | 1908 1911 1919 1934 | Old age pensions Unemployment and health insurance Housing subsidies Unemployment Assistance Board |
| (4) | Institutional welfare state 1945 –? | End of Poor Law and setting up of wide range of comprehensive services to meet need | 1944 1945-8 1946 | Education Act Comprehensive insurance and assistance service set up National Health Service Act |

war Keynesian era. In social policy the decisive change came earlier with the Liberal reforms of 1906–11. Why should this be the case?

We can explain this earlier shift with reference to two factors. First, the changing economic context, in particular the intensification of inter-imperialist rivalries, meant that the state became more concerned about the reproduction of labour power, both in terms of its physical attributes and its qualities of skill. Thus educational policies and legislation to improve the health of the younger generation received considerable impetus.

In the second place, social policy came to be seen as having a legitimating and integrating as opposed to repressive role. The impetus to such changing attitudes came both from above and below: from the dominant class, the ideology of social imperialism justified ameliorating the conditions of the domestic working class, to forge unity in the struggle with other nations. From below, the working class was growing in organization and in the early years of the twentieth century took the momentous decision to form the Labour Representation Committee, later to become the Labour Party, to pursue the interests of the labour movement in parliament. For the first time the class struggle was brought directly into the legislative arena by identifying class with party — albeit an essentially reformist and bourgeois party in organization and ideology.

The demand for reform and a break from the penal Poor Law led the Liberals to introduce the 1911 National Insurance Act, which introduced health and unemployment insurance. The radical nature of this step can be gauged from the fact that it went against almost all established opinion in the welfare field. Even Fabian socialists such as the Webbs regarded it as anathema that workers should have *rights* to benefits without first having to demonstrate moral improvement!

Nevertheless, we refer to this only as an *embryonic* welfare state for three reasons:

(i) the limited coverage of the population — only certain sections of workers were covered by unemployment insurance, and in the case of health, the worker but not his family was eligible for benefit. Pensions were reserved for those of good character. The moral overtones of the Poor Law were far from dead and buried.

(ii) The limited scope of state intervention — the emphasis is largely on services in cash. Fully free and comprehensive health and education services await the post second world war period.

(iii) The limited scope of direct *state* responsibility: health insurance was largely run by Friendly Societies and intense lobbying during the passage of the Bill opened the door to the commercial insurance companies.

During the inter-war period, the emergent welfare state grew through the extension of existing services, in particular national insurance, and the addition of new ones, most notably public housing in 1919. The inter-war years are sometimes seen as a period of gradualism when ideas that were to form the basis of more radical changes after the second world war were being developed. An alternative approach would be to see it as a time when new ideas — for a comprehensive health service for example — failed to see the light of day once working-class strength had been weakened by unemployment, the collapse of the 1926 General Strike and the failure of the Labour Party to develop an alternative economic programme to Tory tax-cutting policies, a failure shown in stark relief in 1931 when the Labour government split over whether social security benefits should be cut.

The major reorganization and extension of the welfare state occurred after the second world war, and much has been written about the effects of 'total war' in creating a sense of national solidarity (Titmuss, 1976), and in strengthening the labour movement and awakening it to the possibility of demanding better conditions in the post-war world. The reforms initiated by the war-time coalition and post-war Labour government took Britain into the era of what Mishra calls 'institutional welfare'. In the institutional welfare state, there is an extensive range of statutory social services covering the majority of the population, with voluntary agencies playing a secondary role (Mishra, 1977). We shall now consider in more detail how this transition is reflected in the growth and power of the administrative state apparatus.

## The growth of the state apparatus

Earlier in this chapter, we defined the institutions of the state as: the government, the administration, the coercive apparatus, the judiciary, sub-central government and the representative assemblies. The making and implementation of welfare policies is most directly the responsibility of the government, the administration and the representative assemblies, with an important role in some areas being played by the judiciary. In the next two sections we shall be looking at the way in which the emergence of the welfare state has been associated with changes in the character and size of these institutions and led to a changing balance both between the centre and the localities and the executive and the representative assemblies.

If we compare the situation at the beginning of the nineteenth century to that of today, we can observe that the most striking changes to emerge are: the phenomenal growth of the administration at national and local level, the creation of a national system of local government, and the centralization of power. This latter point is not meant to suggest that local government is powerless: far from it. But that an increase in local powers and duties has been more than matched by an increase in central control and supervision over their operation.

The early Victorian state had no need of a vast administrative apparatus since its role was largely concerned with the creation and sustenance of an appropriate juridical framework within which individual capitalists could interact. Policy making could by and large be made by the government and parliament, implemented by the judiciary. Looking at central government departments only seven — Foreign Affairs, the Exchequer, Home Office, Agriculture, Posts and the Scottish and Lord Chancellors Offices — can be traced back to the early nineteenth century. Whilst at local level few of today's authorities — whether or not they boast ancient charters or antiquated regalia — bear any relation to the system of counties, parishes and boroughs which formed the local administrative organization until the late nineteenth century.

Clearly, however, the state was acquiring new functions even then, and until well into the nineteenth century the administration grew by the *ad hoc* creation of new authorities. Initially such changes occurred at local level as new bodies were set up to deal with the tasks thrown up by an urbanizing, industrializing society — the Improvement Commissioners to deal with paving and cleansing; the Turnpike Trusts to undertake the maintenance of roads. A major break occurred in 1834 when the Poor Law Amendment Act required the establishment of locally elected Boards of Guardians acting under the strict supervision of the central Poor Law Commission. This was the first move in a continuing process of administrative growth and change in which the central government has attempted to reconcile the conflicting demands of local democracy and autonomy as against central control to ensure uniformity and control of the public purse.

Until 1870, which as we have seen marked the beginning of a change in the attitude of capital towards state intervention, centralization and administrative reform from above was resisted — the Poor Law Commission was acceptable because it implied that relief would be equally *restrictive* in different parts of the country. But a similar attempt to set up a Central Board of Health in 1848 foundered in the face of powerful resistance to such extensions of central power, and health together with the limited activities of the central state in relation to education, was entrusted to a kind of catch-all body, the Privy Council.

All these authorities coexisted in a glorious confusion that was particularly pronounced and anomalous at local level. From 1870 onwards, a process of rationalization and reform can be observed, coinciding with the gradual break from *laissez-faire* ideology. In 1871, the Local Government Board was created to supervise local activities in the field of health, housing and poor relief, whilst between 1870 and 1894 local government was reformed — the Acts of 1888 and 1894 creating the two-tier system of counties and boroughs, urban, or rural district councils, alongside independent county boroughs responsible for all services in the major cities. This system survived without major modification until the 1960s. Then London government was reformed to take account of the growth of the conurbation, and in 1974 local government in the rest of the country was completely reorganized, introducing a two-tier system of authorities: counties and districts, or metropolitan counties and metropolitan districts in six major conurbations. In this process many small authorities were abolished and the number of local councils drastically reduced. The creation of larger authorities with greater resources strengthens local government: but at the same time it facilitates central control, since Whitehall has to deal with fewer bodies. This is a matter of significance when we come to the proposals to reform the grant system, which we shall discuss further below.

At national level, new central departments responsible for social policy have been spawned as the Local Government Board became too unwieldy — the Ministry of Health in 1919, the various Ministries responsible for pensions, national insurance and social assistance in 1946 and 1948, and the Ministry of Housing and Local Government in 1951. This process of fission reflected the period of growth of social services: new departments came into being as services were felt to be too important to remain buried in larger departments, without separate ministerial representation in parliament. More recently we have seen a process of fusion as ministries have been recoupled into new super-departments, the Department of the Environment (DOE) and Department of Health and Social Security (DHSS) in particular. Some fission may re-occur (the Ministry of Transport has now split from the DOE), and the hopes that amalgamation of itself would create greater coordination between services has rarely been realized. Nevertheless, the process has resulted from the desire to increase expenditure control and policy coordination in the vastly expanded social services, and it seems unlikely that it will receive a major reverse despite the failure to live up to initial expectations.

This process of expansion and reorganization at local and national level has been accompanied by a change in the central-local relationship. The process of centralization which has occurred tends to provoke reactions either of complete boredom, or passionate concern at the demise of an ancient democratic institution. Neither approach appears fully justified. Local government may be boring — and indeed low voting figures in local elections suggest that few appreciate its significance; but it does matter, as debate over selective schooling and the sale of council houses for example has shown.

On the other hand, local government is very much the creature of central government. But this has almost always been the case. Since its creation in its modern form in the late nineteenth century, British local government has never enjoyed the freedom and autonomy of, for example, authorities in the USA, and central government has always had the final say — as the Poplar Poor Law Guardians found to their cost in the early 1920s when they were gaoled for defying the central government by paying higher rates of public assistance. More recently, the suspension and surcharging of the Councillors of Clay Cross who refused to implement rent increases for local authority housing as required under the 1972 Housing Finance Act shows that nothing has changed.

Nevertheless, it is undeniable that central control over local government is increasing. In the mid 1960s, Griffith described central departments as adopting either a *laissez-faire*, regulatory or promotional attitude towards local authorities (Griffith, 1966). Since then, the areas where central departments adopt a 'live and let live' approach, or merely prescribe regulations have diminished because areas such as health, described as *laissez-faire* have been taken away from local authorities (NHS reorganization 1974) whilst welfare and children's departments have been amalgamated to form mammoth Social Service Departments (1970 Social Services Act) which are more amenable to central control.

Griffith tended to equate central control with *promotion* of a service. This was not to say that all controls were aimed at stimulating activity — many controls simply reflect the Ministry's desire to know what is happening and monitor spending — but that they arose where a promotional stance was being adopted.

This was not a fully accurate picture in the 1960s: in areas such as council housebuilding detailed control was often associated with restrictions both on the number and quality of houses built. Since then, this restrictive role has become more pronounced as the Treasury has attempted to grasp the reins of local spending. Financial control has traditionally been achieved through central government's control over local borrowing (loan sanction) and the level of Rate Support Grant subsidy which meets about two-thirds of local spending. In recent years this system has been strengthened by the introduction of cash limits which specify expenditure in cash rather than volume terms. The present government is further tightening the screw through its proposal to reform the grant system, replacing the Rate Support Grant with a new block grant representing the difference between what the central government thinks each authority should spend, and the standard rate poundage it should levy. Authorities who spend more than the government's estimate of their local needs cannot do so with impunity: there is a clawback procedure whereby Whitehall takes away a proportion of central government grant in line with rate increases above the standard-rate poundage. Block grants give local authorities more freedom to switch money between services and so have traditionally been regarded as enhancing local autonomy. The stringent financial penalties in the new legislation mean, however, that it is only freedom *from* certain restrictions that is being given, and not freedom *to do* what authorities want.

This process of financial centralization has alarmed local councillors of all political persuasions. Central-local relations are part of a general phenomenon of limited conflict between different elements of the state apparatus. Such conflicts are tolerable if the working-class is relatively quiescent, but in periods of working-class challenge the state has to think more strategically. This demands a process of centralization, the creation of what O'Connor calls 'a class-conscious political directorate to coordinate the activities of nominally independent government agencies' (O'Connor, 1973, p. 67). Beyond a certain point working-class challenge may induce an opposite, decentralizing process, as we saw with the proposal for Scottish devolution. Until now, however, the dominant trend has been one of centralization.

Conflicts between central and local government can be of two main kinds: local authorities may fail to introduce services which have been conceded by central government under the pressure of working-class demands, or they may be provided on too generous a scale. In the first case legitimation is threatened, in the second accumulation. (For a further discussion see Dale, 1980.) The source of the first type of conflict is often the position of locally based fractions of capital who may come to dominate local councils and pursue short-term, anti-reform policies which may be detrimental to the long-term interest of capital as a whole in social stability. The most extreme example of such a conflict is what has occurred in Northern Ireland: discriminatory control of local services by the Unionist Party sparked off mass unrest in the civil-rights movement of the late 1960s which has led to the removal of almost all major social services from locally elected bodies.

Northern Ireland is a dramatic example, and its history and politics are rather different from those of Britain. Nevertheless, it is an example of a more general phenomenon. When working-class demands have been strongly articulated, concessions have usually been accompanied by measures to ensure that services are provided with some degree of uniformity over the country as a whole. A major shift of this character occurred after the second world war, when income maintenance and the hospital service, previously wholly or partly under local control, were nationalized.

The era of expansion is now however at an end, and the growth of social expenditure is seen by national capital to jeopardize accumulation. Local authorities may however not willingly cut expenditure along the lines suggested by central government. This may be due to the closer association between some groups of Labour councillors and the local labour movement, an association which the journey to Westminster weakens. Local councillors are also in much closer contact with producer groups in the social services who play an important role in lobbying for the maintenance of social expenditure. Finally many authorities exhibit a kind of municipal ideology — a remnant of the Victorian 'civic Gospel' whereby local town halls seek to command legitimacy through the provision of a high standard of service and asserting their independence from central government.

Thus centralization has been the result of class struggle both because concessions are increasingly fought for and won at national level and have to be provided nationally; and because once concessions have been made the central state seeks to control the rate of expansion of services given the tendency for many local authorities to be more generous than capital finds acceptable.

So far we have considered geographical centralization. Alongside this has been a process of concentrating power in the executive rather than the representative assemblies.

### Who decides — politicians or bureaucrats?

In this section we shall look at two further aspects of the concentration of power: the increase in the power of the administration *vis-à-vis* representative bodies, and the centralization of power within the administration, resulting from the enhanced position of the finance departments at central and local level.

The insight that the development of capitalism and the growing role of the state leads to a shift of power to the administrative bureaucracy is not peculiar to marxism: Weber observed this process at work in Germany after the first world war. What however is peculiar to marxism is the view that the bureaucratic form is determined not by the technical necessity of dealing with complex problems, but the political role played by the bureaucracy in articulating and prosecuting the interests of the dominant class. Bureaucracy is not exclusively a capitalist phenomenon, witness its role in the USSR and Eastern Europe where it has been variously described as a layer separate from the (dominant) working class, or a new class. These issues are clearly very problematic and cannot be resolved here, where we shall concentrate on the bureaucracy's role under capitalism.

The higher civil service in Britain influences the actions of the state in two ways: civil servants influence ministers during the policy making process; they then control the implementation of policy, and in the process redefine the aims set by the legislature. In this second process of implementation the judiciary may also play a significant role: for example, in the field of security of tenure for private sector tenants, it has been argued that the legislation has been fundamentally undermined by judges who have redefined the concept of 'tenancy' thus allowing landlords to evade the provisions of the Rent Act (Arden, 1979).

Returning to civil servants, one has only to read politicians' memoirs such as the Crossman diaries (Crossman, 1975) to appreciate that ministers, if not the prisoners of their top civil servants, are at least strongly influenced by their personalities and prejudices and they play an important role in the control of the political agenda. Among their key functions are those of advising ministers, working out the implications of policies, negotiating with pressure groups, and preparing ministerial briefs for parliamentary intervention. The way in which civil servants carry out these functions is crucial for ministerial perceptions of feasibility: if civil servants calculate that a particular policy would lead to 'administrative chaos', does this amount to sensible advice or virtual blackmail?

This is a problem that is particularly acute for any government bent on radical reform. The power of officials may also reinforce central power. Officials at national and local level may work together, sharing a common professional identity and approach to policy questions, despite conflict between local councillors and the central state. Thus a council attempting to defy a central government edict, such as that giving public-sector tenants the right to buy council houses, may find that their officers are calmly proceeding with the arrangements to comply. If a radical government or local authority is serious then 'a battle — in fact the class struggle' must be fought within the state apparatus (Miliband, 1977, p. 184).

Thus far we have tended to assume that civil servants will tend to be a conservative force. Miliband argues:

> higher civil servants in the countries of advanced capitalism may generally be expected to play a conservative role in the councils of state, to reinforce the conservative propensities of governments in which these . . . are already well developed, and to serve as an inhibiting element in regard to governments in which they are less pronounced
>
> (Miliband, 1973, p. 108).

The explanation of this conservatism lies according to Miliband in the class and educational background of these people (mainly men), the system of recruitment, and their closeness to the world of business. This last point brings us to the point of asking whether the conservatism of civil servants lies more in their structural position rather than their individual attributes.

Poulantzas describes the bureaucracy as a 'specific category' which 'is able to possess its own unity and coherence, despite the diversity of recruitment and class affiliation of its various strata' (Poulantzas, 1973, p. 335). This internal unity derives from the function of the bureaucracy in putting into practice the role of the state — a state which Poulantzas has already defined as pursuing the interests of the capitalist class. Another way of putting this, avoiding functionalist undertones, would be to argue that the bureaucracy is charged with making the system work, a role which we have already seen leads to business gaining a privileged hearing in the corridors of power. This is reinforced by the fact that the bureaucracy is dependent on tax revenues both to finance its activities and also its very existence. Disruptive change, which is likely to lead to falling economic activity and tax incomes at least in the short term, thus not only undermines the ability of the bureaucracy to put into practice the functions of the state, but also its ability to perpetuate itself through staffing its vast apparatus.

The bureaucracy according to Offe (1974), distills the overall interests of capital from the conflicting pressures directed at the state. It can do this more effectively than politicians who are concerned with their legitimacy in the eyes of the electorate and must maintain the appearance of giving equal consideration to all demands. The bureaucracy is removed from public scrutiny and can maintain more direct communication with capital.

In addition to looking at the role of the bureaucracy, we must also consider the implications of the way in which the bureaucracy carries out its tasks. The bureaucratic organization particularly that of central government is hierarchical, senior staff setting out the rules and procedures for dealing with issues and more junior staff implementing them in a fairly routinized way. The combination of discipline from above and the hope of career promotion up the hierarchy encourage conformity, and a reluctance to depart from or change established procedures. This produces a kind of administrative inertia: a mentality which eschews disruptive changes and tends to take what civil servants may call a long-term view which supposes that any radical government will be short lived, so that in the meantime 'they resume their quiet defence of entrenched departmental positions and policies against political change' (Crossman, 1975, p. 22).

This mode of functioning, beneficial for capital in its stability and continuity, is not without contradictions. Stability also means rigidity and inflexibility, attributes that become dysfunctional when the state is required to respond to new demands and problems. We shall have more to say on this in the next section. Secondly, the strength of the bureaucracy enables it to protect its members, particularly those higher up, as the present Thatcher government has found to its cost in its attempts to cut drastically civil-service employment.

At local level too, the power of officers has been growing as local services have been extended. Since the 1960s in particular, attempts have been made to import corporate management techniques from business into local government administration (Bennington, 1976; Cockburn, 1977). The watchwords of corporate management are 'integration, control from the top, more efficient use of money and labour, forward planning' (Cockburn, 1977, p. 13), and the desired effects a reduction in the number of departments and committees, centralization of power around the chief executive and a Policy and Resources Committee of senior councillors, and a greater stress on technical rather than political solutions to problems, leaving the councillor a smaller role compared with the officer.

Corporate management has been introduced patchily (Stoker, 1980) and has failed to live up to the expectations it aroused precisely because technique is, in the last resort, unable to stifle politics. This has been particularly true of the initial enthusiasm for corporate *planning* which has been largely stillborn. Nevertheless where introduced corporate structures have strengthened the role of senior officers and councillors and provided more effective structures for the implementation of expenditure cuts (CSE State Apparatus and Expenditure Group 1979).

Returning to the central government, we can see that a variety of pressures, similar in many ways to those which encouraged the growth of corporate management, have led to developments in the area of social planning which have shifted the balance of power between departments. Glennerster sees social planning as being made up of two elements: forward planning and evaluation (Glennerster, 1975). In Britain the strength of the executive has led to a stress on the former, with ministers and civil servants being reluctant to countenance effective scrutiny of the output of their activities. The major element of forward planning is the annual exercise in public expenditure projection over the next five years. This system is known as the PESC (public expenditure survey committee) system. This has evolved gradually since the early 1960s when the Plowden Committee recommended some system of enabling the government to contain the growth of public expenditure within whatever limits it had set. As Glennerster points out, most systems of forward planning have been incorporated into the PESC system with a corresponding increase in the power of the Treasury, which has always enjoyed a remarkable position of dominance in the system of central departments.

We shall now turn to some of the tensions between these trends to centralization and the need for the state to maintain its flexibility in a period of growing social crisis.

## The problem of being asked to solve problems

The welfare state is expected to play both a legitimating role, meeting many social needs in response to working-class demands; and a social controlling role, containing social tensions. The forms of intervention developed to undertake these tasks, whilst at the same time not jeopardizing capital accumulation, are creating new contradictions and crises.

We have already referred to the way in which the welfare state is a concession to appease class struggle which may fuel further class struggle. Looking at the welfare state since 1945, we can see that the class struggle around welfare has become more pronounced and the contradiction between meeting the expectations of workers that their needs will be met, and of capital that the welfare state will not be their total loss, has been heightened. In this section, we will consider this problem in the context of the discussion about the form of the state, since it is also true to say that these contradictory expectations have also spawned a series of different kinds of organization, which can neither work together nor solve the problems with which they are faced.

Looking first at working-class expectations of the welfare state, it is probably true to say that only since 1945 has the average person had any consciousness that the state should meet her/his needs 'from the cradle to the grave'. The post-1945 reforms were crucial in establishing this new frame of reference in people's minds. The main subsequent undermining of the Beveridge principles of the time have come from the extension of the private sector, and its support by the state as an alternative to public provision, but this has only achieved great significance in the field of pensions and housing.

Not only does the existence of a comprehensive framework of services fuel expectations that these services will be maintained and strengthened, it also weakens acceptance of territorial inequalities. If as Marshall (1963) suggests people are to receive services on the basis of citizenship, then this must be a more than formal commitment to equality of access: the services must be there so that there can be equality of use. Greater awareness of territorial inequality has been a major factor spawning Scottish nationalism — the first significant electoral challenge to the established political parties in Britain.

On the other side of the coin, the state is faced with mounting social tensions which it expects the welfare state to deflect and contain — a process which must involve both legitimation and repression. The most significant of these social problems are first, unemployment, and in particular youth unemployment — the switch from school to the dole queue breeds cynicism, distrust of authority and threatens basic social values such as the work ethic. Secondly, racial inequalities and the geographical concentration of black people in inner-city areas of poor housing and urban facilities and declining manufacturing employment, encourage fears of racial violence, particularly as British-born black people demand — but fail to get — equal access to the employment and housing markets. Finally, the effects of the women's movement on women's expectations has undermined traditional domestic patterns and led to fears of family breakdown.

In attempting to respond to conflicting expectations, the state has founded three different kinds of organization which have run into different kinds of problems. These three types I shall refer to as: the classic bureaucracy, the professionalized bureaucracy and the state — voluntary-sector partnership.

By the 'classic bureaucracy' I refer to those organizations which most clearly correspond to Weber's ideal type:

> a clearly defined hierarchy where office holders have very specific functions and apply universalistic rules in a spirit of formalistic impersonality
>
> (Warham, 1977, p. 67).

The DHSS, the organization dispensing cash benefits such as insurance and supplementary benefits, most clearly corresponds to this model: there is a clearly defined hierarchy, with those at the bottom applying rules made by their superiors, having little discretion and being the least trained and the lowest paid. As Stevenson points out:

> By and large the civil servant has been trained not to question (at least openly) the decisions of his superiors. Whatever private reactions there may be, the roles are so structured, especially in the lower grades, that authority is accepted without much challenge
>
> (Stevenson, 1973, p. 66).

In fact in the area of supplementary benefits in particular, clerks *do* have discretion, both negative to suspend benefit, or positive to raise the level of benefit. Both the circumstances and the amounts of money involved are, however, specified as tightly as possible.

This 'bureaucratic orientation' is contrasted by Stevenson with the 'professional orientation'. I have called organizations such as the health service, social-service departments, education, 'professionalized bureaucracies' because, although they allow their staff a great deal more freedom than the classic bureaucracy, they nevertheless remain bureaucracies. There are hierarchies, and the workers' role is circumscribed by law and the dictates of public accountability: doctors cannot perform menstrual extraction abortions because of legal stipulations; social workers have to follow certain procedures for taking children into care, and they cannot simply cry 'professional judgement' when they face public criticism of their decisions.

Nevertheless, unlike in the supplementary benefits office, the workers in the 'front line' of these organizations actually dealing with the public, are generally highly trained, and invoke their status as professionals (or aspiring professionals) to justify their enjoyment of a degree of autonomy from supervision by superiors. Several attempts have been made to construct 'ideal types' which capture the essence of professionalism. Forder however rightly dismisses these as a mystification. Rather he sees professionalism as 'an ideology whose function is to legitimate the power, authority, and status of occupational groups' (Forder, 1974, p. 119).

In other words, a professional group is one which has developed an ideology of its own, usually around the concept of serving the interests of the client, and has the power and confidence to win a wide degree of autonomy in decision making in the work situation.

These two types of organization present different problems for the state in its attempt to pursue policies of both legitimation and accumulation. On the one hand organizations such as the DHSS purport to treat all alike — legitimation in terms of fairness — and the existence of rules offers the possibility of appeal and redress. On the other hand, these aspects giving the DHSS legitimacy tend to be outweighed by the way in which the classic bureaucratic mode tends to generate conflict between the client and the organization: the low status and lack of motivation of counter clerks leads to an unsympathetic treatment of claimants; the proliferation of rules seems petty, heartless, if not downright absurd. The lack of discretion means that many social problems, which rarely fit into neat pigeon holes, cannot be dealt with.

On the other hand, the DHSS dispenses vast amounts of money, over which there is quite strict control, a factor of immense advantage to the state. When cash benefits were administered by local authorities some major conflicts over the level of benefits arose. We have already referred to the case of the Poplar Guardians. During the 1930s several authorities were either 'relieved of their responsibility' for transitional benefit or threatened with suspension. Supplementary-benefits workers are socialized into an attitude of 'guarding the public purse' — an attitude which has led to accusations that they treat the money they give out as if it were their own.

The professional orientation leads to the opposite problem. The professional claims to be client centred: but this may lead to them being seen as insufficiently impartial. Workers in the DHSS tend to see social workers as 'do-gooders' who are too emotionally involved and hence are easily taken in by false stories (Spencer and Crookston

1978). This leads to conflict between the two organizations, which is institutionalized in the situation where social workers represent claimants in appeals against DHSS decisions. As Spencer and Crookston query:

> Has bureaucracy gone mad when it necessitates the development of a second bureaucracy to negotiate with the first bureaucracy on behalf of whom the first bureaucracy supposedly serves?
>
> (Spencer and Crookston, 1978, p. 235).

Whilst social workers have the kind of autonomy and broad remit which enables them to respond flexibly to situations, the nebulous character of their role means that they face uncertainty in what they are trying to do, rarely produce concrete results and easily become the butt of public criticism.

Neither social workers nor teachers have direct control over major resources, although they influence the level of expenditure on the social services through their role in discovering unmet needs and their opposition to cutbacks. Doctors on the other hand, directly allocate resources such as drugs and use the concept of clinical freedom to oppose any control over their actions. The Treasury which has to meet the annual drugs bill can thus do little in the face of escalating costs.

The state-voluntary partnership is a newcomer to this list of organizations. Traditionally the social services can be divided into either of the above two types, surrounded by a voluntary sector. In recent years we have seen the voluntary sector coming to play a more prominent role in what can only be described as a close partnership with the state. The prototype of this type of initiative was the American President Johnson's 'Great Society Programme' of the 1960s where the Federal Government went direct to the grass-roots organizations of the ghettos.

In Britain a whole series of initiatives were taken in the late 1960s as part of a new 'poverty programme' (see CDP, 1977). Many involved directing existing state programmes more towards deprived areas. Others such as the Urban Programme extended to supporting more informal initiatives. In the 1970s the focus on poverty in the inner city was retained, and the voluntary sector has been involved with the local authorities in setting up projects in certain cities under the inner city partnerships. Finally, concern with youth unemployment has led to the setting up of a whole series of special programmes such as the Job Creation Programme, which have involved establishing new local independent bodies to organize projects in the voluntary sector.

These initiatives have been set up where the legitimacy of the existing statutory agency was in doubt. They give social policy a human and less monolithic face — but they run into the problems of the voluntary sector: lack of accountability, particularly scandalous in relation to some housing associations, which have been fostered as a direct alternative to council housing, and have received massive state financial support; the tendency towards personality and other conflicts amongst voluntary groups; and the problem for the state of ensuring that in the more informal parts of the voluntary sector radical workers will not use the money provided to develop activities which challenge the very basis of existing state policies.

## Conclusion

In this chapter we have adopted a structural approach to analysing the state on the grounds that alternative theories offer no perspective on why there are consistent biases in the policy output of the state, and the character of its administration — biases which correspond to the limits of state intervention discussed in the previous chapter. On the other hand we have attempted to avoid a functionalist interpretation which would see the structure as totally determining what the state does, thus rendering obsolete any theory of why the state acts in the way it does.

Whilst recognizing that social science has not finally solved the problem of reconciling a theory of change based on creative human action with a theory based on structural causation, we regard historical materialism as the most fruitful approach. Concrete application of this approach to the British welfare state has brought us to the position where we can see on the one hand the way in which the changing economic environment (the changing national and international dynamics of capital accumulation), and the power wielded by the economically dominant class in the economic and cultural spheres, set limits to the state's actions and generate tendencies for it to respond in particular ways. On the other hand the state is not entirely passive: its particular form differs as between advanced capitalist countries and these variations are of significance for the ability of the state to develop policies which modify crisis tendencies. There is no 'ideal' state form for capitalism, since the state is required to undertake activities which are inconsistent and cannot be carried through harmoniously. Nevertheless changes in the character of state organizations and methods of policy making have material effects — crisis modifying or crisis furthering — and we have tried to look at some of these in the British context. In the final chapter we shall try to bring together these analyses of different sources of crisis in an overview of the future of the welfare state in Britain.

# 8

# Needs

## Introduction

Ideological debates are usually associated not only with opposed ideas, but with the adoption of different concepts and linguistic conventions. This is true of the social sciences today. The fragmentation of disciplines and their very different goals and starting points means that each employs a different set of key concepts, and many an academic slanging match is conducted as to their respective validity.

Both economics and social administration are disciplines centrally concerned with the problem of rationing goods and services between individuals. Within social administration need is seen as a central concept (Walton, 1969; Bradshaw, 1972; Forder, 1974); whilst in opposition two economists have disparaged this approach as 'needology' and argued that 'the word "need" ought to be banished from discussion of public policy' (quoted in Williams, 1978, p. 37). The uneasy proximity of economics and social administration has led to an on-going debate between them.

Social administration has tended to take the concept of need for granted, a deficiency which we shall explore further below. It is therefore to philosophy that we must turn to find an analysis of what is implied when we speak of needs rather than, for example, wants or demands. Plant in particular has drawn our attention to the peculiar feature of the concept that it bridges the distinction usually drawn in philosophy between facts and normative judgments: 'To say that "x needs y" is not just to state a fact but it is to imply, *ceteris paribus*, that he ought to get it' (Plant, 1974, p. 76).

There are few, if any, needs whose satisfaction is independent of the type of society in which we live. Even where needs are satisfied at the individual, personal level — the need for love for example — the degree of satisfaction achieved is very much influenced by people's social environment. This is even more obvious when we consider needs whose satisfaction depends on the consumption of socially produced goods and services such as housing and health care. Thus analysis of needs can open the door to critical judgments being made

about forms of social organization which appear to inhibit the satisfaction of needs.

So far we have talked as if needs were simply intrinsic properties of
individuals or arise from thin air. This is unsatisfactory. The societal
dimension needs to be brought in to explain the source of needs as well
as the manner in which they are satisfied.

In the rest of the chapter we shall begin by looking at how needs are
analysed within the frameworks provided by social administration
and neo-classical economics. We shall then set out the approach of historical materialism, which we shall then attempt to apply to the
question of how needs are generated, recognized and to some extent
met in capitalist society.

## Levels of discussion of the concept of need

Before looking at individual approaches, it is useful to consider the
general question of the levels at which discussion of needs can operate.
Three levels in particular can be identified:

(i) The discussion of ultimate or final needs. Here we are concerned
with the ends of human activity to which other activities are directed.
The question can be approached empirically in terms of attempts to
discover what needs people are attempting to meet. This is an
extremely complex question. We may observe with relative ease what
people actually *do*: but it is much less easy to understand what they are
seeking to achieve by their actions. In other words we do not know
which needs they are trying to meet. Unless we can answer this
question by making efforts to identify these aims of human activities,
we cannot say whether society's productive activity is actually
meeting needs, nor which needs it should meet.

(ii) At a second level, needs can be discussed as means towards these
ends. We may refer to these needs as 'intermediate'. In other words we
say that 'x needs y' not as an end in itself, but because y is a way in
which x can satisfy some final need. The nature of the final need thus
dictates whether the provision of y will lead to people feeling that their
need has been satisfied. Thus for example, we may say that x needs a
further period of education. If this is in order to gain access to a better
job and hence greater power, status and material well-being, then the
need is in practice for a recognized but scarce qualification. If the need
is for education in its own right as a means towards the experience of
greater mental and cultural development and interaction with like-
minded people, then the qualification is of less significance and the

content of the courses provided more important.

(iii) A third level of discussion involves the issue of how individual needs should be recognized. Where a good or service is being distributed in a non-market situation how is the provider to decide which individual is in need and should have his/her want satisfied, and how are different kinds or degrees of need to be given priority? Here we have come down to the level of rationing.

## The social administration approach: needs as rationing

The discipline of social administration has largely grown up alongside the growth of state intervention in the market. This intervention involves the attempt to satisfy some wants through means other than the sale of goods and services. The market mechanism discriminates between wants according to ability to pay, and the discipline of economics uses the concept of demand to refer to those wants which are expressed in the market and backed up by purchasing power. The social services use non-market criteria to ration services — in practice a wide variety of devices are used to discriminate between people, many of which are arbitrary and capricious in their effect (Parker, 1967). The politics of housing priorities was thrown into stark relief in the London Borough of Newham for example: in 1975 councillors realized that the effect of the revised points scheme for allocating council housing, which gave greater weight than before to need factors, would be to increase considerably the percentage of families of Asian origin being rehoused. The Housing Department promptly changed the scheme to give greater weight to length of residence in the area. (Reported in *New Society* 20 November 1975.)

Nevertheless the social services do claim to allocate services according to need, and in many cases the importation of other criteria is not deliberate but the consequence of the imbalance between legitimately recognized needs and resources. Furthermore, social administration as a discipline is committed to the centrality of the criteria of need as a rationing device.

It is unfortunate, however, that this concentration on rationing means that the discipline has concentrated almost exclusively on the third level of the discussion of needs. Thus, although Forder refers to final needs insofar as he looks at what he refers to as 'ideal norms' this is simply put forward as one of a shopping list of possible definitions, rather than in terms of the hierarchy discussed earlier (Forder, 1974). This tendency to put the issue forward as simply a list of definitions stems from the orientation towards the problems experienced by administrators and planners in the social services rather than the development of social theory. This is most explicit in Bradshaw, who concentrates only on looking at 'four separate definitions used by administrators and research workers' (Bradshaw, 1972, p. 640). Concepts become handy tools for the practitioner rather than the basis of social theory.

This complete omission of one level of discussion emasculates discussion at other levels. Turning to intermediate needs, these are defined as the social services. The lack of consideration of goals rules out a broad-ranging discussion of needs as *means* to ends. Instead, the starting point is those intermediate needs that society has already accepted. Nevitt states:

> the social-need element in the public provision . . . of goods and services requires no special explanation as the social acknowledgement of a 'need' must be assumed whenever governments provide a service
>
> (Nevitt, 1977, p. 114).

Bradshaw prefaces his own analysis of need with the observation that:

> The history of the social services is the story of the recognition of social needs and the organization of society to meet them
>
> (Bradshaw, 1972, p. 640).

Thus needs present no real problem: they are simply what the state has chosen to recognize. The stage is set then for the main concern of social administration: rationing in the social services.

## A conservative and a radical critique of social administration

Criticisms of the social administration approach have come from two sides. On the one hand, from economics has come what I shall refer to as a conservative critique: conservative because it attempts to replace the concept of need with that of demand because of the implied moral commitment, the 'ought' associated with the former concept. On the other hand is a radical critique, radical because the centrality of the concept of need forms the basis of a critical theory of society.

## The critique of needology

Economics like social administration is centrally concerned with issues of rationing and it is on this terrain that the debate between economics and social administration has been conducted. Culyer in his introduction to a study of the NHS lays claim for economics to the whole ground of rationing theory. He writes:

> in the firm belief that there exists no other framework of thought that can at the same time provide a relevant and thoroughly worked out corpus of analysis through which the problems . . . posed by alternative choices can be elucidated
>
> (Culyer, 1976, p. I).

At the level of rationing theory there is some substance to some of the criticisms of social administration made by economists. Culyer makes two points at the outset of his study. First he argues that academic analysis of social policy has been dominated by 'romantics' or 'sentimental socialists' whose analysis of problems of choice is clouded by a commitment to particular social services in their present form. This is related to a second argument: that need tends to be seen as a need for services. In other words means are confused with ends, or returning to our hierarchy of need, intermediate needs are confused with ultimate needs. This obscures discussion of possible different routes to the same end (Culyer, 1976). This critique has some merit: the dominance of Fabian style reformism, and the close association between social administration academics and the social services certainly blinkers much analysis, and does lead to a rather unrigorous acceptance of the basic social services in their present form.

What alternative then do economists propose as a framework of analysis? Economic analysis has tended to confine itself to the study of markets centring on how a hierarchy of prices for different goods both signals to producers which are the most profitable markets to supply, and at the same time rations goods between consumers. In a market situation the concept of need is redundant and demand — consumer tastes backed up by purchasing power in the market place — is used to analyse how wants are satisfied. In chapters 6 and 7 we indicated how the issue of non-market provision was treated: the theory of public goods and externalities lays the basis for deciding which goods should be provided outside the market, whilst the theory of individual self-interest expressed in individual and group demands in the political system explains what the state actually does.

Nevitt, who occupies the unusual position of being a professor of social administration committed to the methodology of neo-classical economics, uses this approach to argue the case for the use of the concept of demand rather than need in the analysis of social policy (Nevitt, 1977). Demands are individual tastes expressed singly in the market, or by individuals or groups of individuals in the political system, backed up by willingness to pay which, when interacting with a supply schedule, create a price. Needs are a sub-set of demand goods which are recognized by society as being sufficiently important to warrant state intervention either to redistribute income so that individuals can purchase such goods, or to provide them directly. Government recognition of needs comes about through the articulation of demands in the political system, the task of economic theory being to provide guidance as to how much of any good should be provided. This is achieved through indicating the demand and supply functions associated with different goods (both individually purchased and collectively provided goods) thus giving price tags to the demands for state intervention to meet needs. Once the concept of demand is broadened to include demands in the political system as well as demands in the market place, the concept of need becomes less relevant and Nevitt predicts that it may eventually be jettisoned.

Implicit or explicit in all critiques of 'needology' is the view that demand as an economic concept is objective and scientific whilst need is subjective. A closer examination of the theoretical underpinnings of economic theory reveals, however, the hollowness of such claims. Three criticisms in particular can be laid at the door of orthodox economics: its behaviourism, its lack of concern with the social production of wants and the narrowness of what it regards as the economic sphere. We shall look at these in turn.

Economics is concerned with the manner in which the market satisfies demands for socially produced goods and services. These demands are taken at face value: if people are willing, for example, to pay more for education, and the market responds by expanding the private education sector, then the market has satisfied a want. Yet as we have already pointed out in the discussion of a hierarchy of needs, what people *do* is a very incomplete guide to the real meaning of their wants. As Hirsch points out: 'The relevant problem is not only how much is the individual willing to spend on this or that activity, but what for?' (Hirsch, 1977, p. 59).

Once this question is posed, a veritable Pandora's Box of issues is released on a largely uncomprehending world of economists!

A second question which tends to be avoided by economists is that of the source of wants. If the performance of the market is judged on the basis of its ability to satisfy wants, the objectivity of this approach breaks down once it is suggested that the market itself generates the very wants which it satisfies. This problem of the social moulding of needs has largely been ignored by orthodox economists.

Finally the sphere of concern of orthodox economics is incomplete. The focus is on the manner in which demands for socially produced goods and services are satisfied, mainly by the market but in some cases by state provision. Yet the mere purchase of goods does not of itself necessarily satisfy a need or want. In many if not the majority of cases goods are purchased by housewives and are further transformed through her unpaid labour before they become final consumption goods. Once again we are back with the problem that the ability of the market to satisfy consumer demands does not provide an adequate guide to whether it truly satisfies people's wants and needs.

## The needs of people in society

In order to transcend orthodox economics we must bring in the societal dimension to provide answers to those questions which the theory either ignores or explains in an individualist framework. In particular we need to explain the source of wants, the mechanisms whereby wants come to be regarded as needs and the means existing in society for their satisfaction. We shall concentrate on the first two, since the third was considered in chapter 6. Finally we shall see whether a structural analysis of the generation of needs which are not satisfied can form the basis of a critique of society and a perspective on social change. Whilst historical materialism provides some sort of answer to all these issues, versions of idealism also deal with some of them in ways which go beyond the individualism and behaviourism of neo-classical economics.

## The idealist critique of needs in capitalist society

In chapter 3 we looked at various authors grouped together under the general label of reformists, who far from taking needs for granted provide an extremely trenchant critique of the needs generated by the capitalist system. They can be divided into two groups. First there are those such as Tawney and Titmuss who are particularly concerned with what they identify as non-material, universal needs such as that for altruism, and indict capitalism for its repression of these needs. Secondly there are those such as Galbraith and Hirsch who see wants and needs as socially moulded and recognize capitalism's inability to satisfy them, but slip into an idealist method when considering social change.

We shall concern ourselves here with the second group: despite their outspoken and sometimes inspiring critique of capitalism's distortion of human interest, the first group's approach lacks any serious theoretical underpinning. In particular their understanding of the source of wants and needs is totally inadequate, and the basis of their indictment of capitalism becomes the moral convictions of those making it. No avenues to social change are suggested beyond moral exhortation.

Galbraith on the other hand does have a theory of the social moulding of needs couched in terms of the requirements of the giant corporations for stable markets (Galbraith, 1969). The mechanisms involved are, however, discussed in individualist terms: the large corporations persuade people to buy products through their sales strategies involving advertising and product design. In opposition to the domination of the corporations Galbraith has some concept of the 'public interest', which may perhaps be equated with the idea of people's true needs. This whole area remains very vague and ill-defined however, and we do not know whether the public interest is derived from some notion of universal needs, or of what people would themselves choose if they were not bamboozled by the sales efforts of the corporations.

Hirsch (1977) is concerned with the proliferation of wants under capitalism, in particular the way in which the breaking down of class barriers and the impetus to economic equality associated with the development of capitalism lead to those lower down the economic ladder aspiring to consume what is presently enjoyed only by a minority. Such expectations are bound to lead to frustration, since many of the goods sought lose their desirable qualities once they become widely available. Such an analysis shows capitalist society to be caught up in an insoluble contradiction: it must promise desirable rewards, but it cannot fulfil such promises.

Recognition of such a crisis raises the question of how it is to be resolved, and in particular whether it requires the abolition of market society in favour of a society geared to meeting collectively decided needs. Hirsch however remains locked in a reformist perspective, and contents himself with suggesting some limited reforms aimed at qualifying the competition for the most socially scarce goods. In the light of the depth of the crisis which he has identified, his proposals can only be described as mind-bogglingly inadequate!

## The materialist approach to needs

The basis of a materialist approach to understanding needs has been laid by Marx, and extended and developed particularly through the 'critical theory' associated with the German Frankfurt School. This approach to the question combines on the one hand a theory of the development of new needs which is relative, showing how the definite material conditions within which people act govern the manner in which they reproduce themselves, including their needs; and on the other hand a critique of capitalist society on the basis of its failure to satisfy human needs. This duality of a theory which is relative and explains how needs arise, and a theory which attempts to stand outside society and provide a critique of it, is the source of both the richness and relevance of the theory to contemporary society, but also of many problems which we shall consider later.

Despite the many misplaced criticisms of Marx's work as purely deterministic, the materialist method, unlike functionalist sociology, places people and their creative action firmly in the centre of the stage. In particular it is through people's creative action in the form of labouring to produce their means of subsistence that they produce and reproduce their own lives. Materialism thus starts from some notion of universal basic needs — those required to sustain life — and goes on to show how people come into association with each other to create means of production and objects to satisfy these needs. This process of production is the underlying motor force for changes in people's ideas, from their earliest perception only of their immediate physical environment and their most basic needs for biological survival, to the proliferation of their wants and needs.

> The first historical act is thus the production of the means to satisfy these needs (purely biological needs for survival). The second point is that the satisfaction of the first need (the action of satisfying and the instrument of satisfaction which has been acquired) leads to new needs;
>
> (Marx and Engels, 1970, pp. 48 and 49).

Within this theory it is only the biological needs for survival that are taken as given. Consciousness of other needs develops with the development of society, and forms of social organization, together with the state of technology, will condition the way in which needs emerge. People are not entirely imprisoned within social structure, but these set definite limits to their actions. People find:

a mass of productive forces, capital funds and conditions which is indeed modified by the new generation, but also on the other prescribes for it its conditions of life and gives it a definite development, a special character;

(Marx and Engels, 1970, p. 59).

Most needs then are relative to society, and in his work of political economy, Marx set out to analyse the basic structural features of capitalist society. In particular he identified capitalism as generalized commodity production: a system whereby the motor force for production is not the intrinsic use of the output to individuals (their use value) but their exchange value (i.e. their value realized upon *sale*).

This analysis of the 'laws of motion' of capitalism is the basis of a critique of capitalism from two aspects. On the one hand the manner in which capitalism *creates* new needs; on the other hand, its inability to *satisfy* needs.

The drive to sell more and more commodities means that markets and hence wants, must be created:

Under private property . . . every person speculates on creating a *new* need in another, so as to drive him to a fresh sacrifice, to place him in a new dependence and to seduce him into a new mode of *gratification* and therefore economic ruin

(Marx, 1964, p. 147).

This characterization of capitalism is echoed today in, for example, Galbraith's critique of advertising: but, as we have already suggested, whereas for Galbraith it is an unsightly blemish on the body of capitalism, for Marx it is intrinsic to capitalism's inherent drive for profit. This descriptive analysis of capitalism is linked to a powerful critique of its effects on the human condition. The needs created by capitalism are indicted as 'inhuman, unnatural and *imaginary* appetites; (Marx, 1964, p. 147). This view perhaps needs to be balanced a little: Marx expressed tremendous admiration for the achievements of capitalism in expanding the productive forces available to people and the consequent possibilities for satisfying needs. He also saw in the associated division of labour the basis for the development of social theory and philosophy. Nevertheless, the point is strongly made: the needs generated within capitalist society cannot be taken as a yardstick to measure the satisfaction of human needs in any other society, and furthermore, many such needs not only *would* not exist in another type of society, but they *should* not exist.

Having shown how needs are created, Marx also discusses capitalism's failure to satisfy them. What capitalism defines as need for the worker is 'a bestial barbarization, complete, unrefined, abstract simplicity of need' (Marx, 1964, p. 148). There are virtually no limits to the degradation that can be imposed on the dominated class, as Marx saw in the Irish famine, when the Irish peasantry was reduced to starvation. Thus the worker's needs are reduced to those of bare survival, combined with the lowest form of pleasure: the gin palaces of Victorian England. Where workers acquire the means to satisfy further wants they are exhorted to be thrifty — to save rather than to enjoy: 'The worker may only have enough for him to want to live, and may only want to live in order to have (that)' (Marx, 1964, p. 150).

So far we have discussed material needs. Marx was also extremely concerned with people's non-material needs. The human need for culture is revealed in all societies: even very primitive communities have their own sense of identity embodied in their myths, religious practices, music and dances. Marx was particularly concerned with one particular need, for human association, which he saw as being expressed through labour. Under capitalism however, labour is alienating. People are alienated from the products of their labour because of the system of private property and commodity production, and labour itself is alienating: it is an act which is forced upon the worker rather than being undertaken to satisfy a need. Capitalism is contrasted with communist society where the satisfaction of human needs is the aim of production, and labour itself becomes fulfilling. In particular, through the abolition of the division of labour people are no longer limited to engaging in a single area of production, but can undertake diverse activities thus enriching their skills and personalities.

In Marx therefore we have a theory of how needs develop, but also a critique of the needs generated by capitalism and its failure to satisfy them. This presents no real problem when we are dealing with those basic human needs which are to a large extent independent of society. For example, we can have no difficulty in indicting capitalism for its failure to give everyone an equal chance to satisfy their basic need for survival, a failure that is revealed, for example in infant mortality statistics of 13.7 per 1,000 live births in England in 1977, 16.1 in Scotland, and 17.2 in Northern Ireland (Royal Commission on the NHS 1979). When we move on to the area of socially conditioned needs, however, the mingling of facts and values poses problems. Can we argue that the needs created by capitalism are a distortion of true human needs without invoking some universal, absolute standard of human need which is external to society? Turning to non-material needs, the notion that labour is alienated must imply the converse, that non-alienated labour is possible in a society where there is a right relationship between people.

In the final analysis normative judgment cannot be avoided. Nevertheless such judgments have to be made every day of our lives and it is not for academics to refuse to participate, but rather to show how theories of society and people can help inform such judgments.

In the case of Marx's theory of need, two points can help illuminate his indictment of capitalism. First, the analysis that capitalism must create consciousness of new needs but cannot satisfy them indicates that capitalism as a system tends towards contradiction and crisis. Marx was no armchair theoretician but an active participant in working-class struggle. In other words his analysis led him not to abstract calls for people to change, but to an active involvement informed by his analysis of crisis tendencies in capitalism. Secondly, the notion of human freedom, expressed through people's ability to control their environment was central to Marx. Commodity production places people at the mercy of apparently impersonal forces. What is in fact a social relation between people appears as a relation between physical objects:

> It is nothing but the definite social relation between men themselves which assumes, here, for them, the fantastic form of a relation between things

> (Marx, 1976, p. 165).

In other words, in market society people's decisions about what to produce appear to them not as acts which have been collectively decided, but as consequences of the operation of the price mechanism which 'dictates' what should be done.

People's freedom thus involves on the one hand, the development of the productive forces, giving them greater control over nature; and on the other hand, a society in which people can come together to make conscious, collective decisions about their own lives. Capitalism by its very nature cannot satisfy this second condition.

This approach has been taken further and made more explicit by writers of the Frankfurt School, especially Marcuse and Habermas. Their writings are centrally concerned with the contradiction between on the one hand an insistence on humanity's ability to make decisions freely and rationally, and on the other the observation that capitalist society is irrational, and is associated with irrational acts by people. They attempt to resolve this contradiction by arguing that a form of social organization is possible where people can come together and agree on their true needs. Thus, Marcuse argues that capitalist society implants false needs in people. True needs cannot, however, be imposed from the outside by some philosopher king:

> In the last analysis, the question of what are true and false needs must be answered by the individuals themselves, but only in the last analysis; that is, if and when they are free to give their own answers
>
> (Marcuse, 1964, p. 6).

Such a view that needs and interests are what people would freely choose in a non-oppressive society is echoed by Lukes in his discussion of a radical view of power and interests (Lukes, 1974a) and Habermas (see the translator's introduction to Habermas, 1975).

By adopting this approach we can avoid the charge that, in discounting present-day expressed needs, we inevitably move to a dictatorship in which an individual or group imposes its view as to what people should want from above. The key question now becomes how we can create and recognize a non-oppressive society in which people will have a free choice, such that it will actually be possible to *discover* what true needs are. Marx believed that a revolutionary struggle led by the working class could create a society in which the basis of oppression — private ownership of the means of production and the cultural and political dominance of those holding economic power — could be removed. Only in a society in which socialist production relations and political democracy have replaced capitalism can we argue that people are genuinely free to come to a decision as to what are truly human needs.

## Capitalism and the generation of new needs

Capitalism revolutionizes the forces of production. In other words it both changes the manner in which people come together to undertake production and the quantity and character of their output. This process generates new needs in a number of ways. In the first place, if we take needs as referring to desirable end states, or 'ideal norms', we may argue that the results of capitalist development are that we require a new input of socially provided goods and services simply to arrive at the same end state. In this case we can say that increases in the consumption of goods and services which are often referred to as new needs are not really this at all. They represent not new final needs, but new means of satisfying the same final needs. On the other hand, we may also argue that as production increases, totally new possibilities for satisfying previously unthought of needs open up. In this sense capitalism generates completely new needs.

Returning to the first group: the need for more socially provided goods to reach the same end state arises for a whole series of reasons. We shall consider three which appear particularly significant: diswelfares, the decline of informal and domestic systems of service and support, and thirdly, the manner in which the consumption of more and more material goods becomes ever more important in the pursuit of non-material ends.

## Diswelfares

Titmuss was one of the first writers within social administration to note that

> for many consumers the (social) services used are not essentially benefits or increments to welfare at all; they represent partial compensations for disservices, for social costs and social insecurities which are the product of a rapidly changing industrial-urban society. They are part of the price we pay to some people for bearing part of the costs of other people's progress
> (Titmuss, 1968, p. 133).

The greatest 'diswelfares' of the industrial revolution may perhaps be seen as, first, the loss of security associated with the capitalist mode of production, in particular the manner in which market relations take away the right to a livelihood, and the right to security against loss of home; and secondly, the effects of urbanization. Whilst particular groups have suffered more than others during the development of capitalism, from the hand-loom weavers in the early years of the nineteenth century onwards, it would be wrong to ignore the fact that these diswelfares have to some degree affected all those who neither own nor control the means of production.

Let us examine these diswelfares in more detail. All three can in some way be traced back to the key features of capitalism: that impersonal market relations penetrate every area of life, including the relationship between employer and worker, which is reduced to a simple cash-nexus. The capitalist buys the worker's ability to work through payment of a wage and controls what she or he does, seeking to use that labour power to produce the maximum output of goods. As historians point out, this is very different from the pre-capitalist master-servant relationship:

> the proletarian . . . must be distinguished from the 'servant' or pre-industrial dependent who has a much more complex human and social relationship with his 'master', and one which implies duties on both sides
>
> (Hobsbawm, 1969, p. 85).

The capitalist controls not only the hiring and firing of workers, but also their activities in the production process. The drive to extract more output from workers has led to an ever more complex division of labour, with the worker performing the most simple and repetitive tasks. The early years of the industrial revolution were associated with the break-up of craft skills with the beginnings of the factory system. More recently, the increasing technical and scientific sophistication of production has led to a polarization of the distribution of skills between managerial and scientific workers on the one hand, and production workers on the other. As Braverman points out:

> The break-up of craft skills and the reconstruction of production as a collective or social process have destroyed the traditional concept of skill and opened up only one way for mastery over labour processes to develop: in and through scientific, technical and engineering knowledge. But the extreme concentration of this knowledge in the hands of management and its closely associated staff organizations have closed this avenue to the working population
>
> (Braverman, 1977, p. 443).

In these ways industrial capitalism led to workers losing both security — no longer did they have any right to a livelihood — and the self-respect which came from pride in craft skills.

These changes were associated with the shift from a predominantly rural society where the worker could derive part or all of his livelihood from rights in a parcel of land, to an urban-industrial one. In 1750 England's largest city was London with a population of 675,000. It was a city based on commerce, and had no rivals in terms of size, the vast majority of the population living in the countryside. During the next century there grew up dramatically a whole series of new *manufacturing* cities — Manchester, Liverpool, Leeds, Glasgow. In the city the market determined what happened to land and property: the allocation of land according to market forces and the need to house workers cheaply and close to their places of work produced the kind of appalling living conditions so vividly described by Engels and other observers. Whereas under feudalism each person had some rights to land,

> by the beginning of the nineteenth century the new industrial working class were almost totally deprived of legal methods of obtaining long-term rights in property
>
> (Nevitt, 1971, p. 2).

Thus much of what we refer to as the welfare state consists of mechanisms giving partial compensation for, or insurance against, the diswelfares of urban-industrial capitalism. During the nineteenth century the rich avoided these diswelfares through their control of the means of production, their reliance on family connections, and their ability to buy services. Yet even they could not fully avoid the ravages of cholera. The regularly employed worker gained limited protection in certain areas through membership of a trade union or friendly society, whilst the poor bore the full brunt of market forces. During the twentieth century the state has taken over the function of compensating and partially shielding people from the full rigour of the market. In particular, a system of social insurance and assistance provides a partial substitute for the wage during periods of unemployment or sickness, and child benefits compensate families since their children are no longer a source of income; a system of cash benefits for housing and legal regulation of private sector rents and security have given the majority of the population some form of housing rights, either by virtue of ownership (for owner occupiers), or rights as statutory tenants. Legislation giving most private tenants security against arbitrary eviction was introduced in 1915 and despite subsequent amending legislation, covers the majority of working-class private tenants today. Council tenants have had to wait until 1980 for similar rights. Finally, anti-pollution and public-health and slum-clearance legislation have all attempted to reverse the high social costs of urban development. Loss of status and self-respect on the other hand, is something for which the welfare state cannot provide a ready redress. Whilst Marshall (1963) argues that rights to social services constitute a set of citizenship rights enjoyed equally by all members of society, Pinker (1971) suggests that reliance on social services leads to loss of self-respect — people feel the stigma of being receivers rather than givers.

So far we have discussed the diswelfares arising from the social relations of capitalism and have laid particular stress on their impact in the early days of industrialization. An optimist would have expected a combination of economic growth and the compensatory actions taken by the state to have transformed the situation today. In practice things are less simple: chapter 6 has already criticized the fallacy that economic growth solves poverty. Economic growth also creates diswelfares for social groups who see themselves as secure, even privileged. For example, economic growth has vastly increased the diseases of affluence — cardio-vascular disorders, for example, account for some 628 deaths per 100,000 population in Britain compared with 64 per 100,000 in the less developed Philippines (*Social Trends*, 1975). In the urban sphere the promise of suburban owner-occupation has not been without contradiction as mortgage rates soar, and the decline in public transport services leaves house-wives trapped at home and intensifies urban congestion and pollution. Whilst these diswelfares cannot compare with those experienced by the miner who has contracted lung disease, or the low-income family in a high-rise flat in the inner city, they nevertheless point to the manner in which the relentless pace of change under capitalism con-stantly creates new problems and sources of dissatisfaction which the state can do no more than very partially ameliorate.

## The changing role of women and the family

The family in the pre-industrial era served both as a unit of pro-duction, a unit of reproduction, and a means of maintaining non-pro-ductive dependents. The separation of work and home, and the huge technological advances of capitalism have had enormous conse-quences for the role of the family. In particular the family has lost its first function, the burden of the second and third functions has increased enormously, whilst increased mobility, and the changing role of women have left the family less equipped to carry them out. The result has been the extension of state social services to care for the dependent population, and the further penetration of commodity pro-duction into areas of reproduction which were previously the exclu-sive preserve of domestic labour — unpaid domestic labour of house-wives in the case of the working class, and paid domestic servants in the case of middle-class families, at least until the inter-war years.

These are not necessarily symptoms of the *decline* of the family, but of it being unable fully to meet the new demands being placed on it. Many studies indeed show that the family still shoulders the main burden of caring for the non-productive population, and with relatively little state help (Moroney, 1976).

The increase in the burden of dependency under capitalism has a number of causes. First, medical advance has extended the average expectation of life at age one to 69 for men and 75 for women, an increase of 14 years and 18 years respectively compared with 1901 (*Social Trends*, 1979). At the same time the young and old have been excluded from assuming a productive role in modern industry for a whole series of reasons — in particular, a revulsion at using the weaker members of society in the exhausting and sometimes dangerous conditions of modern industrial production, the desire of the working class to limit the labour supply and so prevent downward pressure on wages, and finally the extension of the education system. The resulting 'dependency ratio' is a crucial figure for social policy. Today 24 per cent of the population are below the school leaving age, and a further 17 per cent are over pensionable age (*Social Trends* 1979).

At the same time as maintaining these dependents, the demands made on the housewife in terms of the reproduction of labour power have also intensified. As workers' expectations about the satisfactions of private life rise, the housewife has to work harder as cook, decorator and home-maker — a trend reflected in many women's magazines.

Social change has left the family ill-equipped in many ways to assume these burdens. In particular, increased geographical mobility has separated elderly people from their children, and the absorption of women, especially married women, into the workforce, has placed enormous strains on women as they attempt to perform dual functions as both productive and domestic workers. In 1976 about half of married women worked and they constituted about a quarter of the labour force (*Social Trends* 1979). The results are labelled as 'social problems': the increasing number of elderly people living alone, the problem of children left with unregistered child-minders while parents are at work. The magnitude of these problems may be exaggerated — only a very small percentage of children under school age have mothers working full time. Nevertheless, since these children are often already living in deprived circumstances, inadequate and unstimulating day-care may be a disaster for their future development.

Both the state and the market have responded in some way to what are regarded as 'new needs' generated by these changes. New social services have been developed and existing ones extended to provide support for the elderly — but the enormous costs of providing a comprehensive service to meet needs leaves many with only minimal support. Similar considerations together with society's extremely ambivalent attitude towards working mothers have created a situation where Britain lacks either an adequate system of child endowment (such as is approached in France), or a system of satisfactory child care (as they have in the Soviet Union). The response of the market has not been to relieve the family of any of its responsibilities, but to develop new products which lighten the burden of domestic drudgery. In particular labour-saving devices such as washing machines are now accessible to virtually all urban families either through individual ownership or through socially provided laundries or laundrettes, and the use of convenience foods means that some of the burden of cooking can be lightened.

## *The consumer society and needs*

What are people looking for when they buy any particular commodity? A conventional economist observing consumer behaviour would find the answer simple — they purchase a commodity because it satisfies their want for that particular good. But to many critics of orthodox economic approaches the answer is not so easy. The consumer may in fact be interested in any of various characteristics associated with the good in question. These characteristics may be intrinsic to the particular good — e.g. food satisfies hunger, so a person may consume a meal because he or she is famished. But on the other hand a person may eat a meal in a restaurant because the sharing of meals is a means of being sociable. Finally he or she may eat in a fashionable, expensive restaurant in order to gain esteem and visibly demonstrate to onlookers his or her superior socio-economic status.

Consumption of material goods thus becomes a means to nonmaterial ends. One such end is the display of position, whereby consumption takes the form of 'conspicuous consumption' with the aim not of satisfying one's need but of impressing others (Veblen, 1934). The general level of living, social custom, fashion and other such factors will determine which particular goods, and in what particular quantities will be consumed in an attempt to satisfy those nonmaterial ends. Returning to needs we may say that consumption generally has three aspects;

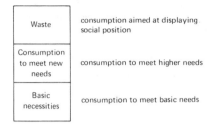

Here we distinguish between three types of need. At the lowest level are basic needs and basic necessities, by which we mean those goods and services which are essential to the maintenance of life — basic food, clothing, and shelter. We may also include non-material needs in this category — the need of children, for example, for adult love and care, and the need for some cultural expression. The satisfaction of such needs does not rely heavily on economic production, although it represents an opportunity cost in terms of production: whilst parents feed or play with their children they cannot be at the same time labouring to build a shelter; participation in religious ceremonies takes people away from work in the fields.

Once society progresses above subsistence level, necessities both material and non-material tend to proliferate, and material and non-material needs become ever more intertwined. In our scheme we have made a distinction between consumption to meet new needs — needs which come to be recognized as the level of society's productive capacity is raised, creating a higher output of consumption goods, and permitting a shortening of the working day so that more time can be spent on pursuits not directly connected with labour; and consumption geared to display and governed by fashion and snobbery, 'conspicuous consumption' in Veblen's terminology.

The critique of capitalism operates at all levels. In the first place not all members of society are able to satisfy their basic needs for survival, a point to which we have already alluded. This discrepancy is even more marked when we come to consider the satisfaction of new needs. In the second place, many would argue that much consumption is not for the satisfaction of new needs, but is a form of waste. If this is so then the progressive aspect of capitalism's expansion of the productive forces must be seen to be severely qualified. Indeed since production requires labour time, we may have arrived at a situation where workers are spending more then half their waking hours involved in alienating work; they are thereby denied the chance to satisfy other needs such as for sporting, cultural or social activities, yet much of what they produce is wasteful, and part of the motivation for working long hours is to gain income to buy wasteful products themselves.

In practise it is of course extremely difficult to distinguish between new needs and waste. Veblen attempts to analyse the way in which the product of society has been used in societies beyond the most primitive, and concludes that it is virtually all absorbed into forms of wasteful consumption:

> The need for conspicuous waste, therefore, stands ready to absorb any increase in the community's industrial efficiency or output of goods, after the most elementary physical wants have been provided for
>
> (Veblen, 1934, p. 110).

A scathing indictment, indeed, of economic 'progress', which suggests that all that has happened is that prosperity has increased the input of consumption needed to enable people to show the rest of the world that they are superior to those beneath them. Insofar as the average level is rising all the time, 'the normal, average individual will live in chronic dissatisfaction with his present lot' (Veblen, 1934, p. 31).

This notion of endemic dissatisfaction is also developed by Hirsch (1977) although his critique of the illusions of the consumer society is less blunt and more subtle.

Hirsch distinguishes between conspicuous consumption and consumption to meet new needs, but shows how they are both subject to 'social scarcity': in other words, however much the economy grows, not everyone can enjoy them, because their desirable characteristics depend wholly or partly on not everyone having access. He identifies, first, *pure social scarcity*. This is analogous to Veblen's conspicuous consumption, since satisfaction derives purely from the fact that only an elite enjoy them. Second, however, is 'incidental social scarcity': here the consumer seeks satisfaction from the intrinsic characteristics of the good, and consumes in order to meet a need. But as consumption becomes more widespread, the possibility of the consumer finding the satisfaction he or she seeks diminishes. This may be due to physical crowding — a private motor car does not provide quick, efficient and relatively tension-free mobility if roads are crowded by other motorists — or social crowding — educational qualifications as a route to more pleasant and creative work lose their efficacy if the majority of the population has the same qualification. Thus, Hirsch argues, people constantly strive to gain the consumption goods enjoyed by the privileged few, but find that the promised land is an illusion: once they can afford the goods in question, they no longer yield the same satisfaction.

What Hirsch's analysis suggests is that the growth in the output of society does create new needs, although it also leads to wasteful conspicuous consumption. What is interesting to ask is whether the 'incidental social scarcity' which blocks the satisfaction of these new needs for the majority is inevitable, or whether it is especially acute in market society. Hirsch himself implies that the latter is the case. In market society there is a constant tendency for goods and services to be provided on a commercial basis, rather than informally or on a collective non-commercial basis. This means that increasingly people can only try to satisfy their needs in ways which are compatible with the dictates of private enterprise. This has two important consequences. First, there is a tendency to underproduce goods and services for which it is impractical to introduce a user charge; and secondly decisions taken piecemeal — the individual's decision to buy a car for example — lead to end results which are seen as undesirable by virtually everyone.

Thus we are back with the idea that the productive potential of capitalism to meet people's needs cannot be realized because of the domination of the social relations of the market. Although Hirsch does not raise the question of an alternative to this domination, his analysis nevertheless poses the question as to whether the construction of a democratic non-market society, in which open collective decision making is the means whereby priorities are decided, is a necessary condition for ameliorating the endless frustration of attempts to satisfy needs under capitalism.

## Class struggle and the articulation of needs

In this section we move from a general discussion of needs back to looking at the welfare state, which represents state intervention in response to demands that particular needs should be met. These demands have come from two sources: first pressure from some of the more enlightened, reformist members of the capitalist class for certain working-class needs to be met as a necessary element in the reproduction of capitalist relations of production; and secondly, pressure from the working class and other oppressed groups.

In chapter 7 we argued that the early nineteenth-century state was more concerned with dismantling restrictions to free trade and the free movement of labour than meeting workers' needs. Nevertheless, even during the first half of the century there was an exception in the form of legislation from 1833 onwards, albeit very limited and piecemeal, which banned the employment of young children in some industries, and restricted the hours of work of older children, women and, rather later, men. In the middle years of the century the issue of public health was taken up by philanthropists and reformers such as Edwin Chadwick, the architect of the Poor Law Amendment Act of 1834, in a campaign for legislation to set up local boards of health to provide a clean water supply and system of sewage disposal.

Both these issues touched on the most basic need of the working class for physical survival. In unregulated factories and sweatshops workers were prey to disease, exhaustion and early death, whilst the lack of any urban amenities in the grossly overcrowded city slums brought periodic epidemics of diseases such as cholera which threatened to spread also to the homes of the middle class. When it comes to the physical survival of the working class, capital has an interest in ensuring that basic needs are met, once the vast reservoirs of surplus agricultural labour have been largely drained. In addition there was a strong concern in Victorian society about the moral consequences of excessive work, especially of women and children. Despite this, the campaigns to get hours of work limited and for public health legislation had to be fought long and hard by a combination of Tory philanthropists, prominent doctors and churchmen, and more enlightened representatives of the rising capitalist class.

Policies motivated by concern at physical reproduction have re-surfaced several times since, particularly when wars have focused the attention of the state on the physical quality of the population. The appalling state of fitness of recruits for the Boer War is widely regarded as having stimulated the Liberal government to introduce legislation to enable school meals to be paid for out of the rates in 1906, and setting up a system of medical inspection in schools in 1907.

So far we have argued as if the working class played little role in the development of social policy. This would not be quite accurate when we speak of the campaigns for the Factory Acts, but in general it is true to say that in the early and mid- nineteenth century working-class pressure played a secondary role in the process of state recognition of needs. From the end of the nineteenth century, however, the situation was reversed: despite the continuing role of reformers and philanthropists such as Charles Booth, Seebohm Rowntree and William Beveridge, the most important force impelling the state to extend welfare provision has been working-class pressure. This is not to argue that the working class has directly controlled the form in which policies have been implemented, but that the balance of class forces has more often than not been the main factor determining whether the state will initiate reform.

In chapter 7 we discussed the way in which class struggle tends to assume different forms in capitalist society and that different types of organization often take up different political issues. In this section we shall argue that the character of the class struggle in Britain and the dominance of certain types of organization and demands have had important consequences for which range of needs the welfare state meets, and how it meets them.

Looking at the class struggle in Britain what stands out most is the dominance of a well organized but reformist labour movement based on the trade unions and the Labour Party. The British working class lacks a revolutionary tradition, and the socialist parties set up during the last two decades of the nineteenth century were a mixed bunch: the Fabians were essentially middle-class reformers with little sympathy with the working-class movement. The Social Democratic Federation and the Independent Labour Party had firmer roots in the reality of the class struggle, but never gained mass support. The result is that the dominant politics of the British working class is not socialism, but 'labourism', a widely albeit loosely used term to refer to a kind of corporate class-consciousness which accepts the basic class structure of capitalism, but within it promotes the interests of the working class.

The main political expression of labourism is the Labour Party — formed as the Labour Representation Committee (LRC) in 1900, and assuming its modern title in 1906. The Labour Party's significance lies in its role as the electoral expression of the interests of the labour movement, indeed the founding conference of the LRC was convened not by socialist groups, but by the Parliamentary Committee of the TUC . This organic link with the trade-union movement remains today, giving the party solidity and permanence.

The Labour Party made its first electoral breakthrough in 1906, when it gained 30 seats, compared with the two gained by the LRC in 1900. Since then the Labour Party has had both a direct and indirect effect on the development of the welfare state: direct through its role as the party of government, in 1924, and 1929 to 1931 (on both occasions without an overall majority), and between 1945 and 1951,

1964 and 1970, and 1974 and 1979. Indirectly its role in opposition has been important as a focus for working-class grievances against the policies of governments more clearly committed to the policies of capital.

Social democratic ideology has generally accepted a distinction between trade unionism and politics, such that trade unions are encouraged to support the Labour Party electorally and through conventional pressure-group tactics, but discouraged from using industrial strength for political ends.

Compared with the role of the Labour Party in alliance with the trade unions, other forms of class struggle — movements of oppressed groups in particular the women's movement, and community action — have had a much smaller impact on the welfare state. These movements are concerned with problems that are experienced particularly acutely by women and the non-working population who are either excluded from the trade unions, or are largely unrepresented in positions of power within them. They have organized themselves outside formal union structures very often, in claimants' unions, women's groups, and tenants associations, but face many difficulties in bringing effective pressure to bear on the unions and the state.

Their limited success stems from some of the particular problems such movements face in organizing, problems which do not face the trade unions. First, women at home and non-workers are isolated and therefore more difficult to organize than workers brought together in one place of work. Secondly, they lack the glue of immediate material self-interest to maintain group cohesion. Thirdly, issues of ideology are more likely to confront and divide them. Whilst one might expect ideological differences to be a divisive factor in the Labour Party, it has in practice managed to survive as a coalition of viewpoints held together by the aspiration for parliamentary power. It is interesting in this context that it was the electoral challenge of Scottish nationalism which led to the first split in the Party. In contrast, the women's movement, from the Suffragettes onwards, has had to grapple with the problem of whether it wants equality on male terms — an equality defined variously as the right to occupy any position at present held by a man, or the recognition by society of the equal importance of areas of feminine competence — or whether to challenge the structures of patriarchy themselves, which dictate not only who shall fill which positions, but what qualities are demanded of their incumbents, and to some degree, which positions there are to be filled. Such issues have often led to splits in the movement.

Finally there are dilemmas in deciding how to organize. If conventional pressure-group tactics directed at the state are to be employed, then in order to gain legitimacy it may be necessary to downplay ideological questions and develop a formal organizational structure with a dues-paying membership and paid officials. Acquiring such a mantle of respectability may however inhibit the use of militant tactics, and lead to the development of a cautious leadership which is unable to mobilize mass support when new possibilities open up. Piven and Cloward (1979) discuss this dilemma in relation to the American welfare-rights movement.

In Britain what we have tended to find is more formal organizations operating through conventional pressure-group tactics at national level, with more loosely organized groups relying more on spontaneity and disruptive tactics active locally. In the housing sphere organizations such as the National Tenants Association operate nationally, while locally individual tenants' groups have conducted a whole variety of campaigns — from taking councils to court over damp houses and flats, to some rent strikes in the aftermath of the rent rises imposed under the 1972 Housing Finance Act. These struggles have tended to remain isolated and sporadic however and have only succeeded in gaining piecemeal and limited concessions in particular localities.

An alternative to pressuring the state is to try to gain trade-union support, using their numerical and industrial strength to reinforce campaigns. Linking the struggles of the users and the providers of the social services is the desired aim of many socialists (Cockburn, 1977), but the examples of such unity that can be cited are relatively few. Historically the most famous and successful example of trade unionists and housewives in joint struggle occurred in Glasgow in 1915, when massive protests against rent rises forced the government to introduce rent control and some security against eviction for tenants. More recently we can cite the example of NUPE's action against private pay beds in NHS hospitals, and the decision of the TUC to organize a national demonstration in 1979 to protest against the Corrie Bill to limit abortion rights.

This fairly lengthy discussion of class struggle may appear to have moved us rather far from the discussion of needs. The point we wish to make, however, is that if an important motor force for the recognition of needs is the class struggle, then the particular character of that struggle will influence which needs are recognized, and how.

The consequence for state policies to meet need of the dominance of a reformist labour movement are: first the needs of certain oppressed groups have been under-recognized. Despite knowledge, for example, that many men used severe physical violence against their wives, the state by and large turned a blind eye until women, many associated with the women's movement, began to establish refuges for battered women and pressure local authorities for financial support. Secondly the trade unions and the Labour Party have largely accepted dominant values even though these reinforce divisions within the working class. Thus the TUC delegation to the Beveridge committee on social insurance were 'contemptuous of "dodgers", of the "very poor" and "of the type of person who will not join a Friendly Society" ' (quoted in Ginsburg, 1979, p. 95).

Finally, the manner in which the labour movement has relied on a reformist Labour Party to translate demands into action has had several consequences for the manner in which needs are met. In particular, policies have only been introduced insofar as they do not threaten the interests of capital; the implementation of policies to meet needs has been entrusted to bureaucracies which are almost completely insulated from working-class control.

## Rationing individual needs

We conclude this chapter with a discussion of the area which is the traditional concern of social administration, the rationing of resources between individuals, a process which is seen as necessitated by the unfortunate fact of life that 'needs are potentially infinite; resources always limited and therefore scarce' (Parker, 1967, reprinted in Butterworth and Holman, 1975, p. 204). The discussion so far should, however, lead us to adopt a critical stance towards such a bland acceptance of the parameters of rationing for three reasons.

In the first place, the view that all needs are necessarily infinite has been qualified by the discussion earlier this chapter of the social generation of needs. Looking at the social services, we can see that many fall into the categories discussed on pages 224-9, namely new ways of satisfying existing needs made necessary by demographic, economic and social change. In this group we would include most income-maintenance services; many of the services which care for the dependent and non-working population; some health services, such as those required to cope with work-related diseases or the rising incidence of road accidents (for a discussion of the social production of health and ill-health see Doyal, 1979); and many of the services made necessary by urbanization — the provision of public open space and subsidized public transport for example.

Some of these new ways of satisfying existing needs are made necessary by the development of urban-industrial society, and cannot be seen as peculiarly related to the capitalist mode of production. Other needs would certainly be less likely to appear as major problems in a non-market society. A planned economy geared to full employment would reduce the need for many insurance and assistance payments; a society organized to prevent avoidable ill-health would find certain categories of demand for curative treatment reduced or eliminated.

Other social services fall into the category of meeting new needs. Health services enable many people to enjoy a much greater level of physical well-being than would have been dreamed of at the turn of the century. Whilst the need for health is not of course new, the changing content we give to the notion of 'health' as new possibilities for treatment open up, makes it meaningful for us to speak of new needs.

It would be difficult to characterize any of the social services as conspicuous consumption, but elements of waste can be said to arise when goods subject to social scarcity are provided. Much educational provision, for example, is consumed with the aim of gaining a qualification which will enable their holder to avoid unpleasant, routine, low-paid jobs, rather than from a desire to study. As qualifications become more widely available they lose their role as a passport to affluence, increasing for example the number of women graduate typists. Even semi-vocational qualifications may be demanded more as a means of creating barriers to entry to certain jobs than because they are intrinsically necessary for performance of such jobs. Both these factors are tending to depress the demand for places in universities at the present time, as potential students realize that they may safeguard their future security better by applying immediately for a job, and employers reconsider policies of seconding workers onto training courses.

A second modification of the traditional view of rationing concerns the assumption of limited resources. Clearly there are physical limits to non-renewable resources as the ecological pressure groups remind us. The limits imposed on social expenditure in Britain today need not be accepted, however, as given. We have already discussed in chapter 6 how social-service costs and the limits on expenditure are conditioned by the imperatives of capital accumulation. Even without abolishing the capitalist mode of production, however, a radical government would have considerable scope to stretch resource limits: nationalization of the drug companies would lower NHS costs, whilst a policy of stimulating economic revival through state investment would not remove the conflict between resources for production versus resources for reproduction, but it would ameliorate the demand for expenditure cuts as a route to revitalizing profits which we are hearing now.

In addition the problem of rationing should not be understood only in terms of the limits on social expenditure, but also in terms of the availability of alternative avenues to satisfying needs. Thus, for example, the rationing of public housing is very much affected by whether it is the only form of housing available to low-income families. At present rationing is extremely severe in housing because of the decline of the private rented sector and the fall in new building in the private as well as the public sector — 1979 saw the lowest level of housing starts since the early 1950s. The possibility that the market might satisfy more social needs is raised by, for example, the workers plan produced by the Lucas Aerospace shop-stewards combine committee, which sought to show how the firm could switch from producing armaments, which are profitable but satisfy no needs, to producing socially useful products. Unless the production of armaments becomes unprofitable, it is unlikely that such firms will consider changing course without state intervention, possibly nationalization. Even so, such changes could be brought about without abolishing capitalism.

Our final critique of the traditional problematic is that it fails to recognize that rationing has aims other than simply the satisfaction of needs. In particular it may have a social controlling role. It reinforces dominant values — social security upholds the work ethic by treating the retired more generously than the unemployed, and the financial dependence of women on men through the cohabitation rule which denies supplementary benefit to women living with men; the more economically productive may be favoured, for example in the provision of sheltered employment for the disabled or the allocation of public housing to key workers; discrimination is practised by local authorities allocating housing against those with a shorter period of local residence, or the homeless, examples of a more general phenomenon of the state buying off one group of workers against another.

Judge (1978) distinguishes between two levels at which rationing occurs; financial rationing is to do with the macro-level allocation of resources between competing claims, whilst service rationing involves decisions about which consumer shall have access to which goods and services. Much useful research has been undertaken into how the rationing process operates at both levels (for example Parker, 1967; Glennerster, 1975; Judge, 1978; Foster, 1979). However, the absence of a broader context leads to the parameters of the rationing process being too easily taken for granted. In discussion of service rationing in particular, attention tends to be focused on the front-line staff, the managers of the system, without sufficient analysis of the constraints within which they operate, and how such constraints should be explained. If we look at the allocation of housing for example, discriminatory policies relate in part to the fact that councils have to let houses in which nobody wants to live. In Manchester, for example, only a tiny minority of waiting-list applicants will consider some overspill estates, whilst those in inner-city deck access developments are voting with their feet whenever they have the chance to leave. In addition it is too easily assumed that there are rational, technical answers to apparently arbitrary decisions. Whilst the search for more efficient and equitable procedures is a valid one, it all too easily ignores the underlying contradictory functions of the social services which are inevitably reproduced to some degree or other in the actions of the social-service bureaucracies.

# 9

## The future of the welfare state

### Is Britain in a state of crisis?

A glance through titles of books on politics and economics published since the mid 1970s, from both right and left-wing viewpoints, reveals a liberal use of the term 'crisis' — from a marxist perspective, for example, *Capitalism in Crisis* (Gamble and Walton, 1976); *Legitimation Crisis* (Habermas, 1975); *The Fiscal Crisis of the State* (O'Connor, 1973); and from the pro-market Institute of Economic Affairs *Crisis 1975* and more ominously *The Coming Confrontation: Will the Open Society Survive to 1980?* (Seldon, 1978b). All share in common the view that advanced capitalist societies are reaching some form of turning point with profound and far reaching implications for future developments. In this final chapter we shall examine the symptoms and causes of Britain's problems, and ask whether they do in fact measure up to some notion of crisis. We shall then consider some strategies for change that have gained support, considering their implications for the future shape of the welfare state. Finally we shall examine the practice of the present (1979—?) Conservative Government. Is it dismantling the welfare state as we presently know it, and what effects will its actions have on British society?

When politicians and media pundits speak of Britain's crisis, they adopt two leitmotifs: the economy is unmanageable and the people are ungovernable. The symptoms of the crisis are, in the economic system, high inflation and rising unemployment; industrial militancy from both sides of industry (the 1970s has seen groups who have not come out for decades, such as the miners, the firemen and the steel-workers, engaged in prolonged strikes often using aggressive picketing tactics, whilst employers have used a variety of tactics to weaken both shop-floor power and the national cohesion of the unions); finally a growing sense of cynicism and erosion of traditional values and hopes for the future. Keynesian style economic policies and the extension of the welfare state have left the middle classes and the aspiring middle classes resentful at high taxation, and the erosion of wage and salary differentials and the extension of the role of the state, whilst the collapse of the long post-war boom has eroded the material basis of

Labour Party reformism, leaving the labour movement without any broadly agreed perspective.

Society is often theorized as consisting of several interconnected systems: economic, political, moral/ideological. It is the way in which seemingly insoluble problems plague all these systems that gives British society an air of crisis. Furthermore, any corrective measures applied to one system seem only to make things worse elsewhere. We are faced with intractable economic problems, industrial unrest, and widespread personal frustration feeding different forms of contempt for traditional values and respect for laws: tax evasion is one symptom among certain strata of the population — the IEA has even coined a new term 'tax avoision' to indicate that high taxation is leading to 'an unconscious rejection of the moral difference between legal avoidance and illegal evasion' (Seldon, 1978b, p. 25); whilst more socially visible anti-social behaviour such as vandalism and petty larceny grows elsewhere. These are all symptoms of crisis, symptoms which seem to be connected. To grasp both their causes and connections we must return to some sort of holistic view of society which sees it as a set of interconnected parts. The most penetrating and original analysis of crisis to adopt such an approach is that of Habermas (1975).

Habermas argues that modern capitalist society is divided into three interacting systems, each requiring a certain input, and each having a particular output. These systems are an economic system based on an input of capital and labour producing an output of consumable goods and services; a political system requiring an input of mass loyalty or legitimation and an output of laws and administrative decisions; the outputs of the economic and political systems are simultaneously an input into the third system, the socio-cultural system, whose output is the normative structure of society — a system of shared values and meanings. Each system suffers a crisis if its output is inadequate in terms of the demands being placed upon it: if the economic system produces too few goods and services we have an economic crisis; if the political system cannot produce coherent political/administrative decisions we have a rationality crisis; if traditional values and beliefs are eroded or expectations accelerate too fast, we have a motivation crisis. A fourth source of crisis Habermas refers to as a legitimation crisis — this occurs where changes in the political system need to be legitimated, but existing sources of legitimation are inadequate. The relationships between these systems are illustrated in Figure 9.1.

In Habermas's schema, developments in the economic system form the starting point for analysis, but the lynch-pin of the system as a

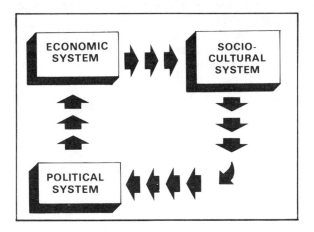

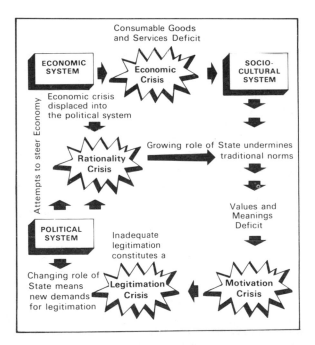

Fig. 9.1 *Crisis tendencies in advanced capitalism.*

whole is seen as the arena of legitimation, an emphasis which is clear from the title of his book, *Legitimation Crisis*. This requires explanation. Under capitalism, the economic and political systems are distinct. At the same time, the economic system is riven with contradictions and tends towards periodic accumulation crises, marked by slumps — the collapse of profits, production and employment. In an attempt to stave off crises the state has become more and more deeply involved in the economy — both regulating the activities of economic agents and producing or organizing the production of various inputs for accumulation. This has the effect of repoliticizing areas of life which were previously left to the decentralized workings of the market, leading to new demands for legitimation — areas such as wage and price fixing become the subject of open, collective decision making rather than subject to the 'laws of supply and demand'. Without mass quiescence this change will provoke more widespread and concerted conflict than was associated with the more opaque market transactions. At the same time, the state is faced with all sorts of conflicting demands from the economic system — in effect the contradictions of the economic system simply reappear in new forms in the political system. There is thus an inevitable tendency for the political system to fail to produce a rational system of administrative decisions. At the same time the state is encroaching more and more on areas traditionally outside the political sphere. This creates disturbances in the socio-cultural system. It is this system and the legitimation system which are fundamental to social integration. The inability of these systems to sustain basic bourgeois values and loyalties undermines the general acceptance of society as it is presently organized and intensifies social conflict.

Here then is a framework which enables us to see the connections between these various crisis symptoms. Theorists differ radically, however, in their understanding of the cause of economic crisis and its relation to the growth in the role of the state. Some see the state as having misguidedly intervened in the economy, both causing economic decline and creating a crisis of over-government: they believe that their prescriptions will banish simultaneously the interconnected crises we have looked at. Others see inevitable crisis tendencies being generated in the economic system: action taken by the state to ameliorate the situation makes it worse elsewhere. The system is caught in insoluble contradiction. The crisis can only be resolved if a more fundamental transformation of society takes place. We shall now look at these different theories and proposals.

## Theories of crisis and problems of crisis management

We shall divide these approaches initially into two broad categories: market and non-market theories and solutions. By market theories we mean those which postulate that the cause of the economic crisis is the encroachment of the state on the market. If only market relationships can be released from the fetters of state intervention, economic output can be restored, and at the same time the erosion of traditional values and aspirations will be halted and unnecessary conflicts, induced by the politicization of economic relations, will be ameliorated. Those who adhere to market theories do not dispute Habermas's view that state intervention in the economy has contributed to crisis tendencies elsewhere, but regard this as an unnecessary intrusion which can be rolled back, thus restoring harmony. This view is associated with bodies such as the Institute of Economic Affairs, and the monetarist theories held by many prominent members of the Conservative Party.

In opposition stand non-market theorists, who see Britain's economic problems as being more deeply rooted in the economic system, and soluble only by further moves *away* from a free-enterprise market economy. The most coherent non-market theories are variants of marxist political economy, which suggest that there are inbuilt tendencies towards crisis in the capitalist system of production, and that growing state intervention, far from being some half-baked intrusion, has been a necessary attempt to stave off the periodic slumps which have plagued the capitalist economy. As Habermas points out, however, such action cannot *solve* the economic contradictions of capitalism, they merely postpone and displace their appearance. The solution to the crisis is therefore to be understood in terms of the transformation of the system of production to some form of socialism.

Not all theories which fall in the non-market camp accept the marxist's assumption that the crisis is insoluble within the present system. There are non-market theories which believe that the crisis can be solved this side of socialism, albeit with the state playing a far more prominent role than it does in most contemporary capitalist societies. Such theories are generally associated with corporatist policies of varying hues. We shall look at these various theories in more detail.

*Market theories — the monetarists*

In the earlier section we spoke of two symptoms of economic crisis:

inflation and unemployment. To those of the monetarist persuasion, the key problem is inflation — the debasement of the value of the currency: whilst monetarists argue that official figures for unemployment give an inflated picture (see, for example, Wood, 1972b), they generally accept that a higher rate of unemployment is a necessary price that has to be paid in order to achieve monetary stability. The central tenet of monetarism is that inflation is caused by the money supply increasing more rapidly than the level of output. Such a discrepancy will *always* lead to inflation, although the timing and precise magnitude of changes in the price level depends on various complicating factors. For instance, an increase in the money supply may initially stimulate the level of output, so delaying an inflationary spiral. But then inevitably that spiral will assert itself as output fails to keep pace with the overall level of demand in the economy.

Monetarists reject the notion that trade unions, pursuing excessive wage claims, cause inflation. They may affect *relative* prices, if individual manufacturers raise their prices so as to recoup high wage settlements: but if the money supply is held constant, then this will simply deflate prices elsewhere in the economy as consumers' purchasing power is reduced by the higher prices in the high-wage sector. If high wage claims are *generally* conceded in a framework of monetary stability, then some firms will simply go bust. Clearly if trade unions were to moderate their wage claims, the harsh medicine of unemployment and bankruptcy can be avoided. But monetarists believe that fear of unemployment will more effectively exert a downward pressure on wages than direct state intervention through some form of prices and incomes policy.

This preference for the market rather than the state as regulator is largely explained by the monetarists' faith in competitive private enterprise. Monetarists operate within an individualist economic framework, and place faith in unfettered market forces, both as the foundation of economic strength and basic values and aspirations. Friedman, the doyen of monetarism, claims that

> Steady monetary growth would provide a monetary climate favourable to the effective operation of those basic forces of enterprise, ingenuity, invention, hard work and thrift that are the true springs of economic growth

> (Quoted in Harris and Sewill, 1975).

Many monetarists go no further than making such statements of belief which point the way to what should be done. Others, however, have realized that the situation is less simple. In order realistically to see what *can* be done, some analysis is required of *why* there has been a constant tendency for the government to inject too much money into the economy (Brittan, 1978). Brittan attempts to supply such a political analysis: our democratic system is based on competition between political teams for votes. Bidding tends to take the form of promises involving increased public expenditure, yet the electorate is not willing to pay for this through rising taxes. The gap must be filled by the injection of money. Attempts to stave off the inflationary consequences of such action through prices and incomes policy founder in the face of the incompatible demands of producer groups (Brittan, 1975; 1978). Inflation is thus built into our system of liberal democracy.

A change in the parameters of what the state is expected to do is a necessary underpinning of monetarist policies within the framework of liberal democracy. Thus monetarism becomes much more than a fetish of the money supply, but a philosophy of minimal government, no longer called *laissez faire* as in the nineteenth century, but a 'social market economy' (see Gamble, 1980). Unfortunately monetarists have little to say on how the changes in attitudes and behaviour on which the social market economy rests can be brought about, beyond the present government's exhortations in favour of free enterprise, and against state intervention. This raises the question of whether monetarism *is* possible in a liberal democratic society: does monetarism represent a diminution of the role of the state? Or does it mean less intervention directly in the economy, less welfare, but a growth in the repressive apparatus of the state to hold back demands for social expenditure and wage claims?

Monetary theories gained ground in the Conservative Party during the 1970s. The 1970 Conservative Government under Edward Heath came to office committed to allowing greater scope to market forces, but was, according to monetarists, 'panicked' into increasing state intervention (an incomes policy, subsidizing unprofitable industry) and expanding the money supply, by social unrest and rising unemployment. (See for example, Harris and Sewill, 1975.) Others have argued that Heath was never a monetarist but fell within the camp of traditional Toryism (Gamble, 1980). Whatever interpretation is accepted, it is clear that the monetarists (Thatcher and Joseph, in particular) have gained the ascendancy in the 1979 Conservative Government. We shall see later how likely it is that they will stick by their beliefs. What do these beliefs entail for social policy?

In the first place, firm control of the money supply is seen as key. The money supply is generally defined as notes and coins in circulation plus bank deposits. This definition is given the tag '$M_3$' and is distinguished from '$M_1$' which refers only to notes, coins and *current* accounts in banks. The government can influence the money supply through its power to print money, and its impact on the level of bank deposits. This latter is affected by government borrowing from banks who can expand their credit and thereby 'create' money. Monetary policy therefore requires a reduction in the public sector borrowing requirement (PSBR). This could be achieved by a massive increase in taxation, but as we have seen, the preferred monetarist solution is swingeing cuts in public expenditure. Certain categories of expenditure are particularly vulnerable, while others may indeed grow. If we use O'Connor's categories of social investment, social consumption and social expenses, we can immediately see that the latter category is likely to increase: higher 'natural' levels of unemployment mean that the surplus population to be maintained out of public funds will grow, whilst the attendant social conflict means higher expenditure on the repressive apparatuses of the state — a fact recognized by the present Conservative Government which came to office pledged to spend more on law and order.

Social investment and social consumption expenditures must decline — both so that lower overall expenditure targets can be reached, and because of the monetarists' belief that the overall role of government should be limited. We have already discussed social consumption expenditures in chapter 6 and argued that they represent a necessary part of the reproduction of labour power. It is inconceivable for a modern capitalist state to argue that workers no longer require health care, education for their children, housing aid — except in the context of a massive change in the balance of class forces, such as occurred in Chile after the colonels' coup. What may, however, be attempted is a shift of certain services or parts of services into the private sector, with reliance on voluntary or state insurance, and a reduction in services caring for the dependent population.

Such policies would have a number of advantages for the state: public expenditure would be reduced as workers paid for the social services out of their wages rather than through taxation, and the unpaid labour of housewives substituted for paid social-care workers; the large, almost monolithic social services would be fragmented, thus reducing the power of the producer groups running these services, who at present form a very powerful lobby for increased public expenditure; fewer women would be in a position to take paid employment outside the home, thus softening the effects of rising unemployment on the male workforce; finally, such policies would accord with the ideological offensive which the monetarists must wage against the idea that the state has responsibilities for individual welfare.

Such a shift in policy, if it is to succeed in qualitatively reducing public expenditure and the role of the state, involves far-reaching changes to the structure of the welfare state. It would rudely shatter the parameters of feasible change which have held since 1945. The problem the Conservative Government faces is that, in a democratic system, such policies will lead to fierce opposition, and at the next election a Labour Government, more radical than the last, will be returned. Can the Conservatives take such a risk, or, put another way, which will have to give — democracy or monetarism?

## Non-market solutions within capitalism

Economic policy after the second world war was dominated, until the 1970s, by Keynesian policies of demand management. Unlike the monetarists, the true inheritors of orthodox neo-classical economic theory, Keynes did not believe that the market mechanism could be left to produce an optimum, equilibrium level of output and employment. The novelty of his approach was his focus on economic *aggregates* rather than conducting his analysis at the level of the interactions between individual firms. In particular, he drew attention to the manner in which insufficient total demand in the economy could lead to long term stagnation of output and employment. Keynes saw that the state had a central role to play in the management of aggregate demand, and post war governments have all used a series of tools to maintain the economy at a level of 'full employment' — including both monetary and fiscal policies and control over social-security payments.

Whilst Keynesian-style demand management has been remarkably successful in maintaining prosperity in the post-war world, the onset of rapid inflation in the 1970s has faced economists with a severe dilemma, which has contributed to the revival of monetarism: do Keynesian policies inevitably fuel inflation? The Keynesian explanation of inflation is expressed either in terms of 'demand pull' or 'cost push', indicating that the cause lies either in too much expenditure (by consumers, firms and the government), or an autonomous increase in prices due to increases in wages or profits. An upward movement of prices induced by excess demand could be initiated by, for example, large and widespread tax cuts, or a massive increase in government purchase of armaments; cost-push inflation may arise when money wages rise more rapidly than output, or firms broaden their profit margins.

The policy conclusions drawn from the Keynesian paradigm were that the economy could be kept in balance by 'fine tuning': concern over inflation largely centred on the problem of wages, and whether a moderate amount of unemployment might have to be accepted as the price of wage stability. This general framework was rudely shattered in the 1960s by two seemingly intransigent problems: low investment and inadequate modernization of industry on the one hand, and high wage demands on the other. Joan Robinson, a prominent Keynesian economist, pointed out:

> It was easy to predict that if we stumbled into near-full employment with institutions and attitudes unchanged, the balance of power in wage-bargaining would tip in favour of the workers, so that a vicious spiral of wages and prices would become chronic. Yet it took about fifteen years of experience for the point to really sink in
>
> (Robinson, 1966, p. 19).

In response to these problems, Keynesians have had to move beyond Keynes. 'Fine tuning' of demand is no longer enough: the state must now intervene in some way other than on the demand side, and move to control the price of labour power. The 1960s saw the adoption, first by a Conservative government, of some limited notion of planning, (see Shonfield, 1965), and both Labour and Conservative governments have introduced incomes policies despite pre-election denials that they would contemplate any such thing.

This extension of the role of the state goes far beyond anything envisaged by Keynes, and many writers have argued that what we are moving towards is a form of corporatism. (See for example, Pahl and Winkler, 1974; Panitch, 1977; Winkler, 1977; Crouch, 1979.) Corporatism does not necessarily involve the jackboots of Mussolini's fascism or Hitler's Nazi dictatorship. The essential features of corporatism are: an economy based primarily on private ownership, but where there is considerable state control over prices, wages and investment decisions, combined with a political structure which incorporates the trade unions and business organizations in national planning. Such a structure can evolve out of a liberal democratic regime, where it takes on a rather different form from the authoritarian dictatorships of Hitler or Mussolini. In particular, as Crouch points out,

> Corporatism in a liberal society means coming to terms with autonomous organizations which will never be entirely successfully subjected to ideological hegemony and which must always do something to represent their members. Relations between the state and these organized interests are therefore always likely to be characterized by bargaining
>
> (Crouch, 1979, p. 23).

We have already suggested that moves in the direction of planning (i.e. influencing private investment decisions directly, rather than indirectly via traditional Keynesian instruments) and incomes policies, represented corporatist developments instituted by both the Conservative and Labour Parties. The advent of the Thatcher group to dominance in the Conservative Party has, however, opened up a clear split in policy between a Conservative Party bent on reducing the role of the state and a Labour Party continuing in a corporatist direction. This latter path is seen most clearly in the proposals of some of the left wing of the party.

The 'alternative economic strategy' espoused by Benn and the Tribune Group of MPs, involves a system of wage and price controls and planning involving what are referred to as 'planning agreements': basically tripartite agreements between large monopoly firms, their workers and the state. These would require firms to supply information and enable the state to monitor and influence their investment decisions. Public power would be further reinforced through large-scale public enterprise initiated by a National Enterprise Board with wide-scale powers and funds.

It may seem curious that corporatism should be associated with the *left*, since it is a policy which is ultimately to do with maintaining the capitalist system at a time of acute class conflict. This paradox can be explained in two ways. In the first place, even the left wing of the Labour Party has an outlook which is reformist rather than revolutionary. The state is seen as neutral, so that extensions to the role of the state under a social democratic government are seen as unambiguously progressive.

In the second place, corporatism itself is a contradictory phenomenon. Almost all academic analysts agree that it is ultimately to do with the question of maintaining class rule — yet it is a strategy with immense dangers for the capitalist class and both potential gains or losses for the working class. Corporatism takes state intervention to its ultimate limit under capitalism, politicizing all areas of social life, and thus opening up the danger of escalating social conflict. This is the danger that the monetarists already see in 'overgovernment': under a more developed corporate state the situation would be far more acute. At the same time, workers may be able to extract many more concessions from the state than they can at present. If the relationship between the state and the unions is one of bargaining, then unions will generally demand some form of *quid pro quo* for any concessions that are made. This kind of thing was seen in the mid 1970s when the Labour government attempted to operate a voluntary incomes policy by agreeing a 'social contract' with the unions: in return for TUC promises of wage restraint, various concessions on social and economic policy were made.

These aspects tend to make corporatist structures unstable: if the unions are to be coopted, concessions have to be made which may harm capital. But if such concessions are not made, then the central trade-union organizations will be unable to police their members and maintain a stable incomes policy. The long-term tendency will then be for societies to become more authoritarian and repressive in style.

British capital is not yet ready for a more developed corporatist approach: the *Economist*, a thoughtful but outspoken advocate of the interests of capital, argued in April 1979 that a government under Margaret Thatcher presented tremendous risks. These risks were that her government's inflexible policies, and her own rather insensitive political style would push the working class to the left leading to the return of a left-wing Labour government in 1984. Nevertheless, Thatcher was given qualified approval on the grounds that the Labour Party was simply ineffective: its policies were a form of watered-down Conservatism, but it lacked the ability actually to confront the trade unions. The only real alternative was presented by Benn: corporatism in a left-wing mould. This was rejected because it entailed a move away from private enterprise. Hence:

> The *Economist* votes for Mrs Thatcher being given her chance. And what shall we be recommending in 1984? We shall endorse Mrs Thatcher for that vital second term only if she has proved she can govern a whole country . . .
>
> (*Economist*, 28 April 1979, p. 17).

The key question for the next few years is precisely whether

Thatcher can move towards monetarist policies in this 'sensitive and flexible way'. If she fails, and assuming an election in 1984, a Labour Government will be elected in which the left wing has a far stronger position. The corporatist path will be resumed. Such a government would massively increase public expenditure, particularly in the area of social investment, to regenerate accumulation. It would also be under strong pressure — pressure it would find hard to resist — to increase social consumption expenditure — i.e. to rebuild and restore the social services. This role of 'sharing out' the national income between capital and labour, investment and consumption, would be riven with conflict. Neither corporatism nor monetarism offers a way out of the crisis.

## Socialist transformation

Events over the past decade have moved Keynesians more towards the traditional preoccupations of marxists: with capitalism as a system of *production*.

Capitalism involves a system of production for profit, involving the accumulation of more and more capital as a basis for expansion of output. A crisis of capitalism is essentially an interruption in this process of accumulation, leading to stagnating output and employment — in other words, a slump such as the world experienced in the 1930s. Why should such interruptions occur? Since profit is the motive force of capitalism, the key to understanding the ills of capitalism is the rate of profit. If the rate of profit is too low capitalists will not invest, and numerous economists have devoted attention to demonstrating empirically that just such a profits squeeze has occurred in Britain. (See especially Glyn and Sutcliffe, 1972.)

Explanations for this phenomenon vary, however. Essentially, low profit rates are explained by either a low rate of exploitation of labour power or problems in the sphere of exchange, such that potential profits cannot be realized because goods are unsaleable. These are not two separate types of crisis-inducing phenomena: capitalist expansion of production has been based on two inter-linked processes — the creation of new markets through the penetration of capitalist relations into every corner of the world, and constant innovation whereby new technologies are developed to raise labour productivity.

Nevertheless, economists disagree as to where to locate the key contradiction of capitalist production: some accept Marx's controversial dictum of an inevitable tendency for profits to decline in the long term, because the substitution of machines for living workers in the labour process lowers the rate at which surplus value is produced. This emphasis on productivity means that less or no emphasis is given to wage claims as a cause of inflation. This contrasts with those who argue that class conflict has led to workers seizing a greater share of what is produced than is compatible with high profit rates. This approach does not necessarily mean that workers are to be *blamed* for the crisis since they are a part of a system which is inevitably riddled with class conflict. Others take an 'under-consumptionist' approach, arguing that the key problem lies in the sphere of the realization of profits, because capitalist production leads to the over-supply of goods in relation to available demand. This is exacerbated in the present era of monopoly capitalism since the giant corporations have to plan their huge technology investment programmes for long periods ahead, and the securing of adequate markets becomes a more risky business in circumstances where mistakes cost more. Such problems are intensified for the mature capitalist countries by the development of new economies: Japan and South Korea for example.

The debate gets exceedingly complicated and confusing. We would suggest (tentatively) the following approach. The development of new industrial powers has intensified international competition, creating barriers to growth for individual states, especially for the older, less dynamic economies such as Britain. This means that capitalists are reluctant to invest, unless they can be sure of a very high rate of exploitation — meaning low wages and high unemployment. The strength of the labour movement in Britain means that this is not possible without a decisive weakening of the trade unions. There is thus a tendency towards a slump in output and employment which the state attempts to avert by expanding demand via fiscal and monetary policies. This causes inflation — and because it means employment levels can be maintained, reinforces union strength. Inflation leads trade unions to demand wage increases to maintain their living standards. Thus far we have discussed the crisis without mentioning the growth of state expenditure. As was suggested in chapter 6, this cannot be regarded as a *cause* of the crisis, but its expansion, in the context of tendencies to slump-flation, has certainly made the situation worse.

Turning to the remedies proposed in the previous sub-sections, we can see that the monetarist 'solution' simply represents the abandonment of policies which have cushioned us from the underlying tendencies towards a slump. If Thatcher, Joseph *et al.*, enforce monetarist policies in their full rigour — strict control of the money supply, cuts in overall public expenditure, non-intervention *vis-à-vis* 'lame duck' firms, and a severe cut in or withdrawal of subsidies to nationalized industries — we shall see widespread bankruptcies, and a massive increase in unemployment. The monetarist dream, that a revitalized, free-enterprise economy will rise like a phoenix from the ashes is hardly credible in an era of giant monopolies and fierce international competition, whilst the consequences in terms of human misery and social unrest are incalculable.

Monetarist policies will hurt not only the working class, but many capitalists as well. It is perhaps not surprising then that many commentators believed in the mid 1960s that Labour was the party which was best equipped to hold the present system of welfare capitalism together. Gamble and Walton, writing in the mid 1970s argued:

> It is apparent that the Conservatives suffer from a growing isolation, whilst Labour commands a greater degree of acceptance in the political establishment than at any previous time . . .
>
> (Gamble and Walton, 1976, p. 197).

The Labour Party is unable, however, to inflict the kind of reversal on the trade-union movement which is required if profitability is to be maintained. The capitalist class is caught in a trap: there is an inescapable conflict between policies required to restore accumulation and the requirement that the government rules by consent. The alternatives under capitalism are continuing economic stagnation, or the sacrifice of liberal democracy to the restoration of profitability. Only the transformation of society to a planned economy geared to the satisfaction of need can overcome this Hobson's choice.

### A note on new technology

So far we have discussed economic policy without reference to the momentous pace of technological change, and in particular the likely effects of the widespread introduction of microprocessors. These tiny silicon chips can be used in two ways: to create new products, and to revolutionize production processes — through the displacement of human labour by machines, and by simplifying technology so that less complex labour processes using fewer workers result. The likely effects on unemployment are disputed: will profits rise and new products be created so that new investment can create jobs to replace those lost? Or will there be a massive increase in unemployment?

There seems every reason to adopt a pessimistic approach: whilst microprocessors create some new products, these often replace existing ones, and it seems unlikely that markets will expand sufficiently to generate investment to replace lost jobs. If long-term unemployment increases, inequalities will widen. Returning to our three strategies, any market solution will essentially leave the distribution of income where it falls, the main role of the state being simply paying out the dole, with some attempts at retraining unemployed workers to get a better fit between the labour supply and employment. This is a further reason to expect fully-fledged monetarist policies to provoke a massive upheaval. If a strategy of planning agreements were introduced, the state would be able to mitigate some of the effects of the introduction of microprocessors, but ultimately it would have to go along with the plans put forward by the monopolies. Whilst in a planned economy the state would have greater control over the rate of technological change and could introduce measures such as work-sharing to avoid a polarization between workers and non-workers, the constraint of competition with the international capitalist economies would remain.

## Monetarism vs welfare: the Tory welfare state

In the first part of this chapter we spelled out what monetarism or more broadly a 'social market economy' implies for the welfare state: an overall cutback in social expenditure achieved through the introduction of charges, hiving off parts of services to the private sector, and reduced public support for the dependent population. In this part we shall examine what changes the new Conservative government, elected in May 1979, has announced or already made to the welfare state along these lines. We are inevitably faced with the problem that the situation is changing daily. Nevertheless, whether or not the Tories stick to a monetarist approach our review of their first year in office should form a useful case study of the problems inherent in such a course. We shall begin by looking at monetary and expenditure policies, before looking at the major social services: housing, health, personal social services, social security and education.

### Monetary policy and the cuts

Earlier in this chapter we referred to 'market' and 'non-market' approaches to solving Britain's economic crisis. The need for cuts in public expenditure is accepted by all those who adopt a market approach. This is most obviously apparent in the policies of the Conservative Party, but the Labour leadership in the government of 1974 to 1979, unable to make a clear choice between the radical corporatist approach of the Bennite left of the party, or the market approach to economic policy demanded by, among others, the International Monetary Fund, moved indecisively from an initial increase in public expenditure, to a massive retrenchment between 1976 and 1978. Nevertheless, these cuts — $2\frac{1}{2}$ per cent in 1976–77 and another 6 per cent in 1977–8 — were seen by Labour as an unpalatable necessity at a time of economic crisis. Expenditure rose again in 1978–79 and from 1979, a modest increase of 2 per cent per year until 1982–83 was planned.

The economic and political views of the Conservative Party — a firmly market-oriented approach to economic growth, underpinned by monetarism and a belief in tax cuts and a rolling back of the role of the state — lead us to expect a far more stringent and consistent attack on public expenditure during the coming years.

In their first year in office, the Conservatives have introduced two budgets. The first, in June 1979, announced net cuts of £1,618 million, which financed a net cut in taxation and slight reduction in the PSBR. Many of these cuts were aimed at Labour's planned increases in public expenditure. They were intended to produce a stabilization of overall expenditure in 1980–81, rather than an absolute reduction. This led to charges of 'phoney monetarism' and demands for 'real cuts' from many Conservative MPs, and in March 1980 a second budget and White Paper announced further cuts of £900 million for 1980–81, leading to an absolute reduction in overall expenditure in that year, and in later years until 1984 (see HMSO, 1980, Cmnd 7841).

Within these overall cuts, a considerable redistribution of expenditure is occurring. In particular while spending on defence and law and order is surging ahead, education is being cut and the latest plans for housing show expenditure being slashed by nearly half by 1984, a truly staggering cut. Health and social security are generally enjoying slight increases, although, in the case of social security rising needs means that the value of benefits in particular unemployment benefit, is not being maintained, whilst rigid adherence to cash limits below the level of inflation mean that in services such as health and personal social services, nominally enjoying an increase in provision, old people's homes will continue to be closed, facilities for the disabled cut, and hospital waiting lists will grow whilst wards remain closed.

Apart from effects on the consumers of the social services, the cuts also affect the producers, both labour and capital. Labour is affected by any cuts in jobs. In 1979–80, wages and salaries accounted for 30 per cent of overall public expenditure and 70 per cent of local-authority expenditure: any significant reduction in overall expenditure cannot but affect staffing levels. Capital, on the other hand, is affected by reductions in the purchase of goods and services from the private sector and public investment in areas such as roads and house building, where reliance is placed almost exclusively on private contractors. During the cuts of the mid 1970s, it may be argued that capital suffered more than labour in the public sector: expenditure on wages and salaries rose by only half a per cent from 1975–76 to 1977–78, but public investment fell by 24 per cent. Whilst capital investment, especially house building, is projected to fall even further during the period to 1984, the government is now also launching an attack on staffing levels. The future of the government's expenditure policies depends crucially not only on the reactions of the social-service users such as parents, and tenants, but also on the ability of the trade unions in the public sector and construction to defend their jobs.

### Restructuring the welfare state

> more pruning of public expenditure isn't good enough, the trees always grow again. Difficult policy decisions to cut out completely (or charge for) existing areas of government activity must be made (Conservative MP Terence Higgins, *Guardian*, 14 January 1980).

The theme of restructuring, as opposed simply to cutting, the welfare state is now a familiar one in social-policy literature. Gough (1979) alludes to two aspects to which we have already referred — the quest for managerial efficiency in the social services, and the shift in emphasis to policies aimed at controlling and incorporating those at the margin of the economy. In addition he suggests that moves are being made to adapt policies, in for example education and social security, more closely to the needs of capital, and to reprivatize areas of welfare provision.

In this section we shall consider this theme of restructuring from a slightly different perspective. The question we are posing is whether Conservative policies represent a real departure from the hitherto accepted parameters of what the state is expected to do to promote the welfare of citizens. Implicit in Higgins's remarks quoted at the outset of this section is the view that such a shift is necessary if a consistent, long-term reduction in public expenditure is to be achieved. Is this what the Thatcher government is attempting and can such an approach succeed?

We saw earlier how the more perceptive supporters of a monetarist approach realize that it is not enough simply to talk of cutting expenditure: it is also necessary to get to the root of the problem, namely the inevitable susceptibility of governments in a democratic system to political pressure for increased expenditure. Economic policy is ultimately a question of politics: expectations are firmly entrenched that state social services will cushion people from the impact of ill health, and unemployment, and provide opportunities for access to decent education and housing. Can these expectations be undermined sufficiently to enable a monetarist strategy to succeed?

Two elements are important in this task. First the Thatcher government is aided by its ability to tap sources of resentment to the welfare state through attacks on 'abuse' of the social services, and appeals to conservative values of individual and family rather than collective responsibility for meeting needs. Secondly, however, the government has to do more than direct the spotlight on 'welfare scroungers': it has to reassert the primacy of market principles of distribution in areas where they have given way to the notion of state-provided services distributed free at the point of consumption. This involves the kind of major changes to the social services suggested by Higgins: requiring people to pay more for state services not only to raise revenue, but to stress their individual responsibility for meeting their needs and remove the relatively easy access enjoyed in a free service; and reprivatizing areas of provision, a means of simultaneously benefitting capital, and enforcing individual choice and responsibility exercised through the market place, as opposed to collective choice and responsibility exercised through the political process.

In the remainder of this section we shall consider how far Conservative policies represent a radical shift back towards the market, as opposed simply to an intensification of existing trends noted by Gough, towards adapting social policy more to the needs of capital.

Looking at the significance of Conservative plans for the social services, three things stand out. First, the private sector of welfare had already grown considerably before 1979, such that in some areas, it has little scope for further expansion. Secondly, where major changes in the private/public sector balance are being proposed, as in housing, it is in areas where state responsibility for meeting needs was *already* ambivalent. Finally, in areas where the public sector holds, with public approval, a virtual monopoly of provision, the political obstacles to producing any major change are revealed by the vagueness of government proposals.

The two largest areas of private welfare provision are in the area of social security (retirement pensions) and housing. Looking first at social security, more than eleven million workers are members of occupational pension schemes (Government Actuary, 1978). Such private insurance arrangements were given explicit recognition as an alternative to a state earnings-related pension under the 1973 Social Security Act, passed by the Conservative government led by Heath. Whilst this scheme was modified by Labour's 1975 Social Security Pensions Act, the basic concept of a 'partnership' between the state and the private sector was retained — the pension funds were reasonably happy with the 1975 Act, and the Conservative Party, then in opposition, promised that any future government would leave it intact, (see Kincaid, 1978). There has been no suggestion that other insurance benefits could be provided by private enterprise, and there seems little scope for further expansion of the private sector in the area of social security. Conservative policy in this area is primarily concerned to intensify an existing trend towards adapting policies to the needs of the labour market by keeping the value of benefits for potential labour-market participants low relative to those for other groups. Thus in 1978, under a Labour government, the supplementary-benefit scale rate for a single pensioner was 28 per cent higher than for an unemployed person. Similar discrepancies existed between unemployment insurance and retirement pensions. Under the Conservatives, the gap is widening, a process accelerated by the decision announced in the March 1980 budget to up-rate some benefits such as unemployment and sickness insurance by less than the rise in the retail price index, whilst maintaining the value of the retirement pension. Finally, the decision to abolish the six months earnings-related supplement to unemployment and sickness benefits, apart from lowering the standard of living of unemployed workers, pushes more into the supplementary-benefits system, where the enforcement of work incentives is much more vigorous.

In the area of housing, the picture is slightly different, and Conservative proposals, in particular the sale of council houses, represent a more radical departure from existing policies. Housing, however, has always occupied a rather uneasy position straddling the private and public sectors. Until the 1960s there seemed to be two clear policy approaches, with the Conservatives advocating home ownership for the majority and a residual public housing sector for the poor, and the Labour Party espousing a social democratic approach of mixed communities within the public sector. More recently, however, the Labour Party has abandoned this approach and accepted home ownership as the preferred form of tenure. It has also moved away from the idea of a public-sector monopoly of rented housing: the 1974 Housing Act gave considerable impetus to housing associations, a 'third arm' which spans a spectrum from provision which is indistinguishable from that of the private landlord, to that which meets needs which many local authorities regard as too contentious to deal with. What the Conservatives are doing is to take this trend towards greater private provision qualitatively further by selling off the public-sector housing stock. Whilst sales of council houses were not unknown under Labour governments, they were the result of local decisions. Certain mainly Conservative-controlled authorities took advantage of the considerable local autonomy allowed in this area to pursue vigorous sales policies, a situation which caused some concern to the government, and led to the announcement of some national restrictions in Spring 1979. Under the Conservatives' housing legislation tenants of three years standing have the right to buy their houses at a discount of a third off market price, rising to a half for those with longer periods of residence. At the same time, public-sector building programmes are being slashed, and a new subsidy system will effectively force authorities to raise rents for remaining tenants.

Our criteria for judging policy changes set out at the beginning of this section was whether, in the long term, they reduced pressure on governments to increase public expenditure. The new proposals for council-house finance may have this effect insofar as those people who can choose between renting and buying a house are more likely to buy if rent levels are escalating. The crucial question, however, is whether Conservative policies will enable people on average or below incomes to find housing outside the public sector. The sale of council houses may win votes, but it is irrelevant to this problem. The only proposals to address themselves to the issue of expanding an alternative supply of housing, namely the provisions allowing temporary 'shorthold' lettings in the private rented sector, are more likely to create fear and insecurity among tenants than new opportunities for those without homes. The new government is creating the conditions for a housing crisis — precisely what they did at the end of the 1950s, with disastrous results for them in the 1964 elections.

The NHS is widely seen as one of the most popular among the social services, a factor which sets political limits to changes that can be made to its characteristic as a public social service, covering a wide range of health services, mainly free at the point of consumption. At the same time it is an area where there is particular concern about the pressure of demand in relation to resources: both actual demand, but also, given medical advance and the existence of much untreated illness, potential demand.

These factors have led to the NHS being somewhat cushioned from the cuts. Expenditure is to be allowed to grow slightly over the next few years, although the inadequate allowance for inflation in present cash limits means that there will nevertheless be cuts in provision. At the same time, charges for prescriptions and dental treatment are being increased.

The whole issue of charging is confused by a fundamental problem as to its aims: is it simply a means of raising revenue or is it also intended to deter people from using the service thus reducing expenditure? The government clearly believes that there is an association between the method of financing the service and the demands that people make. Speaking in Parliament on the subject of the NHS the Social Services Secretary argued that:

> Our people have been encouraged by successive generations of politicians to believe that they are always entitled, as of right, to have their every health expectation promptly and expertly satisfied. I believe that that is a sheer impossibility
>
> *(Hansard*, 23 January 1980).

He went on to argue that in view of the pressure on resources, the government was setting up an investigation into health-services finance, with a view to increasing the insurance element.

Again, it is hard to see how this will relieve the pressures the government is experiencing. If a move towards insurance means no more than that the NHS is financed by a specific, ear-marked tax, then the essential features of the NHS will be retained, and it is unlikely that pressure for resources will abate. If however, a proper *insurance* scheme is introduced, then there will have to be limits set to the state's liability under the scheme to meet health bills and some part of the population will be excluded because they have not made contributions. The inevitable corollary is some form of two-tiered service —

for the insured and the non-insured — and a requirement that individuals above certain income levels top up their health bills out of their own pocket. This would represent a move towards the kind of health system operating in the United States — precisely at a time when the international trend is more towards the kind of system enjoyed in Britain. Politically, it seems highly unlikely that this central plank of the welfare state could be abandoned in this way: talk of insurance remains vague and rhetorical.

The final area of major social expenditure is education. Changes are being introduced which bear the clear imprint of Conservative philosophy, in particular the repeal of legislation requiring local authorities to end selection and reorganize secondary schools on comprehensive lives, and the introduction of a scheme to pay private-school fees for a small number of children selected on the basis of academic tests. Such proposals help legitimate both unequal schooling and inequalities in the job market. But once again, it is hard to see how they fit into a strategy of root and branch reform aimed at reducing pressure for public expenditure.

In conclusion, what the Conservatives are trying to achieve is an increase in the share of national output accruing to capital relative to labour. Any government which attempts to rely on market incentives as the primary means of securing economic growth is likely to pursue such a strategy in some form or other. What is peculiar about monetarism is the severity of the attack on workers' living standards which it implies. Whilst the capitalist world generally is experiencing a recession, Thatcher's policies of sharply reduced state intervention and strict monetary control add domestic fuel to this international trend. Treasury forecasts are for a fall in GDP, of around $2\frac{1}{2}$ per cent in 1980, lasting into 1981, followed by a very slow rate of growth of around 1 per cent a year until 1983. Thus labour is to receive a reduced share of a smaller cake, and both private consumption and social consumption must be held back. This can only happen within the Tories' timetable if the labour movement experiences a major defeat, both in the area of trade-union rights, and the citizenship rights of access to social services. Our review of social policy suggests that, despite the mutilation of certain social services, particularly housing, the basic structure of most will remain impoverished but intact. It is factors such as these which make the future of Conservative policies, in particular whether monetarism will be retained or modified, very uncertain at the time of writing. Nevertheless whether or not the Conservatives perform a U-turn on issues such as incomes policy, the prospects for the welfare state become hardly brighter. Is there a strategy within which it can be defended?

## The future of the welfare state

We have already argued that neither monetarism nor traditional social democracy is capable of defending the welfare state. In the present context of capitalist crisis any strategy for defending and extending the social services which is not part and parcel of developing and organizing around a programme for socialism will find it difficult to make headway. Similarly, a socialist policy to defend the welfare state must also show how its bureaucratic and repressive aspects can be transcended. Only in this way can the interests and struggles of both the producers and the consumers of the social services be united.

At present no agreement exists as to an appropriate socialist programme or method of organizing. The left wing of the Labour Party supports the alternative economic strategy (AES) of selective nationalization, increased public investment and import and price controls; whilst the far-left groups attempt to build disciplined Leninist organizations around a revolutionary programme. More recently, the authors of *Beyond the Fragments* (Rowbotham, Segal and Wainwright, 1979) have suggested a third alternative — a non-parliamentary strategy based on a loose association between different types of organization involved in class struggle.

All the strategies involve immense problems. The attraction of the AES is that it gives workers a credible set of alternative policies to fight for. Its weakness is that whilst in theory it has the potential of being a stepping stone towards a policy of socialist transformation, the practice of the left of the Labour Party is reformist, and no attempt is made to mobilize the working class outside parliament. In addition the emphasis on production in the demands of the AES leaves little scope for linking together struggles around production and reproduction. Apart from restoring cuts, the AES has little to say about the welfare state.

The far left, on the other hand, has a better grasp of the role of extraparliamentary class struggle, and a more realistic appraisal of the forces opposed to socialism and the limitations of any national strategy for change. However, in overstressing the role of reformist leaders in holding back the working class, it underestimates the structural reasons why workers fail to challenge capitalism. The isolation of left groups thereby reinforces a tendency to produce advanced slogans which fail to relate to workers' existing consciousness.

The arguments of Rowbotham *et al.* seem to offer a fruitful way of building a much broader based anti-capitalist coalition, linking the demands of workers, community activists, clients of the social services and other oppressed groups, and rooting the movement firmly in their actual struggles. Nevertheless their ideas are at a very embryonic stage.

In conclusion, whilst the absence of clear perspectives in the face of the present onslaught on the welfare state is disheartening, the positive feature of the present period is that the left as a whole is beginning a long and sometimes painful process of reappraisal. It began in the 1960s in response to the anti-imperialist struggles of the Third World. It continues today, in the face of the limits of both left reformism and revolutionary isolationism.

# Postscript

In this book we have tried to draw out the ways in which capitalism sets systematic limits to the development of the welfare state.

In the present period of crisis, these limits are even more apparent, and in chapter 9 we have argued that defence of the welfare state requires its transformation in the context of a programme of fundamental social change towards socialism. A sceptical reader may challenge this conclusion — after all the word 'socialism' has been used to describe a variety of social systems from capitalist welfare states to the command economies of the USSR and Eastern Europe. Talk of a 'transition to socialism' is simply hot air. We have argued, implicitly or explicitly, that neither of these two systems should be regarded as socialist — the first represents a particular form of capitalism, whilst the post-revolutionary command economy experiences new contradictions, different from but no less acute than those of capitalism. In this postscript we shall attempt to give some sense to a concept of a socialist society, which can avoid the contradictions of both capitalism and the command economies. The hotly contested issue of why the democratic ideals of the *Communist Manifesto* have failed to find expression in today's post-revolutionary societies, lies beyond the scope of this book.

In chapters 6 and 7 we discussed how the basic features of capitalist production necessarily set limits on the area of democratic decision making. In particular, capitalism involves private ownership/control of the means of production, the division of capital into separate, competing units and production of commodities for sale on the market rather than to meet needs. Within such a system, the state has to leave crucial areas of decision making to private economic agents, or risk being blamed for jeopardizing economic growth. Socialism on the other hand involves common ownership/control of the means of production. The first stage of common ownership involves the centralization of economic power in the hands of the state, although Marx believed that under the highest stage of social development, communism, the state itself would become an anachronism.

The fusion of state and economy under socialism lays the basis for extending the area of democratic decision making relative to the liberal democracies of capitalist society. Factory managers are no longer merely private economic agents, able to dispose of means of production and labour power at will. They use their technical, economic knowledge, to implement collectively decided priorities, rather than in the pursuit of profit for a particular group. The main limitation on the sphere of potential democracy in an economically developed country becomes not the role of national capital, but the constraints arising from participation in the international market. It is this factor which led the marxists before Stalin to argue that, whilst the process of socialist construction could *begin* in any single country, it could only be completed on a world scale.

Socialism can only resolve the contradictions of state intervention in capitalist economies if the two principles of economic planning and political democracy can be made compatible. This demands a process whereby the political steering of the economy is achieved in a way that is consistent with the values that guide the democratic expression of interests. We have seen how the crisis-ridden progress of a capitalist economy and the struggle of class-interest in directing intervention, force the capitalist state to walk a tightrope while it is suffering from hiccoughs. Socialism can only be achieved when the anarchy of the market is supplanted by state control of the economy. At the same time a democratic set-up is required in which a collective recognition of interests, without irresolvable conflict, is possible.

How can this be achieved? Any answer to this presupposes a conception of a society in which peoples' individualism, and interest-group conceptions of interest, are supplanted. In short it demands a society without ideology, both in the sense of the material production of misleading and partial ideas about existing society that we have argued is an essential feature of capitalism, and in the sense of the attempt by dominant groups to impose a conception of society that is in their interest. In theory, a planned economy can eliminate the first. How far is it possible to eliminate the danger of the second? It would be naive to suggest that the power of influential bureaucracies is not a major feature of contemporary post-revolutionary societies, and that it stands in the way of any truly democratic decision making. Here we can only give an answer in terms of an abstract conception of the goal of desirable social arrangements: the process whereby these are to be achieved (if at all) we cannot specify. To do so would be to construct a sterile determinism which prejudges the future as if it were history.

We would suggest that the hallmark of socialism is an order in which peoples' conception of society is based on a viewpoint which transcends narrow self-interest, and conceives society as a totality. This would dissolve the self-interest of the market, and the need for personal control over resources to achieve personal ends. Marx argues, in the *Critique of the Gotha Programme*, that this can only be achieved in an economy of abundance, where the sum of social production exceeded the demands made on it (1972b, p. 17). Because capitalism has unleashed the productive forces of social labour, and at the same time sets in train a process which will culminate in the collective use of those forces, many socialists would argue that the viewpoint of totality stands at the end of the present epoch of history. We are not sure. We regard it as the ideal immanent in present social forms, the criterion by which they are to be judged and found wanting.

If humanity has an interest, that interest is in control over the use of, and access to, things that people need. People can only be described as free when social arrangements make it possible for their needs to be met. Our society makes it impossible for this to be achieved, because it is founded on quite other principles. At the same time its contradictions both demand progress, and place barriers in the narrowing down of peoples' conception of interest to a personal compass, and the denial of a viewpoint of totality. Personal interest always involves the risk of conflict. The ideal conception of communism suggests a vision of freedom. We do not know if this is possible. We do know that the notion of socialism as democracy plus a planned economy, represents a possibility of the realization of greater freedom than the welfare state. The rest is history.

# References

Abel-Smith, B. and Townsend, P. 1965: *The Poor and the Poorest*. London: Bell.

Abrams, M. 1973: 'Subjective Social Indicators'. *Social Trends*, CSO.

Anderson, P. 1965: 'Origins of the Present Crisis'. In Anderson P. (ed), *Towards Socialism*. London: Fontana.

Arden, Andrew 1979: 'High Court Guerillas'. *Roof* **4**(4).

Arrow, K. 1971: 'Gifts and Exchanges'. *Philosophy and Public Affairs* **1**(4).

Atkinson, A.B. 1974: *Unequal Shares* (Revised Edition). Harmondsworth: Penguin.

Bachrach, P. and Baratz, M. 1970: *Power and Poverty*. New York: Oxford University Press.

Bacon, R. and Eltis, W. 1978: *Britain's Economic Problems*. London: Macmillan.

Baker, J. 1979: 'Social Conscience and Social Policy'. *Journal of Social Policy* **8**(2).

Barker, D. 1972: 'Negative Income Tax'. In Bull, D. (ed) *Family Poverty* (second edition). London: Duckworth.

Batley Community Project 1974: *Batley at Work*. Batley: CDP.

Beechey, V. 1977: 'Some Notes on Female Wage Labour in Capitalist Production'. *Capital and Class* (Autumn).

Beer, M. 1953: *A History of British Socialism* (2 vols.). London: Allen & Unwin.

Bennington, J. 1976: *Local Government Becomes Big Business*. London: Community Development Project Information and Intelligence Unit.

Berger, P. and Luckman, T. 1971: *The Social Construction of Reality*. Harmondsworth: Penguin.

Beveridge, W. 1942: *Social Insurance and Allied Services*. London: HMSO, Cmnd. 6404.

Beveridge, W. 1944: *Full Employment in a Free Society*. London: Allen & Unwin.

Blackburn, R. (ed) 1972: *Ideology in Social Science*. Harmondsworth: Penguin.

Block N. and Dworkin, G. 1974: 'IQ, Heritability and Inequality, Parts I and II'. *Philosophy and Public Affairs* **4**(1).

Blowers A. and Thompson, P. 1976: *Inequalities, Change and Conflict*. Milton Keynes: Open University Press.

Boulding, K. 1967: 'The Boundaries of Social Policy'. Reprinted in Birrell, W., Hillyard, P., Murie, A. and Roche, D. 1973, *Social Administration*. Harmondsworth: Penguin.

Boyson, R. 1971: *Down with the Poor*. London: Churchill Press.

Bradshaw, J. 1972: 'The Concept of Social Need'. *New Society* (30 March).

Braverman, H. 1977: *Labour and Monopoly Capital*. New York: Monthly Review Press.

Brown, M. 1976: *Introduction to Social Administration in Britain*. London: Hutchinson.

Breton, A. 1974: *The Economic Theory of Representative Government*. London: Macmillan.

Brittan, S. 1975: 'The Economic Consequences of Democracy'. *British Journal of Political Science* **5**(2).

Brittan, S. 1978: 'Inflation and Democracy'. In Hirsch, F. and Goldthorpe, J.H., *The Political Economy of Inflation*. London: Martin Robertson.

Butterworth, E. and Holman, R. (eds) 1975: *Social Welfare in Modern Britain*. London: Fontana.

Byrne, D. and Williamson, W. 1972: 'Inter-Regional Variations in Educational Provision'. *Sociology* **6**(1).

Carrier, J. and Kendal, I. 1973: 'Social Change and Social Policy'. *Journal of Social Policy* **2**(3).

Carrier, J. and Kendal, I. 1977: 'The Development of Welfare States'. *Journal of Social Policy* **6**(3).

Castells, M. 1977: *The Urban Question*. London: Edward Arnold.

Coates, K. and Silburn, R. 1970: *Poverty: The Forgotten Englishmen*. Harmondsworth: Penguin.

Cockburn, C. 1977: *The Local State*. London: Pluto Press.

Collard, D. 1968: *The New Right*. London: Fabian Society.

Conference of Socialist Economists 1977: *On the Political Economy of Women*. London: CSE.

Conference of Socialist Economists State Apparatus and Expenditure Group 1979: *Struggle over the State*. London: CSE.

Connerton, P. (ed) 1976: *Critical Sociology*. Harmondsworth: Penguin.

Corrigan, P. and Leonard, P. 1978: *Social Work Practice Under Capitalism*. London: Macmillan.

Counter Information Service 1976: *Your Money and Your Life*. London: CIS.

Coventry Community Development Project 1975: *Final Report* (vols. I and II). Coventry: CDP.

Crosland, R. 1953: *Britain's Economic Problem*. London: Jonathan Cape.

Crosland, R. 1964: *The Future of Socialism*. London: Jonathan Cape.

Crosland, R. 1974: *Socialism Now*. London: Jonathan Cape.

Crossman, R.H. 1972: *A Politician's View of Health Service Planning*. Glasgow: University of Glasgow Press.

Crossman, R.H. 1975: *The Diaries of a Cabinet Minister Vol. I Minister of Housing 1964–66*. London: Hamish Hamilton/Jonathan Cape.

Crouch, C. 1979: 'The State Capital and Liberal Democracy'. In Crouch, C. (ed), *State and Economy in Contemporary Capitalism*. London: Croom-Helm.

Culyer, A. 1973: *The Economics of Social Policy*. London: Martin Robertson.

Culyer, A. (ed) 1974: *Economic Policies and Social Goals*. London: Martin Robertson.

Culyer, A. 1976: *Need and the National Health Service*. London: Martin Robertson.

Dale, J. 1980: 'Class Struggle, Social Policy and State Structure: Central-Local Relations and Housing 1919–1939'. In Melling, J. (ed), *Housing, Social Policy and the State*. London: Croom-Helm.

Davis, K. and Moore, W. 1967: 'Some Principles of Stratification'. In Bendix, R. and Lipset, S. (eds), *Class, Status and Power*. London: Routledge & Kegan Paul.

Department of Health and Social Security 1978: *Social Assistance*. London: HMSO.

Department of Health and Social Security/Islington Borough Personnel Department 1978: *Liaison between Local Offices and Social Services*. Mimeo.

Deutscher, A. 1964: *The Age of Permanent Revolution*. New York: Dell.

Devine, P. 1974: 'Inflation and Marxist Theory'. *Marxism Today* (March).

Dilthey, W. 1976: *The Rise of Hermeneutics*. In Connerton (ed) 1976.

Donnison, D. 1967: *The Government of Housing*. Harmondsworth: Penguin.

Donnison, D. 1979: 'Social Welfare after Titmuss'. *Journal of Social Policy* 8(2).

Donnison, D. *et al.* 1965: *Social Policy and Administration* (first edition). London: Allen & Unwin.

Donnison, D. *et al.* 1975: *Social Policy and Administration Revisited* (revised edition). London: Allen & Unwin.

Donnison, D. 1976: 'Liberty, Equality and Fraternity'. In Timms, N. and Watson, D. (eds) 1976, *Talking about Welfare*. London: Routledge & Kegan Paul.

Doyal, L. 1979: *The Political Economy of Health*. London: Pluto Press.

*Economic Trends*. Monthly, London: HMSO.

Emmet, D. 1966: *Rules, Roles and Relations*. London: Macmillan.

Field, F. *et al.* 1977: *To Him Who Hath*. Harmondsworth: Penguin.

Finer S. 1952: *The Life and Times of Sir Edwin Chadwick*. London: Methuen.

Fogarty, M. 1976: *Pensions, Where Next*. London: Centre for Studies in Social Policy.

Forder, A. 1974: *Concepts in Social Administration*. London: Routledge & Kegan Paul.

Foster, P. 1979: 'The Informal Rationing of Primary Medical Care'. *Journal of Social Policy* 8(4).

Fox, R. *et al.* 1973: 'Body Temperatures in the Elderly'. *British Medical Journal* 1(5847).

Freire, P. 1976: *Education*. London: Writers' and Readers' Publishing Cooperative.

Friedman, M. 1962: *Capitalism and Freedom*. Chicago: Chicago University

Press.

Fromm, E. 1963: *The Sane Society*. London: Routledge & Kegan Paul.

Galbraith, J. 1969: *The New Industrial State*. London: Hamish Hamilton.

Galbraith, J. 1973: *Economics and the Public Purpose*, Boston: Houghton Mifflin.

Galbraith, J. 1977: *The Affluent Society*. London: Hamish Hamilton.

Gallie, W. 1956: 'Essentially Contestable Concepts'. *Proceedings of the Aristotelian Society*, supp. vol. no. 48.

Gamble, A. 1980: 'Economic Policy'. In Layton Henry, Z.(ed), *Conservative Party Politics*. London: Macmillan.

Gamble, A. and Walton, P. 1976: *Capitalism in Crisis, Inflation and the State*. London: Macmillan.

Gauldie, E. 1974: *Cruel Habitations*. London: Allen & Unwin.

George, V. 1968: *Social Security and Society*. London: Routledge & Kegan Paul.

George, V. and Wilding, P. 1971: 'Social Values, Social Class and Social Policy'. *Social and Economic Administration* **6**(3).

George, V. and Wilding, P. 1976: *Ideology and Social Welfare*. London: Routledge & Kegan Paul.

Geras, N. 1972: *Marx and the Critique of Political Economy*. In Blackburn, R. (ed) 1972.

Giddens, A. (ed) 1972: *Durkheim*. Cambridge: Cambridge University Press.

Giddens, A. 1976: *New Rules of Sociological Method*. London: Hutchinson.

Ginsburg, N. 1979: *Class, Capital and Social Policy*. London: Macmillan.

Glennerster, H. 1975: *Social Service Budgets and Social Policy*. London: Allen & Unwin.

Glennerster, H. 1976: 'The Right Debate'. In Glennerster H. (ed), *Labour's Social Priorities*. London: Fabian Research Series 327.

Glennerster, H. and Pryke, R. 1965: *The Public Schools*. London: Fabian Society.

Glyn, A. and Sutcliffe, B. 1972: *British Capitalism Workers and the Profit Squeeze*. Harmondsworth: Penguin.

Goldmann, L. 1969: *The Human Sciences and Philosophy*. London: Jonathan Cape.

Goldthorpe, J. 1962: 'The Development of Social Policy in England, 1800–1914'. *Transactions of the Fifth World Congress of Sociology* vol. IV.

Gough, I. 1975: 'State Expenditure in Advanced Capitalism'. *New Left Review* **92**.

Gough, I. 1978: 'Theories of the Welfare State'. *International Journal of Health Services* **8**(1).

Gough, I. 1979: *The Political Economy of the Welfare State*. London: Macmillan.

Gould, T. and Kenyon J, 1972: *Stories from the Dole Queue*. London: Temple-Smith.

Gouldner, A. 1971: *The Coming Crisis of Western Sociology*. London: Heinemann.

Government Actuary 1972: *Occupational Pension Schemes 1971*. London: HMSO.

Government Actuary 1978: *Occupational Pension Schemes 1975*. London: HMSO.

Griffith, J.A.G. 1966: *Central Department and Local Authorities*. London: Allen & Unwin.

Habermas, J. 1965: *Inaugural Lecture at Frankfurt University*. Mimeo.

Habermas, J. 1975: *Legitimation Crisis*. Boston: Beacon Press.

Habermas, J. 1976: *Legitimation Problems in Late Capitalism*. In Connerton, P. (ed) 1976.

Habermas J. 1978: *Knowledge and Human Interests*. London: Heinemann.

Hall, P., Land, H., Parker, R., and Webb, A. 1975: *Change Choice and Conflict in Social Policy*. London: Heinemann.

Handler, J. 1968: 'The Coercive Child Care Officer'. *New Society* (3 October).

Harris, J. 1977: *William Beveridge*. Oxford: Clarendon.

Harris, R. and Seldon, A. 1979: *Over-ruled on Welfare*. London: Institute of Economic Affairs.

Harris R. and Sewill B. 1975: *British Economic Policy 1970–74 — Two Views*, London: Institute of Economic Affairs.

Hartman, H. 1979: 'The Unhappy Union between Marxism and Feminism: towards a more progressive union'. *Capital and Class* (Summer).

Hay, J. 1975: *Origins of the Liberal Welfare Reforms of 1906–14*. London: Macmillan.

Hay, J. 1978: 'Employers' Attitudes to Social Policy and the Concept of Social Control, 1900–1920'. In Thane, P. (ed), *The Origins of British Social Policy*. London: Croom-Helm.

Hay, J. 1979: *The Development of the British Welfare State, 1880–1975*. London: Edward Arnold.

Hayek, F. 1949: *Individualism and Economic Order*. London: Routledge & Kegan Paul.

Hayek, F. 1968: *The Confusion of Language in Political Thought*. London: Institute of Economic Affairs, Occasional Paper No. 20.

Hayek, F. 1972, 1976, and 1979: *Law, Legislation* and *Liberty* (3 vols.). London: Routledge & Kegan Paul.

Heisler, H. 1977: *Foundations of Social Administration*. London: Macmillan.

Herrnstein, R. 1973: *IQ in the Meritocracy*. London: Allen Lane.

Hill, M. *et al.* 1973: *Men out of Work*. Cambridge: Cambridge University Press.

Hill, M. 1974: *Policies for the Unemployed*. London: Child Poverty Action Group.

Hirsch, F. 1977: *The Social Limits to Growth*. London: Routledge & Kegan Paul.

HMSO 1980: *The Government's Expenditure Plans* (2 vols). London: HMSO

Cmnd. 6721.

Hobsbawm, E. 1964: *Labouring Men*. London: Weidenfeld & Nicolson.

Hobsbawm, E. 1969: *Industry and Empire*. London: Pelican Books.

Holland, S. 1975: *The Socialist Challenge*. London: Quartet Books.

Holloway J. and Picciotto, S. 1977: 'Capital Crisis and the State'. *Capital and Class* **2**(summer).

Holloway, J. and Picciotto, S. 1978: *State and Capital*. London: Edward Arnold.

Holman, R. 1973: 'Poverty, Welfare Rights and Social Work'. *Social Work Today* (6 September).

Holman, R. 1978: *Poverty*. London: Martin Robertson.

Home Office 1970: *CDP Objectives and Strategy* (Press Release).

Humphries, J. 1977: 'Class Struggle and the Persistence of the Working Class Family'. *Cambridge Journal of Economics* **1**(3).

Hutchinson, T. 1970: *Half a Century of Hobarts*. London: Institute of Economic Affairs.

Institute of Economic Affairs 1975: *Crisis 1975*. London: IEA.

Islington Personnel Dept/DHSS 1978: *Relationships between the Social Services Dept. and Local Offices* (SB). London: HMSO.

Jay, M. 1973: *The Dialectical Imagination*. London: Heinemann.

Jencks, C. 1973: *Inequality*. London: Allen Lane.

Jones, D. *et al.* 1974: *Community Work One*. London: Routledge & Kegan Paul.

Jones, K. *et al.* 1975: *Opening the Door*. London: Routledge & Kegan Paul.

Jones, K. *et al.* 1978: *Issues in Social Policy*. London: Routledge & Kegan Paul.

Jordan, W. 1974: *Poor Parents*. London: Routledge & Kegan Paul.

Joseph, Sir Keith 1972: Speech to Pre-school Playgroups Association, Mimeo.

Judge, K. 1978: *Rationing Social Services*. London: Heinemann.

Judge, K. 1979: Review Article, *Journal of Social Policy* **7**(3).

Kaim-Caudle, P. 1973: *Comparative Social Policy and Social Security*. London: Martin Robertson.

Kerr, C. *et al.* 1960: *Industrialism and Industrial Man*. Cambridge, Mass.: Harvard University Press.

Kincaid, J. 1975: *Poverty and Equality in Britain*. Harmondsworth: Penguin.

Kincaid, J. 1978: 'The Politics of Pensions'. *New Society* (16 February).

Klein, L. 1968: *The Keynesian Revolution*. London: Macmillan.

Klein, R. 1974: 'The Case for Elitism'. *Political Quarterly* **45**.

Klein, R. 1975: 'Social Policy and Public Expenditure 1975'. *Inflation and Priorities*, London: Centre for Studies in Social Policy.

Lenin, V. 1963: *Selected Works* (3 Vols). Moscow: Progress Publishers.

Leonard, P. 1976: 'The Function of Social Work in Society'. In *Timms and Watson* (eds), 1976.

Levi, M. 1979: *On the Marxist Theory of the State*. Mimeo.

Lindblom, C. 1977: *Politics and Markets*. New York: Basic Books.

Lindenfeld, F. 1973: *Radical Perspectives on Social Problems*, New York:

Macmillan.

Lipsey, D. 1979: 'The Reforms People Want'. *New Society* (4 October).

Lockhead, A. (ed) 1968: *A Reader in Social Administration*. London: Constable.

Lockwood, D. 1964: 'Social Integration and System Integration'. In Zollschan, G. and Hirsch, W. *Explorations in Social Change*. London: Routledge & Kegan Paul.

Lukacs, G. 1971: *History and Class Consciousness* (2nd edition). London: Merlin Press.

Lukes, S. 1970: 'Methodological Individualism Reconsidered'. In Emmett, D. and McIntyre, A. *Social Theory and Philosophical Analysis*. London: Macmillan.

Lukes, S. 1973: *Individualism*. Oxford: Blackwell.

Lukes, S. 1974a: *Power, A Radical View*. London: Macmillan.

Lukes, S. 1974b: 'Relativism, Cognitive and Moral'. *Proceedings of the Aristotelian Society*, supp. vol. no. 48.

Lukes, S. 1976: 'Socialism and Inequality'. In *Blowers and Thompson* (eds), 1976.

Lukes, S. 1977: *Essays in Social Theory*. London: Macmillan.

Macbriar, A. 1962: *Fabian Socialism and English Politics*. Cambridge: Cambridge University Press.

Macpherson, C. 1962: *The Political Theory of Possessive Individualism*. London: Oxford University Press.

Macpherson, C. 1968: 'Elegant Tombstones'. *Canadian Journal of Political Science* 1.

Macpherson C. 1973: *Democratic Theory*. Oxford: Clarendon Press.

Macpherson, C. 1978: *Property*. Oxford: Blackwell.

Madge, N. and Rutter, S. 1976: *Cycles of Disadvantage*. London: Heinemann.

Manchester Housing Workshop 1980: *Hulme Crescents: Council House Chaos in the 1970s*. Manchester.

Marcuse, H. 1956: *Eros and Civilization*. London: Routledge & Kegan Paul.

Marcuse, H. 1964. *One-Dimensional Man*. London: Routledge & Kegan Paul.

Marcuse, H. 1976. 'Repressive Tolerance'. In Connerton, T. (ed), 1976.

Marsden, D. and Duff, E. 1975: *Workless*. Harmondsworth: Penguin.

Marshall, T. 1963: 'Citizenship and Social Class'. In Marshall, T. *Sociology at the Crossroads*. London: Heinemann.

Marshall, T. 1977: *Social Policy*. London: Hutchinson.

Marx, K. 1964: *The Economic and Philosophic Manuscripts of 1844*. New York: International Publishers.

Marx, K. 1968: *Selected Works*. London: Lawrence & Wishart.

Marx, K. 1972a: *Capital* Vol III. London: Lawrence & Wishart.

Marx, K. 1972b: *Critique of the Potha Programme*. Peking: Peking Press.

Marx, K. 1973: *Grundrisse*. Harmondsworth: Penguin.

Marx, K. 1974: *Capital* Vol II. London: Lawrence & Wishart.

Marx, K. 1975: *Early Writings* (Coletti ed.). Harmondsworth: Penguin.

Marx, K. 1976. *Capital* Vol I. London: Penguin.

Marx, K. and Engels, F. 1962: *On Britain*. Moscow: Foreign Languages Publishing House.

Marx, K. and Engels, F. 1969: *Basic Writings* (Feuer, L. ed). London: Fontana.

Marx, K. and Engels, F. 1970: *The German Ideology*. London: Lawrence and Wishart.

Marx, K. and Engels, F. 1972: *Communist Manifesto*. Peking: Peking Press.

McLellan, D. 1978: *Marx*. London: Fontana.

Meadows *et al.*, 1972: *The Limits to Growth* (Club of Rome Report). London: Earth Island.

Miliband, R. 1973: *The State in Capitalist Society*. London: Quartet.

Miliband, R. 1977: *Marxism and Politics*. Oxford: Oxford University Press.

Mill, J.S. 1846: *A System of Logic* (2 vols). London: Parker.

Mills, C.W. 1970: *The Sociological Imagination*. Harmondsworth: Penguin.

Milne, A. 1962: *The Social Philosophy of English Idealism*. London: Allen & Unwin.

Ministry of Pensions and National Insurance 1966: *The Financial and Other Circumstances of Retirement Pensioners*. London: HMSO.

Mishra, R. 1977: *Society and Social Policy*. London: Macmillan.

Moorhouse, B. *et al.*, 1972: 'Rent Strikes' In Miliband, R. and Saville, J. (eds), *Socialist Register*. London: Merlin Press.

Moroney, R. 1976: *The Family and the State — Considerations for Social Policy*. London: Longman.

Myrdal, G. 1960: *Beyond the Welfare State*. London: Duckworth.

National Community Development Project 1977: *Gilding the Ghetto*. London: NCDP.

National Consumer Council 1976: *Means-Tested Benefits*. London: HMSO.

*National Income and Expenditure*, Annual. London: HMSO.

Navarro, V. 1978: *Class Struggle, Medicine and the State*. London: Martin Robertson.

Nevitt, D. 1971: *Fair Deal for Householders*, Fabian Research Series No. 297. London: Fabian Society.

Nevitt, D. 1977: 'Demand and Need.' In Heisler H. (ed), 1977.

Newton, K. 1976: *Second City Politics*. Oxford: Clarendon Press.

Nozick, R. 1974: *Anarchy, State and Utopia*. Oxford: Blackwell.

O'Connor, J. 1973: *The Fiscal Crisis of the State*. New York: St Martin's Press.

Offe, C. 1974: 'Structural Problems of the Capitalist State'. In Beyme, K. (ed). *German Political Studies* vol. I. New York: Sage.

Offe, C. 1976: *Industry and Inequality: the achievement principle in work* and social status. London: Edward Arnold.

Olin Wright, E. 1978: *Class Crisis and the State*. London: New Left Books.

Packman, J. 1969: *Child Care, Needs and Numbers*. London: Allen & Unwin.

Pahl, R. and Winkler, J. 1974: 'The Coming Corporatism'. *New Society* (10 October).

Panitch, L. 1977: 'The Development of Corporatism in Liberal Democracies'. *Comparative Political Studies* **10**(1).

Parker, J. 1975: *Citizenship and Social Policy*. London: Macmillan.

Parker, R. 1967: *Social Administration and Scarcity*, reprinted in Butterworth, E. and Holman, J. (eds), 1975.

Parkin, F. 1971: *Class, Inequality and Political Order*. London: MacGibbon Kee.

Parsons, T. 1937: *The Structure of Social Action*. New York: McGraw-Hill.

Parsons, T. 1951: *The Social System*. London: Routledge & Kegan Paul.

Parsons, T. 1954: *Essays in Sociological Theory*. New York: Free Press.

Parsons, T. 1961: *Structure and Process in Modern Societies*. New York: Free Press.

Parsons, T. and Smelser, N. 1956: *Economy and Society*. London: Routledge & Kegan Paul.

Pinker, R. 1971: *Social Theory and Social Policy*. London: Heinemann.

Pinker, R. 1979. *The Idea of Welfare*. London: Heinemann.

Pirsig, R. 1974: *Zen and the Art of Motorcycle Maintenance* London: Bodley Head.

Piven, F. and Cloward, R. 1974: *Regulating the Poor*. London: Tavistock.

Piven, F. and Cloward, R. 1979: *Poor People's Movements*. New York: Vintage Books.

Plamenatz, J. 1975: *Karl Marx's Philosophy of Man*. Oxford: Clarendon Press.

Plant, R. Lesser, H. and Taylor-Gooby, P. 1980: *Political Philosophy and Social Welfare*. London: Routledge & Kegan Paul.

Plant, R. 1974: *Community and Ideology*. London: Routledge & Kegan Paul.

Plowden Report 1976: *Children and their Primary Schools*. London: HMSO.

Popper, K. 1962: *The Open Society and its Enemies* (2 vols). London: Routledge & Kegan Paul.

Popper, K. 1969: *Conjectures and Refutations*. London: Routledge & Kegan Paul.

Poulantzas, N. 1969: 'The Problem of the Capitalist State'. *New Left Review* **58**.

Poulantzas, N. 1973: *Political Power and Social Classes* (transl. O'Hagan, T.), London: New Left Books.

Powell, E. 1972: *Still to Decide*. Tadworth, Surrey: Eliott Right Way.

Rawls, J. 1973: *A Theory of Justice*. Oxford: Oxford University Press.

Rein, M. 1977: *Social Science and Public Policy*. Harmondsworth: Penguin.

Reisman, D. 1977: *Richard Titmuss*. London: Heinemann.

Rex, J. 1970: *Key Problems in Sociological Theory*. London: Routledge & Kegan Paul.

Rex, J. 1972: 'Class', *New Society* (5 October).

Rimlinger, G. 1971: *Welfare Policy and Industrialization in Europe, America, and Russia*, New York: Wiley.

Robinson, J. 1964: *Economic Philosophy*. Harmondsworth: Penguin.

Robinson, J. 1966: *Economics an Awkward Corner*. London: Allen & Unwin.

Room, G. 1979: *The Sociology of Welfare*. Oxford: Blackwell.

Rose, S. *et al.* 1973: 'Science, Racism and Ideology'. In Miliband, R. and Saville, J. (eds), *Socialist Register*. London: Merlin Press.

Rowbotham, S. Segal, L. Wainwright, H. 1979: *Beyond the Fragments*. London: Merlin Press.

Rowntree, S. 1902: *Poverty, A Study of Town Life*. London.

Royal Commission on the Distribution of Income and Wealth 1975: Report No.1. London: HMSO, Cmnd 6171.

Royal Commission on the Distribution of Income and Wealth 1979: Report No.7. London: HMSO, Cmnd 7595.

Royal Commission on the NHS 1979: Report. London: HMSO, Cmnd 7615.

Runciman, W. 1972: *Relative Deprivation and Social Justice*. Harmondsworth: Penguin.

Samuel, R. *et al.* 1962: 'But Nothing Happens'. *New Left Review* **13–14**.

Seldon, A. 1978a: *Charge!* London: Temple-Smith.

Seldon, A. (ed) 1978b: *The Coming Confrontation — Will the Open Society Survive to 1989*. London: Institute of Economic Affairs.

Shonfield, A. 1965: *Modern Capitalism*. Oxford: Oxford University Press.

Sidgewick, P. 1966: 'Herbert Marcuse'. In Miliband, R. and Saville, J. (eds) *Socialist Register*. London: Merlin Press.

Simmel, G. 1971: *On Individualism and Social Forms*. Chicago: University of Chicago Press.

Singh, A. 1977: 'UK Industry and the World Economy — A Case of de-Industrialization'. *Cambridge Journal of Economics* **1**(2).

Skidelsky, R. 1977a: Review of J. Harris. *New Society* (10 November).

Skidelsky, R. 1977b: 'The Political Meaning of the Keynesian Revolution'. In Skidelsky R. (ed), *The End of the Keynesian Era*. London: Macmillan.

Slater P. 1977: *Origins and Significance of the Frankfurt School*. London: Routledge & Kegan Paul.

Sleeman, J. 1973: *The Welfare State*. London: Allen & Unwin.
Sleeman, J. 1979: *Resources for the Welfare State*. London: Macmillan.
Smelser, N. 1959: *Social Change in the Industrial Revolution*. London: Routledge & Kegan Paul.
Smelser, N. 1964: 'Towards a Theory of Modernization'. In Etzioni, A. (ed), 1964, *Social Change*. New York: Basic Books.
Smith, A. 1930: *The Wealth of Nations*, Cannan (ed). London: Methuen.
Social Audit 1974: *Smokeless Fuels*. London: Social Audit Ltd.
*Social Trends*, Annual. London: HMSO.
Spencer, H. 1852: 'A Theory of Population'. *Westminster Review* NS1.
Spencer J. and Crookston, L. 1978: *The Relationship between Local Authority Social Services Departments and the Supplementary Benefits Organisation Part I: The Report*, First draft of a report prepared for the DHSS.
Stedman-Jones, G. 1971: *Outcast London*. Oxford: Clarendon Press.
Steedman, I. 1977: *Marx After Sraffa*. London: New Left Books.
Stevenson, O. 1973: *Claimant or Client*. London: Allen & Unwin.
Stoker, G. 1980: 'Corporate Management and the Local State.' Unpublished paper to Leicester Group of the Conference of Socialist Economists.
Supplementary Benefits 1976: Administration Paper No. 5. London: HMSO.
Supplementary Benefits Commission 1978: Annual Report, 1977. London: HMSO, Cmnd 7392.
Sweezy, P. 1947: 'Keynes, the Economist'. In *Harris, S.* (ed). *The New Economics*, New York: Knopf.
Tawney, R. 1922: Labour Party Working Party on Education.
Tawney, R. 1923: *The Affluent Society*. London: Bell.
Tawney, R. 1929: *Equality*. London: Bell.
Tawney, R. 1936: *Religion and the Rise of Capitalism*. London: Murray.
Tawney, R. 1972: *R. H. Tawney's Commonplace Book* (ed. Winter, J. and Joslin, D.). Cambridge: Cambridge University Press.
Taylor-Gooby, P. 1978: 'The Boring Crisis of Social Administration'. *Times Higher Educational Supplement* (17 February).
Thane, P. 1974: 'A History of Social Welfare'. *New Society* (29 August).
Thane, P. 1978: *Origins of British Social Policy*. London: Croom-Helm.
Therborn, G. 1978: *What Does the Ruling Class Do When it Rules*. London: New Left Books.
Thompson, E. 1978: *The Poverty of Theory*. London: Merlin Press.
Timms, N. and Watson, D. 1976: *Talking About Welfare*. London: Routledge & Kegan Paul.
Titmuss, R. 1950: *Problems of Social Policy*. London: HMSO.
Titmuss, R. 1960: *The Irresponsible Society*. London: Fabian Society.
Titmuss, R. 1961: *Social Policies and Population Growth in Mauritius*. London: Methuen.

Titmuss, R. 1962: *Income Distribution and Social Change*. London: Allen & Unwin.

Titmuss, R. 1964: *The Health Services of Tanganyika*. London: Pitman.

Titmuss, R. 1968: *Commitment to Welfare*. London: Allen & Unwin.

Titmuss, R. 1973: *The Gift Relationship*. Harmondsworth: Penguin.

Titmuss, R. 1974: *Social Policy*. London: Allen & Unwin.

Titmuss, R. 1976: *Essays on the Welfare State*. London: Allen & Unwin.

Townsend, P. 1963: *The Last Refuge*. London: Routledge & Kegan Paul.

Townsend, P. 1970: *The Fifth Social Service*: London: Fabian Society.

Townsend, P. 1971: *The Concept of Poverty*. London: Heinemann.

Townsend, P. 1973: *The Social Minority*. Harmondsworth: Penguin.

Townsend, P. 1974: Inequality in Health Services. *Lancet* **2**(15 June).

Townsend, P. 1979: *Poverty in the United Kingdom*. Harmondsworth: Penguin.

Treasury 1979: *Economic Progress Report 110 June 1979*. London: Treasury.

Tressell, R. 1955: *The Ragged-Trousered Philanthropists*, London: Lawrence & Wishart.

Vaizey, J. 1973: *The Future Economy of Cities*. Mimeo.

Veblen, T. 1934: *The Theory of the Leisure Class* New York: Random House.

Wainwright, H. 1978: 'Women and the Division of Labour'. In Abrams, P. (ed), *Work Urbanism and Inequality*. London: Weidenfeld & Nicolson.

Walton, R. 1969: 'Need', *Social Services Quarterly* **43**.

Warham, J. 1977: *An Open Case, The Organisational Context of Social Work*. London: Routledge & Kegan Paul.

Webb, B. and S. 1909: *Break Up the Poor Law!*, (Part I of the Minority Report of the 1909 Commission). London: Fabian Society.

Weber, M. 1948: *From Max Weber* (Gerth, H., and Mills, C. eds). London: Routledge & Kegan Paul.

Weber, M. 1964: *The Theory of Social and Economic Organizations*, (Parsons, T. ed.). London: Collier Macmillan.

Wedderburn, D. (ed) 1974: *Poverty, Inequality and Class Structure*, Cambridge: Cambridge University Press.

Weir, S. 1976: 'Red Line Districts'. *Roof* (July).

Westergaard, J. and Resler, H. 1975: *Class in a Capitalist Society*. London: Heinemann.

Wilding, P. 1972: 'Towards Exchequer Subsidies for Council Houses, 1906–14'. *Social and Economic Administration* **6**(1).

Wilensky, H. 1975: *The Welfare State and Equality*. Los Angeles: University of California.

Wilensky, H. 1976: *The New Corporatism*. New York: Sage.

Wilensky, H. and Lebeaux, C. 1965: *Industrial Society and Social Welfare*, 2nd Edition. New York: Free Press.

Williams, A. 1978: ' "Need" — an Economic Exegesis'. In Culyer A. and Wright K. *Economic Aspects of Health Services*. London: Martin Robertson.

Willis, P. 1978: *Learning to Labour*. Farnborough: Saxon House.

Wilson, E. 1977: *Women and the Welfare State*. London: Tavistock.

Winkler, J. 1977: 'The Coming Corporatism'. In Skidelsky, R. (ed), *The End of the Keynesian Era*. London: Macmillan.

Wolfe, A. 1979: *The Limits of Legitimacy*. London: Macmillan.

Wood, A. 1972a: 'The Marxian Critique of Social Justice'. *Philosophy and Public Affairs* (Spring).

Wood, J. 1972b: *How Much Unemployment?* London: Institute of Economic Affairs Research Monograph 28.

Woodroofe, K. 1962: *From Charity to Social Work*. London: Routledge & Kegan Paul.

Yaffe, D. 1973: 'The Crisis of Profitability, A Critique of the Glyn-Sutcliffe Thesis'. *New Left Review* **80**.

Index

# Author index

# Subject index